HUNTING FOR GOLD

Hunting For Gold

BY

Major William Downie

AMERICAN WEST PUBLISHING COMPANY

PALO ALTO/CALIFORNIA

Special Contents of This Edition
© Copyright 1971
American West Publishing Company.

Library of Congress Catalog Card
Number 79-169523
ISBN 0-910118-22-1

Note To The Reader

One of the most exciting—as well as one of the most significant—events in the history of the American West happened with the discovery of gold in California in 1848. Told and retold, in fact, in fiction, and in between, the Gold Rush adventure never loses its lustre.

William Downie, like thousands of his contemporaries, sought both escape from the Old World and excitement in the New when he left his native Scotland for San Francisco in 1849. But Major Downie was hardly typical of the prospectors who stormed to the American River country, and later to the gold fields of the Fraser, and later still to the Yukon. For Major Downie the thrill was in the hunt, and the treasures he found and lost were secondary benefits. Not only were his experiences often unique, but his observations, his companions, his way of life, and his uncanny story-telling ability set him apart from his fellow seekers. In 1893 he penned his reminiscences of California, the Northwest, Alaska, and Panama, called his volume *Hunting for Gold*, and had it published by the California Publishing Company of San Francisco. Today, copies of the original (and only) edition are virtually extinct.

This new, American West edition is an exact facsimile of the original, photographed from actual pages of the 1893 edition, obtained from the Library of Congress. To achieve complete authenticity, the Table of Contents remains at the end of the book (starting on page 399); the halftones and line etchings have not been retouched, nor have imperfections in type been altered from the original.

As part of the front matter, we have added an introduction by Robert Becker, associate director of the Bancroft Library at the University of California, Berkeley; following the Table of Contents, we have added an index, prepared by the late Joseph Gaer in 1935 in mimeograph form as part of a California literary research project. The index, in itself, provides a capsule history of Major Downie's travels and has captured the flavor of the original edition.

INTRODUCTION

The nineteenth century undoubtedly seemed a remarkable time to those living through it, but from the vantage point of hindsight, it differed from its predecessors pretty largely in degree. Men covered the earth in greater numbers; they traveled greater distances in less time and generally in more comfort. Communication by cable and wire increased man's contact with, if not his understanding of, his fellow man. Wars tended to be shorter, with greatly improved and more expensive weapons, and with a vastly increased loss of life. In short, the nineteenth century did resemble the eighteenth, save for changes that might just possibly be improvements.

But halfway through the century, in 1848, there did occur the beginning of a phenomenon such as the world had not yet known—the California Gold Rush. It is said to have commenced in the dusty street of a shabby village on the remote shore of the Pacific, when the cry arose, "Gold! Gold from the American River!" For fifty years thereafter throughout the world, men heard and answered similar cries: from Australia's Ballarat in 1851; from British Columbia's Fraser River in 1858; from the Comstock in Nevada and Pike's Peak in Colorado in 1859; from Otago in New Zealand in 1861; from the Salmon River in Idaho in 1862; from Bannack and Virginia City in Montana in 1863 and 1864; from South Africa for placer diamonds in 1870 and for gold in 1873; and from the Klondike in Alaska in 1898. Similar discoveries created smaller rushes in Oregon, Arizona, South Dakota, and western Australia.

In each case the rush was characterized by a common pattern of development; it was initiated by an individual miner or prospector with little capital or equipment, save muscle, ingenuity, hope, and savage determination; it came to maturity with a sudden, overwhelming influx, sometimes worldwide in nature, of goldseekers, a few with experience and skill in the endeavor but the majority with neither. The rush and the level of population then declined with the entrance of large-scale, heavily capitalized industrial endeavor, which itself gradually drifted into eclipse as the entire ore body was worked out. In the meantime, ubiquitous prospectors made further discoveries in equally remote regions, and the same process of development and decay occurred once again.

While it cannot be said that the worldwide mining excitement of the last half of the nineteenth century would not have happened without the California experience, it is nonetheless true that the California pattern can be identified again and again and that California gold hunters participated in most of the discoveries and all of the rushes. Not only was the California Gold Rush the first and possibly the biggest in terms of individuals involved, but it was also basic in many ways to all the rest.

Very few of the forty-niners had had any experience in placer mining. There were some South Carolinians and north Georgians who had mined in the Alleghanies, and there were Mexican miners who brought experience from Sonora and Durango. But this experience largely consisted of using a shovel and pan; there had to be invented the rocker, the Long Tom, the sluice, the hydraulic monitor, and the gold dredge. There had to be discovered the chemistry of gold-bearing ores, more efficient methods of extraction, and more productive techniques of corporate and joint-stock financing. There had to be created the social institutions, the laws of conduct and property, to allay the specter of anarchy that existed in the first Sierra camps when there was no means of enforcing even the most rudimentary rules. Out of necessity there emerged a system of mining claims, of water rights and regulation, of restrictions as to personal behavior. And all these institutions traveled throughout the world from their origin in the California Gold Rush.

The first rush began in the spring of 1848, after the discovery at Sutter's Mill became known, and, with the exception of a few gold-seekers from Oregon and Hawaii, was entirely a local affair, ending with the winter rains. By that time, the president of the United States had announced the presence of gold in quantity in California, and the second California Gold Rush began. By ship, mule, ox, horse, and foot, the horde of emigrants found their way west "to see the Elephant." Many of this remarkable generation over the following decades saw many elephants in many parts of the world.

They dreamed of tearing quick riches from the earth and returning home as wealthy men. Most of them did neither, for a couple of seasons of backbreaking labor in icy Sierra creeks and on parched Sierra hillsides made it apparent that few would get rich in such a fashion. They took whatever they had gained and got out.

Many returned with enough to start a general store, to read for the Law, or to open a crossroads saloon. Still more stayed in California, where they went into business, practiced medicine, ran for the Senate, or took to the plow, discovering slowly the agricultural marvels of a gentle land. They founded villages that in time became great cities. They put up their own money and anyone else's to establish a bank, an express line, a railroad. They dominated the political, social, and economic life of California and indeed all the western states for the next thirty years. From the residents of California before the end of 1855 came: the first seventeen governors (1849–1890); the first eighteen U. S. senators (1849–1886); twenty-nine of the first thirty congressmen (1849–1879); two-thirds of the delegates to the state constitutional convention of 1878; and more than thirty of the first forty appointed regents of the University of California.

This is not to say that the fact of California residence would guarantee success. Many goldseekers returned from the diggings with only enough to buy a ticket home. Some, like Major Downie, lost heavily by misfortune and poor judgment; others succumbed to the temptations of the monte tables and the dreary deadfalls of the red-light districts of Sacramento and San Francisco. Many drifted on to the Fraser, Pike's Peak, or the Comstock. One or another ended his days at the hand of the Apache, against an adobe wall in a sun-drenched Nicaraguan courtyard, or at the end of a rope in the hands of a self-appointed committee of his peers. The gaudy fate which legend has ascribed to the forty-niner came about in many ways but, one must remark, with sufficient rarity to become worthy of notice. Alive or dead, the hell-raising forty-niner of the legend was in large measure a creation of the forty-niners themselves, as will soon become apparent in Major Downie's recollection forty years after.

Born in Glasgow in 1819, William Downie, sailor, lumber merchant, and adventurer, arrived in San Francisco on June 27, 1849. He soon left the coast for the mountains, arriving in Sacramento after an upriver voyage of eleven days, and from there traveled on to the Yuba River to Bullard's Bar. In October, accompanied by seven Negro goldseekers, another white man, and a white boy, Downie set off into the Sierra. The white man had to return because of illness, but the party continued, augmented by an Indian and a Kanaka named Jim Crow, arriving at the Forks of the Yuba before winter set in. Here in the following years grew up the town of Downieville, intermittently Major Downie's home for the rest of his life.

The Oakland *News* of November 28, 1871, contains the following short news item:

> *Yesterday we had a friendly visit from Major William Downie, the founder of Downieville, and who also bore a conspicuous part in the exploration of the Fraser River country. The Major built the first cabin at the forks of the Yuba, sometime in the winter of 1849–50, and around that grew the present town of Downieville, which was named after him.*
>
> *We first saw him there in March of the following spring, when he was a sort of mining generalissimo for a party of Scotch and English sailors, together with some intelligent Irishmen and a sprinkling of Australian people. The amount of gold which that party discovered and dug and spent would be incredible to relate now.*
>
> *We have seen the Major go through with two or three pounds of dust on one Sunday, and after emptying the company sack, the party would sober up, disperse and dig more.*
>
> *In 1854, the Major dissolved partnership with the Messrs. Barleycorn & Co., and became a rigid and influential Temperance man, and afterwards went to Brit-*

ish Columbia and became a confidential explorer for Governor Douglas. There he married a Scotch lady, and returned with his family to Downieville, his old stamping ground....

In 1874, Downie tried his luck in New Granada, or Panama, as he relates, and the following year he was back in Downieville, organizing the Centennial Gravel Mining Company. He died suddenly on December 27, 1893, on board the steamer *City of Puebla* just before disembarking in San Francisco from Victoria, B.C.

Downie's association with British Columbia began with the Fraser River excitement in 1858. He did not follow the earlier goldseekers of that year up the river but chose to remain on the coast, leading a party to prospect the Queen Charlotte Islands. The trip was unsuccessful but it led to his employment, without salary, by Governor Douglas as an explorer, attempting to find a shorter route to the upper Fraser, directly from the Pacific. Downie's description of his travels is a significant contribution to the literature of exploration and displays a sense of compassion for the native inhabitants such as rarely found expression among the forty-niners. After the massacre of the Waddington surveying party and one of Downie's closest friends by a group of Bute Inlet Indians (who were subsequently captured and hanged in retribution), Downie comments:

> *Strange indeed, that it would be thus, that after all the difference between the human being and the savage brute is so small; for it should at all times be borne in mind that although Waddington's party had committed no atrocities on the Indians, yet the usurper of the country had in so many instances caused the Indians to suffer indignities, which even more civilized races would have considered that only blood could atone for.*

The evident satisfaction that Downie found in his British Columbia explorations may explain his otherwise irrational willingness to drop a well-paying claim at a moment's notice to track down a rumored strike somewhere else. Is it not possible that the gold was in reality just an excuse? Could it not be that the real lure was the unknown, the wilderness itself, with an irresistible urge to find out what lay over the next ridge, across the wide valley, beyond the far mountain? Perhaps it was that the purpose of his life lay not in finding, but in hunting for gold.

September, 1971   *Robert H. Becker*

Hunting For Gold

Reminisences of Personal Experience

And Research in The Early Days

Of The Pacific Coast

From Alaska to Panama.

BY

Major William Downie

[FOUNDER OF DOWNIEVILLE, CAL.]

—Press of—
The California Publishing Co.
San Francisco, Cal.
1893

COPYRIGHTED BY
THE CALIFORNIA PUBLISHING COMPANY
ALL RIGHTS RESERVED.

Hope told its flattering tale: "Come seek ye here—
"For courage, Fortune gives you shining gold!
"Remove the treasure's mantel and behold
"The glittering specks that from beneath it peer;

"Leave home and friends, leave all that you hold dear—
"As Jason won the golden fleece of old
"Shall you have your reward—a hundred fold—
"Come, tarry not—your greatest chance is near!"

And so like Jason's Argonauts they went—
Each sinew strained, each hardy muscle bent,
With courage, youth and vigor, who could fail?

Some ne'er returned, their story none could tell—
A few to-day in lofty mansions dwell,
But more, by far, deny hope's flattering tale

Chris M. Waage.

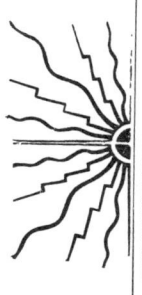 O the surviving members of the advance guard of gold hunters, the California pioneers and their descendants, who are now living throughout the United States, this book is most respectfully dedicated by the AUTHOR

INTRODUCTION

In presenting this book to the public the publishers feel assured that it is almost superfluous, to introduce the author or dwell upon the merit which these pages possess, as originating from the pen of Major William Downie. As one of the very earliest pioneers and gold seekers in California, Major Downie has become a man of universal interest, while to some of his discoveries in the early days is due the fever heat of excitement, which at that period, made the world's great heart palpitate with double-quick pulsation, and sent thousands of daring adventurers across the arid deserts and the stormy main.

Too much cannot be said of the remarkable nature, of which Major Downie is possessed, having been endowed with a physique and general constitution, which at times have carried him through the most desperate circumstances, the subject of these pages is mentally and morally equipped with a temperament which enabled him to successfully withstand the temptations that caused the fall of so many others in the early days; while his native generosity and amiability secured for him many friends, who dearly prized his personality.

As a practical miner, Major Downie is without a peer, and even to this day his authority is acknowledged, and his advice is taken by any working miner, and rarely without benefit to the recipient. These pages tell of the days when this experience was gained; the days on the

Yuba, when, to honor him, his companions called the settlement at the forks, Downieville, the name by which it is known as yet; the days of hardships in the snow-clad Sierras; the adventures in British Columbia and Alaska; and the weird search for gold in the Indian graves of Panama.

It was only after repeated solicitations from his friends that Major Downie allowed his notes to be given out for publication. The material thus provided was entrusted by the publishers to Mr. Chris M. Waage for compilation and revision. Mr. Waage is a journalist and literateur of some note, and he has spared no effort in order to present Major Downie's papers in the most acceptable form, retaining throughout, the simple modest way of relating the story, which characterizes the original manuscript.

In conclusion, the publishers wish to draw attention to the illustrations, which have been chosen with a view to depict the situations as far as possible. Some of them have been reproduced from engravings dating back to the very earliest days, when pictorial art of this class was first introduced into California.

THE PUBLISHERS.

HUNTING FOR GOLD.

CHAPTER I.

Introductory Remarks—At Home in Scotland—First Voyage—A Sailor on the Lakes—Lumber Trade in Buffalo—The Gold Fever—Round the Horn—San Francisco—Expensive Dinners—The Glorious Fourth—Generous Gamblers—Fun with the Immigrants.

I have been asked by many friends to give to the world, through a publication, some of my reminiscences of the early days of gold hunting and adventures on the Pacific Coast, and it is in complying with this oft repeated request that I have penned the following.

Some of the incidents described, may be fairly said at one time to have helped to revolutionize the known world, and for that reason must forever retain a certain interest.

The narrative throughout is based upon personal experiences, observations and conclusions, and is compiled from notes, taken at the time; recollections, corroborated by friends who were with me at the periods referred to; letters, which have passed between myself and friends, and from official reports bearing upon the circumstances related. The correctness of my account is therefore warranted, and, while it is not infrequent to read descriptions of life in the early days, which are highly flavored with unnecessary romance, I claim for my work that in its details it corresponds with actual facts which have now become part and parcel of the history of the western coast of this great continent

I was born in the city of Glasgow, Scotland, in the year 1819. It was the memorable year when the terrible masacre took place at the Manchester reform meeting. James Monroe was then the fifth president of the United States, and George III was king of Great Britain. It was in the days when such names as Shelley, Byron, Scott, Coleridge and Wordsworth shone in the literary firmament; the days of early steamboat traveling, and the days that had not as yet seen the locomotive engines dashing, snorting and fuming through quiet fields. In that same year the steamer Savannah, 350 tons, came from New York to Liverpool in 26 days, and the passage was regarded as a marvel. There were then in the whole of Scotland not twelve steamers, and only the wheels of one stirred the surface of the river Clyde. It seems long ago, and the world to-day seems scarcely the same as in those days.

I was raised in Ayrshire. From quite a boy my mind was bent upon adventure. When I saw the waves rolling in through the North Channel, I knew from my school books that they came from the great Atlantic, and I longed to be on them and sail away to different parts of the great world. So, when I was old enough, I shipped on board a vessel that carried coal between different points on the coast. It was not exactly what I wanted, but it fitted me for a larger undertaking, when a chance should afford itself, and when it came I was ready for it. My first deep-sea voyage was to Australia on a Glasgow vessel. I was in Sidney in the days, when Botany Bay was made the inhospitable home for thousands of condemned prisoners, whose greatest offense in many instances consisted in shooting a jack rabbit in the Squire's covers. I recollect seeing the landing of a cargo of unfortunates who had been consigned to those, then desolate, regions. From Australia we sailed to the

East Indies and visited the Isle of France and from there we went to London.

My next voyage was to America. I shipped at Donegal for Quebec in the old Spring Hill and arrived there, determined to try my fortune in foreign lands, before returning home. I had a varied experience. I first sailed lakes Ontario and Erie. From there I drifted into the lumber business on Grand River, established a store in Dunville at the mouth of this stream, and ultimately, in partnership with a man named J. C. Hayward, became interested in lumber yards on the Buffalo Shipping Canal.

I was stopping in Buffalo at the Love Joy Hotel, when I first heard of the discovery of gold in California. The result the rumors produced was magical. Men of all ages and in all conditions of life got the gold fever, and I among the rest. Some of the tales told were fabulous, and the reports of treasures found in some instances were enough to entice any man of grit and daring to challenge fortune As will be seen further on, many even, who had neither of these qualities, ventured upon the search for gold, prompted merely by the lust for gain, and the hope, perchance, of escaping the yolk of poverty, or the discomfort of narrow circumstances. At the hotel the advisability of going to California to try our luck had become a leading topic among a number of the boarders, and at last I made up my mind to go. Being a sailor I concluded that to travel by sea would be both more comfortable and far safer than to trust ones self to the chances of traversing vast deserts and encountering hostile Indians. So I shipped from Boston for New Orleans on board the brig Monterey.

I well remember the day of my departure for the far West. It was the day before General Zacharias Taylor was elected to the presidency, which was to be his only for one brief year. Political enthusiasm ran high, and much admiration was expressed for the gallant soldier, who had distinguished himself so much during the Mexican war; but I cared little about politics and was anxious to get away.

Arrived at New Orleans the next thing was to secure passage to San Francisco Bay. The small vessels, going by the Panama route, were crowded to their utmost extent, and I concluded to try and work my passage on some ship, going around the Horn. Fortune favored me, and I was not long in finding the desired opportunity. The clipper "Architect," in command of Captain Gray of Baltimore, was lying ready to sail, and a shipping master informed me that just one man was wanted to sign articles at once. I offered my services and the shipping master kindly responded: "Take off that black coat," he said, "and come to the office in the morning."

I did as he told me, and the next morning I signed articles, received two months wages in advance, and a few hours after had made myself perfectly at home on board. This was indeed a piece of good luck, for there were any number of men in those days, who would gladly have worked their passage out for nothing, and I believe I was the only foremast hand who received any wages. Everybody on board with the exception of the officers was bound for the mines. The thirst for gold and adventure had seized everybody, and, when after a long and tedious voyage we ultimately dropped anchor in the Bay of San Francisco, all hands left the ship at once, for such was the custom in '49.

San Francisco at that period looked vastly different to what it does nowadays. A number of the crew stayed together, and we at once made our way for some place, where we could camp for the night. I still remember the names of Perkins, Pierce and Gibson as belonging to our company, and there were more, whose names I have forgotten. It was on the 27th day of June, 1849, that we landed. The weather was mild, and there was no reason to waste money on hotel accommodations, which then were both scarce and expensive, so we determined to camp for the night in Hide Park. The name sounds aristocratic enough, but the place itself was anything but inviting. The location of it was about where now the Palace Hotel rears its lofty walls, and it derived its name from the fact that here the old Spanish settlers piled up their hides and horns, previous to shipping them, and at the time of our arrival the ground was covered with these goods arranged in bales and proper heaps. Here we made ourselves as comfortable as circumstances would permit, and spent the first night in the land of gold, of hope and of opportunity.

After we had spent a few days in our new quarters and got the lay of the land, we all succeeded in getting work. Some of us found employment at handling lumber, others at rolling casks and barrels up the beach as fast as the lighter could bring them from the vessel, while I with three or four others was hired to ballast a brig, which was lying off the Mission. In order to get aboard the brig we had to take a boat, which lay on the beach at the foot of what is now Sansome Street, and I well recollect the first morning, as we were walking down to this spot, encountering several men, who came running toward us and pretended to warn us against going on board the brig, saying "They would do for us there." These fellows, who belonged to the class, known as "Sidney Ducks," reckoned without a host. We told them that nothing could scare us, we had just landed after a long voyage and nothing would please us better than a good live fight. When they heard this, they concluded to leave us alone, and we were no more troubled with their importunities.

Labor was scarce then, as nearly everybody was making for the mines, and work was therefore plentiful. We received from $8.00 to $16.00 a day, but could not afford to engage board and lodging, for which the most exhorbitant prices were charged, and so made the best of it in our own camps. Some of our passengers went to the Parker House to board but had to give it up, as the prices were too high. The Parker House was then the principal hotel in San Francisco. It was situated on Kearny Street, and the expense of staying at a hostelry of that class in '49 may be imagined, when it is stated that a good dinner cost from $8.00 to $12.00. No wonder our passengers found their purses somewhat too small for a prolonged stay at this hotel.

I remember one fellow traveler in particular, who by the time he landed had become thoroughly disgusted with salt beef and hard tack, and made up his mind to go somewhere at once, where he could get a good dinner. He was told that the Parker House was the place for him, and so thither he went, having first put into his pocket a Spanish Doubloon, which was worth about $16.00. The dinner was a pleasant change in the diet of our friend, and, after he had enjoyed it, he went to the counter and threw down the gold piece to pay for the meal. The clerk looked carefully at the coin, put it in the till and gave his customer four dollars in change. "What is that?" asked the stranger. "Your change," replied the clerk, "your change for dinner," and then engaged in conversation with other customers.

As soon as the traveler got an opportunity he again approached the clerk and asked him confidentially to state what they charged for dinner at this establishment.

"Twelve dollars," said the clerk suavely, "twelve dollars—that's all sir."

"See here," said the traveler, holding out the four dollars he had received as change, "if that is so, you may as well take these other four dollars along with it, as I can't get anything in this town for such a small amount."

There are many scenes and incidents, that occured during my first visit to San Francisco, which, although they then puzzled me, now cause me to smile as I remember them. The first celebration of the Fourth of July, which I witnessed in the weird and wondrous West, left an indelible impression upon me. The festivities were minus the more modern Chinese fireworks, but let those who object to this mode of celebration, appreciate the fact that the general tumult and noise was not produced by anything so harmless. In '49 the glorious Fourth was ushered in by drinking to the constitution in bumpers, until the celebrants were half-seas over. Then began the fun. Instead of firecrackers, pistols were used, instead of sending up rockets, men would show their adroitness with the gun by shooting through windowpanes, hitting lighted lamps or candles and offering to shoot off buttons from their friends' garments. One episode caused quite a little excitement. An old Mexican, who had got somewhat mixed in the political situation, hoisted his native flag, but this so annoyed the Americans that they forthwith pulled it down, and the old fellow in his disgust rolled himself up in his colors and went to sleep.

Gambling was then carried on on a large scale all over the city, and Faro and Monte were the most frequent games. The banker would have a little tin cup by his side, in which he would deposit all silver coins under half a dollar. This small change was termed "chicken feed," and when anybody came in looking hungry or thirsty, and seemingly in want of means to satisfy his cravings, the banker would dive into the tin cup and take from it a dollar or more, which he would hand to the stranger that he might get relief. There was a certain spirit of magnanimity and generosity, which inspired all who had plenty of money at that time, and it extended even into those grades of the community, who made a living by preying upon the folly of others. One more incident I must relate, because at the time being it caused much merriment at the expense of a number of "greenhorns," and characterizes life at that period. The steamer from Panama arrived with a large number of passengers, nearly all of whom were bound for the mines. Towards evening of the day when they had come ashore, a number of the boys played a joke on the new arrivals, which none of them could possibly forget, harmless as it was. They marched into town, forming quite a large company. Every man was armed to the teeth, and they were accompanied by a lot of Indians, who carried sacks filled with sand and pebbles from the seashore. The sacks were marked MUCHA ORO, and the whole caravan presented the appearance of being a band of successful miners, returning from the gold fields. The immigrants would stop in amazement, wherever they came upon the company, and ask all sorts of questions relative to this apparently magnificent treasure, some of them expressing their doubts that there would be any more gold left to look for, others talking hopefully of the brilliant prospect before them. Of course the initiated enjoyed the joke hugely.

Such was life in San Francisco in the early days, and such the men, who laid the foundation for a great and magnificent city.

CHAPTER II.

On Board the Milwaukee—No Clearance Papers—Going up the River—Sacramento—Teamsters Talk—Off for the Yuba—First Experience—War upon Foreigners—A Silent Friend—Store Keeping—Lumpy Gold—Restless—Foster's Bar—Sick Men with Great Appetites—In Search of a Partner.

I was now getting tired of life in San Francisco, little as I had seen of it, for indeed the greater part of my time had been taken up with work, and I was saving my money till such time, as I should want it for the purpose of going to the mines. It was not then always an easy matter to hold on to one's cash. Alluring temptations were thrown in the way of the newcomer from all quarters, and the chances of the gambling table induced many a foolish fellow to part with the coin, which might have opened far brighter prospects to him, had he stuck to it, and disbursed it more judiciously. But outside the gambling resorts all manner of devices were invented by cunning schemers, whose designs were to profit by the youth or inexperience of the immigrants, for the purpose of enriching themselves.

The Schooner Milwaukee was getting ready to go to Sacramento, and I took passage on her. She was a small craft of about fifteen tons, carrying a general cargo of merchandise and a number of passengers as well. It was on the 5th of July 1849 that we left San Francisco with the excitement of the great national holiday fresh in our minds, and the effects of patriotic drinks still heat-ing the brow of some of our fellow passengers. I for one was particularly pleased to get away from the reckless city, where it seemed to me that men's passions were worked up to fever heat, and where everything was done to excite them. I had not then even a forecast of the scenes that should open to me. I little dreamed that the quiet of the mountains and the silence of the valleys were even at that hour echoing with the thunder of human emotions; that nature in its holiest solitude was being made the theater, in which was enacted the most powerful scenes of human aspirations, degradation and often vice in its most hideous form. The sentiment of hope was predominant with all of us, and I fully believe that every man on board depicted to himself treasures of his own, greater than any on which Aladin's lamp threw its magic light, and fondly believed that the labor of months would secure to him years of ease and plenty and a life of unbroken satisfaction. Alas for hope! The few verses at the beginning of my narrative express pretty nearly what became of the gold seekers. The tracks of some few led to gilded halls, but far more lead to domicils, where disappointment told her story in the modest larder, while there are many whose tracks were never found; whose voices were stilled in the midst of the brawl, and on whose unknown graves no tears were ever shed.

The traveler who to-day goes to Sacramento, comfortably seated in a railroad car, or even by the little river steamer, can hardly imagine what our journey meant. The accommodations on the schooner were extremely scanty, and in regard to room, the hold and the deck cabin were pretty much on a par, while the deck itself was so full of all sorts of cargo that it was almost an impossibility to get the necessary exercise. If one wished to lie down, he had to remove some of the cargo from the hold, put it on deck wherever he could find space, and rest himself on the barrels below, where he might remain as long as he pleased and could bear the suffocating atmosphere of the limited space. There was no cheering bell that called to meals; no happy conversation over a well laid table for everybody was told to bring his own grub or go without it, and for this kind of a passage we were charged one ounce of gold or the equivalent in silver.

After a good deal of pulling and hauling we got under way and things went all right until we reached Benicia. Here our craft was boarded by Uncle Sam's officers, and, as our captain could show no clearance papers from the port of San Francisco, he was told to return and secure them before we could proceed any further. Consequently the Milwaukee had to come to, and we lay there for three long days, while the captain took a trip back to San Francisco and returned with the necessary documents which enabled us to continue our voyage. It was a tedious undertaking to go up the river. There was very little sailing done, and in order to make any headway at all we had to pull and warp the old hulk most of the way, and everybody took a hand to help along. There was a good deal of impatience manifested at times, but on the whole the crowd put up with the inconveniences fairly well, most of them consoling themselves with flattering thoughts of the Gold Diggings and their expected success there.

After a voyage of eleven days we reached Sacramento. The people we met here were mostly of a different stamp from what we had seen in San Francisco. There was considerably more of comparatively legitimate business done here, as the men came down to this city from the mines to deposit their find and purchase rations. The

IMMIGRANT TRAIN NEARING THE SACRAMENTO RIVER.

teamsters did a tremendous business and took loads of provisions and all sorts of necessaries of life on the gold fields, in all directions, wherever the gold-seekers were, or the storekeepers catered to the adventurers. It was therefore a matter of course that we first consulted the teamsters, as to where we might go with the best chance of success. They in return seemed to agree that the American River was the best place for us. We were told that it was a good deal nearer than the Yuba, and that gold was panning out there as well as on any of the fields.

We were as yet undetermined when I happened to meet Mr. J. Rose, who was going to the mines on the Yuba, with goods. His accounts of the location decided me, and we agreed to work the launch up the Yuba as far as Nye's ranch, which is now known as Marysville. We then procured a case of brandy, preserved meats, and other necessary articles, stowed them away in the stern sheets, and a fair wind springing up, we set sail. The next morning we were at Vernon's, and after a two days voyage arrived at Nye's Ranch, when those of us who were bound for the mines, left the frail craft, and set out on our pilgrimage.

There were three of us, and we were buoyant with happy anticipations as we made our way to Rose's Bar, where we learned that there were diggings further up the river, and determined to push up to Bullard's Bar. Here we bought a rocker for twelve and one-half ounces, and now we stood at the gate that should lead us into the promised land. It seems strange now to think back upon our first experience in trying to find gold, and the primitive manner in which we went to work. The three of us divided the labor, so that one worked the rocker, while the other stirred, and the third used the pick and

SACRAMENTO IN FORTY-NINE.

shovel and carried the dirt in a bag, about a panful at a time. I honestly believe that I could now run one day's work through in one hour, pick, shovel, rocker and all. We used a scoop about the size of a cigar box for wetting the dirt. It had a long handle to it, and when the water was thrown on the dirt it would be stirred up, a process somewhat similar to making mush.

The weather that summer was extremely hot, and the temperature in the middle of the day became almost unbearable, more especially to those who had not yet become acclimated. It was a common thing among new arrivals to take a SIESTA of several hours in the middle of the day, owing to an idea, generally imported from home, that it was not healthy to work during mid-day hours in California.

At Bullard's Bar some of the singular scenes of miners' camp life in those days began to unfold themselves to me, and here, for the first time, I saw a party organized for the purpose of driving away "foreigners". What was implied by the term "foreigners" was not exactly clear to me at that time, and it would be hard for me to explain it even now. The little company so organized, consisted of from twenty to thirty men. They were armed with pistols, knives, rifles and old shotguns, and I remember distinctly that they were headed by a man who carried the stars and stripes in an edition about the size of an ordinary pocket handkerchief.

Not far from where we were working, these brave warriors made a halt and rested for a while, and I took the opportunity to ask one of the men, where they were going, and for what purpose. In reply I was told in tip-top Tiperrary brogue, that the expedition had set out for the purpose of exploring the river thirty miles up and down with a view to driving away all "foreigners." The crowd was a motley one, and as to nationality, somewhat mixed. Irishmen were marching to drive off the Kanakas, who had assisted brave Captain Sutter, of immortal fame, when he was in difficulty with the Californians. They were joined by Dutchmen and Germans, who could not speak a word of English, but were jabbering together in their own harsh jargon, while

CAPTAIN JOHN A. SUTTER.

none of them had ever been in the United States. Then there were a few New Yorkers, who really went out for the purpose of looking after a good claim, already opened, but all had joined hands in the alleged common interest of protecting the native soil (for that was really the only native feature about it), against the invasion of "foreigners."

I never learned whether this expedition met with any success or not, and whether they derived any benefit from their undertaking. I worked along with my partners through the months of August and September, when we began to discuss the advisability of getting out of the mountains. Matters were not altogether satisfactory. I suffered from scurvy, and our food was not of the best, as provisions were getting very scarce and prices had risen in proportion. I had tried to wing-dam some of our claims, so as to find out whether there was anything in the bed of the stream or not, but my efforts had proved futile, as we could not succeed in drying the claims. I cannot say that we felt disheartened at our difficulties, but the circumstances could not be called encouraging, and we recognized the fact.

There was one thing, about this time, which caused me a good deal of trouble and considerably puzzled my imagination It was the mystery with which the miners surrounded all matters appertaining to prospecting. One man in particular put my patience to a test in this regard, and it was his reticence which ultimately caused me to receive a lesson on some of the points of etiquette observed among miners in those days.

The man I refer to was the same who had sold me a rocker for the trifling pay of twelve ounces and a half. I was in the habit of occasionally calling at his camp, and always found him particularly friendly and affable. It seemed, therefore, strange to me that, while he would converse with me freely on all other matters, as soon as I asked him for any information in regard to finding gold, he became as dumb as the proverbial clam. He belonged to a company from Waterloo in the State of New York, and he used to go out prospecting, staying away often from eight to ten days at a stretch. It was more in particular, when he returned from these trips, that I used to visit him. I knew that there was something called Wambo's Bar; that the gold became finer about this locality and ultimately ran out altogether, and I also knew that a Mr. Van——(something) used to go out prospecting with my friend. But to all my interrogations as to where they had been, what success they had met with, or anything else that came natural to me to ask, I received evasive answers, or no response at all, until one day my friend made me acquainted with the code that guided a miner's tongue in those regions.

"Look here young fellow," he said, "if there is a thing a miner don't care to talk about, it is where he has been, and you might say that it is just as good as law among prospectors, that every man keeps mum. Let me give you a bit of advice: When you get to feel that way yourself; that you have struck it rich in a new prospect, don't you advertise your good luck and have a band playing outside your tent to celebrate; but after sundown, when everything is settled in camp, and your nearest neighbor is snoring loud enough to compete with a cathedral organ, you just pack your traps on your back and skip out of camp; and if you should meet anybody on the road, who should ask you where you are going, just tell them that you have had poor luck and are making back for town. But the next morning, bright and early—or as soon as you can reach it—stick your pick into your new claim and work it for all it is worth, before anybody comes to interfere with your happiness."

This visit to my friend settled in my mind the fact that I could find out nothing by inquiry, and that if I wanted to learn anything, I must depend upon my own experience. Just about this time I had my finger badly jammed with a rock and had to go to Foster's Bar to have it dressed, for which I paid one-half ounce, and as

I was partly HORS-DE-COMBAT for the time being and needed a rest, I divided the dust with my mates, and went into store-keeping.

But I soon discovered that store-keeping did not suit me, and I had not been long in it, before I wished to get out again and away to the mines. One morning two men came in to purchase something. They had three mules with them, heavily laden, and they stated that they were on their way to Foster's Bar, but had lost the trail. After they had bought the goods, they paid me in lumpy gold, and left. Now this incident told a tale at the same time as it settled a question that I had often asked myself, and in response assured me that they were washing gold higher up the river.

I made up my mind at once that I was going to have some of that gold myself, and accordingly stored away what goods I had and went to Foster's Bar, where I bought a horse and a mule for the expedition. During the first night, the horse was either stolen from me, or it strayed away, but I was anxious to proceed on my journey at once, provided I could find somebody who would join me, and I made inquiries all through the camps with a view to finding a partner. Foster's Bar, at this period, presented a singular appearance. It was crowded with men, and if one went up to the camps, his olfactory organs would perceive in a somewhat disagreeable manner, the perfumes of pork and slap-jacks, arising from a hundred frying-pans, and causing an odor, which could only be compared with all the soap factories in Ohio, frying out at full blast. There was much sickness about this place at that time, and I do not wonder at it, for the smell of the place was enough to make any body feel out of sorts In almost every tent somebody was sick, and every here and there a squalid-looking individual might be seen crawling on his hands and knees to his tent door, through smoke and dust, (not gold dust however), but even these invalids would devour half-cooked slap-jacks, or whatever grub was at hand, apparently with the greatest relish, for it is a well-known fact, that in 1849, sick people had as good appetites as those who were well and able to work.

It is not to be wondered at, that in this crowd I failed to find companions for my expedition. I had everything ready to go, and had bought a United States rifle and one of Allen's pepper boxes, but I was doomed to disappointment. Twice I had the promise of company, but both times the parties backed out, and the season was now so far advanced that I almost gave up the idea of going this fall, and returned to Bullard's Bar, where, it will be remembered, I had the balance of my goods stored. Among the things, I had here a small quantity of brandy, a liquor highly prized in those days, and also some lime juice, which was used extensively on the diggings as an antidote for scurvy.

I now thought I was settled at store-keeping for the winter, but I was to breathe the mountain air and pursue my search for treasure sooner than I had anticipated.

CHAPTER III.

Off for the Mines Again—The Early Discovery of Gold—A Free Mason of 1820—An Interesting Document in San Francisco—Did the Priests Hold the Secret?—Captain W. H. Thomas' Account—Under the Wild Onions—"Cut-Eye" Foster—A Sickly Man from Massachusetts—Jim Crow is Introduced—Over the Range—Facing the Wilds.

One day some colored men came into my store. They were working below the bar, and after taking a drink they became genial and began to talk about the diggings up the river. I gave them to understand that I was desirous of exploring those regions for the purpose of prospecting, and after a little while they all agreed to join me in the attempt to find gold there. Once more I closed my store. Whatever was of any use to us, I packed, ready for the trip, and wound up my business in short order according to regular California style. We then went as far as Foster's Bar, where we crossed the river, and on the night of October the 5th, 1849, we camped on the hills. Once more I was off in search of treasure, and as I rolled myself in my blanket that evening, I thought of the "lumpy gold," the two men had brought to my store some time ago, strange visions floated across my mind as I closed my eyes, and in my dreams I fancied that I was unearthing untold millions of hidden treasure.

I cannot here refrain from commenting upon the discovery of gold in California. It is a universal idea that gold was first discovered in these parts in the year 1848, and we, who were among the early seekers for

SUTTER'S MILL, COLOMA, CAL.—WHERE MARSHALL FIRST DISCOVERED GOLD.

the precious metal, undoubtedly flattered ourselves that we unearthed secrets which had been hidden from time immemorial. This however was only partly true. It is a fact that we found gold in locations where hitherto it had never been known to exist, but on the whole, California was then known to many as a gold-bearing country.

On that October night, to which I have referred, I, for one, considered that we were among the original discoverers, but I soon had experiences, which persuaded me that I was mistaken. It was not an uncommon thing to fall in with Indians, who offered gold for trade, and it seemed reasonable to conclude that if the Indians knew of its presence at that period, they might have known it long before.

I have since learned that the records of the Monterey Custom House show that between 1838 and 1846, during the Spanish rule, as much as $5 000 in washed gold or gold dust was exported to various parts of the world. During that same period one Don Alfreds Robinson, who came to California in 1828, took $1.000 worth of gold to Philadelphia on behalf of Don Abel Stearns of Los Angeles, and delivered his goods to the mint in the quaker city. The same Don Abel Stearns, who had a store at Los Angeles, which was the most important establishment in the whole region, was a Massachusetts man, who had received the Spanish title. In 1820 he was made a Master Mason in the Washington Lodge of Roxbury, and, probably because of his affiliation with this important craft, he met with the most pronounced success in his career. In 1836, at the age of forty, he married a Miss Bandini, who was then only fifteen years old, and in addition to being esteemed the greatest beauty of California, was the daughter of one of the most prominent Spanish gentlemen. Stearns accumulated a considerable fortune during his time, and a great deal of it was obtained through trading gold from the Indians.

In regard to the cargo of gold which Robinson took to Philadelphia in 1842, there exists a document, representing the certificate of deposit at the mint, and this interesting paper may still be found among the archives in the Pioneers' Hall in San Francisco.

When the question is asked how the fact of the presence of gold could be withheld from the outer world for so long, the answer suggests itself, that the secret was kept through the efforts of the priesthood.

This particular matter has been ably discussed by Captain W. H. Thomas, president of the New England Society of California Pioneers, who paid his first visit to California as early as 1843. In a letter addressed to the BOSTON HERALD the Captain writes as follows:

"This supremacy was at its highest in 1765, when from the missions in San Diego a chain of twenty-four missions was extended northward. Junipero Serra was Priest-President of all the missions in California, and was an intelligent, persevering, enterprising man. He was not only instrumental in founding mission after mission, but he added to the herds thousands of sheep and cattle.

"I have been six times to California and have talked with priests of many nationalities—Mexican, Spanish, Irish and American—and I am confident, from what they say that Junipero Serra knew about the gold ; but he was a singular character, and ruled with a hand of steel, so that gold was a word that no one dared to utter. He had the history of Peru and other foreign countries in his mind, and he knew that an influx of gold-hunters

CARMEL MISSION, NEAR MONTEREY, CAL.

meant terror and destruction and the failure of all his great plans.

"It is claimed that the first discoveries were in 1848, when the whole world was turned topsy-turvy with the astonishing news. I, myself, was in California in 1843, and stayed there three years, and I can positively say that gold was known here then, for I saw it in Monterey. On Sundays the Indians would come into town, naked except for a cloth around their loins, and exchange a little pinch of gold for a drink of ARGUADIENTE or na tive rum. No one knew where they got the gold, but sometimes they would have several dollars' worth of the precious dust. This was an old custom, for at Mission Carmel I interviewed, through an interpreter, an aged Indian, who said that when he was a boy gold was found in the mountains and rivers round about, and the natives would wash out a panful in order to get a good drunk on Sunday, which Christian Indians were forbidden to do He thought that there was still gold in the mountains, but he was so old that he had forgotten where it was.

"In 1844 Andres Castillero, the same person who afterward discovered the New Almaden quicksilver mine in Santa Clara county, while traveling from Los Angeles to Monterey, found near the Santa Clara river a great number of water-worn pebbles, which he gathered up and carried with him to Santa Barbara. He there exhibited them, said they were a peculiar species of iron pyrites and declared that, according to Mexican miners, wherever they were found there was a likelihood of gold being also found. A ranchero named Francisco Lopez, who was living on the Piru creek—a branch of the Santa Clara river—but who happened at the time to be at Santa Barbara, heard Castillero's statements and examined his specimens. Some months afterward, having returned home, he went out to search for strayed cattle. At noon, when he dismounted from his horse for the purpose of resting, he observed a few wild onions growing near where he lay. He pulled them up and in so doing noticed the same kind of pebbles as those to which Castillero had called his attention. Remembering what Castillero had said about them he took up a handful of earth and upon carefully examining it discovered gold. The news of this discovery, at the place which was called San Francisquito, about thirty-five miles northeast of Los Angeles, soon spread. In a few weeks a great many persons were engaged in washing and winnowing the sands and earth in search of gold.

"The auriferous fields were found to extend from a point on the Santa Clara river about fifteen or twenty miles from its mouth over all the country drained by its upper waters, and thence easterly to Mount San Bernardino.

"On May 14th, 1843, Alvardo wrote to the Prefect of the district, reproving him for not having given official notice of the discovery, and directing him to gather and forward an account of all circumstances of interest relating to the gold, for transmission to the Supreme Government.

"From that time to the present day there has been more or less working of these mines, but no places of very great richness have been found, and none to compare with those afterward discovered on the tributaries of the Sacramento and San Joaquin."

The reader will no doubt pardon my deviating from the straight narrative, which I will now resume, but the matter presented in Captain Thomas' letter seems to me well worth quoting. On the morning of the 6th of October, we assembled at the spring and had breakfast, and then a consultation took place among some of us, as to who should join the expedition, and who should stay behind.

The reason for this was that there were about forty Kanakas, who had worked with the colored men at my camp, and who now wanted to join us. But as they had neither money nor rations, they expected to live on our provisions during our prospecting tour, and as we did not propose to make pre-arrangements for a famine in camp, we came to the conclusion that the Kanakas must stay behind. I therefore told them that if they intended to come with us, they must look out for themselves, as we could not spare them any provisions, neither did we know where we were going, nor when we should return, and our chances of starvation were quite as good as our chances of success.

This decided the matter and limited our company to two white men, including myself, a white boy named Michael Duvarney, who proved himself a little hero, and seven colored men. I soon perceived that my caucasian companion—I mean the adult—was not the kind of person to do any good in the wilds of the mountains. I think the poor fellow was from Michigan, and he was one of the most dejected looking objects I ever beheld. I first thought that he was love-sick, but when I saw him spending his evenings at the camp-fire swallowing Brandreth's pills as quickly as a chicken would eat dough, I concluded that it was his stomach, and not his heart which was out of order. At all events, his presence was a decided damper on the whole company, with his melancholy appearance, his pills and his spleen. I soon discovered that the rest thought with me, that our Michigan man was not a fit subject for our company, and when we came to the Slate Range, I advised him to return. A few words about the hardships that awaited us, the chances of being torn to pieces by grizzlies, and other minor matters, which might impede our march to success, soon persuaded our friend, in future, to swallow his pills in more congenial surroundings, and he returned, to the evident joy of all concerned.

While we were camped at Slate Range, one of our men went back for a Kanaka and an Indian. The Kanaka he returned with, was Jim Crow, whose name still lives in those regions, and of whom I shall have more to say later on. After his arrival we moved to the camp of "Cut-Eye" Foster, whom I now met for the first time, and bought and distributed a supply of flour. Foster's camp was then close to ours, in what was then known as Oak Valley, and I tried my best to get all possible information from him. He seemed to think that prospects, in the comparatively unexplored regions, were good, but held that it was now too late in the season to venture so far into the mountains, and as a matter of fact, we saw several white men returning. I felt sure that had my companions belonged to the same race, they would not have desired to go 'till spring, but as it was, we were all determined to push on, and chose our route, not along the river bank, as "Cut-Eye" advised, but across the ridge by way of the present elevation of the Mountain House.

I have a lively recollection of getting ready to go, when some of our men undertook to clean our fire-arms. They took them all to pieces, and having made a roaring fire, placed them upon it. Many of the barrels were charged, and as they became heated they began to go off, and a running fire was kept up for sometime. Shot and bullets were flying in all directions, and everybody hastened to take shelter behind the trees. I was just returning through the woods, and hearing the fusillade, quickened my pace to see what the racket was about, when I was suddenly halted by my own men, who shouted to me to keep behind the trees. For a while I was at a loss to understand the situation, but when I realized it, I could not help smiling, although I made it understood that in future we would clean our fire-arms in a somewhat different manner.

We bade good bye to "Cut-Eye," and made for the wilderness with the winter close at hand, but we relied upon our courage, our determination and our physical strength.

CHAPTER IV.

Through the Woods—Meeting Two Grizzlies—Across the River in a Hurry—McNair's Island—The Color of Gold—Over the Ridge—We Strike the River—A Noise in the Bushes—Round the Point—A Scene that Charmed Us—The Forks at Last—Sullen Miners—Moving Camp—Mules on the Hillside—Camped on the Yuba—Reminiscences of Philo Haven.

We had not gone very far, when we came upon two small trees, which had been blazed to indicate the road to the river at Goodyear's Bar, but we did not care to start at this point and so kept up the divide, until we reached a place where now stands Galloway's Ranch. Here we made a halt and held a consultation as to how to approach the river. Our journey resumed, we struck a blind trail, which left us in the midst of the thicket, but we did not care to go back, and made our way through the chapparal, until at last we reached the top of the ridge, which separates the two canyons, later known as Jim Crow and Secret Canyons. No sooner had we reached this altitude, than we met with an adventure which rather startled us. As our mules were jogging along, carrying the pack, and we came after, puffing and blowing with the exertions of the ascent, a grizzly inquisitively approached the animals and so scared them that they started down the hillside at a rate which would have done credit to any equine racer, and for awhile we wondered whether we should ever have the good luck to see our frying pans, rockers and the rest of the outfit again. I did not see the bear, and up to that time considered myself somewhat unfortunate in regard to seeing the animal so characteristic of California, for he always got out of the way before I could clap eyes on him, even when he succeeded in scaring one of the company. One night however, as I lay rolled up in my blankets and sound asleep, I was

LOOKING FOR THE COLOR

roused by the warm breath of a grizzly, who quickly decamped when I made a sudden motion, and he found that the place was already occupied. But I was not long to remain without an introduction to the King of the California forest.

When we had pulled ourselves together after the scare, and quieted the frightened mules, we started down the hill and ultimately made our camp at a point which has since been called McNair's Island. Here some of the company tried a pan or two of dirt, looking for the color, but it proved pretty hard to raise.

Meanwhile, three of us took a stroll up the river to explore the locality, and in sauntering back to camp, we had the second adventure of the day. Charley Wilkins, who was walking a little ahead, suddenly stopped, and pointing to a moving mass of something which was coming forward from the brush, exclaimed: "What is that?" But he did not wait for an answer, for we all simultaneously perceived that the unshapely object was a huge grizzly, who came to bid us welcome. Never did three men vacate the space they occupied more quickly than we did. We fairly flew towards the river and plunged in, making for the opposite shore at full speed.

The bank was high and steep, and in our endeavors to climb up by holding on to grass or loose rocks, we fell backwards into the water several times, splashing about like young ducks and never even daring to look 'round. When we ultimately got ashore there was not a sign of the enemy, who evidently had never attempted to pursue us.

We now made for our camp, and arming ourselves with the whole arsenal at our command, all hands marched out to kill the bear, but he had gone, leaving nothing but his track. From that day henceforth however I was satisfied that I had seen a grizzly, and no mistake about it.

As soon as we had returned from our fruitless pursuit some of the company went across the river to a point opposite Secret Canyon, where some work had already been done, and here we found the first gold since leaving Bullard's Bar. We moved our camp across to the flat and went prospecting up and down the river. In some few places we found gold, but not in any quantity, as it never ran over a dollar to the pan. The most gold seemed to be at Negro Bar, situated a short distance from Omit's Flat, but, seeing that the locality would not pan out satisfactorily, we decided to strike camp and look for the North Fork. Of this we had heard various reports and, thinking that the best way to find it was by going North, we steered our course up the hill in that direction, leaving McNair's Island behind us. It took us nearly half a day to reach the top of the steep hill, and on our arrival there a poor prospect greeted us, for, although we thought we could see from the lay of the land, where the North Fork must be, it was by no means clear to us how to get there. For the purpose of finding water and also the best way of getting down this dry and barren ridge, we now unpacked our traps, and, dividing ourselves into two parties, we went about reconnoitering the country. I, together with three others, followed the ridge, in what I took to be the direction of the Forks, and when we came to the rocky point above Breyfogle Flat, we suddenly beheld the river shining before us in the sunlight. Ah me, how pleased we were at that sight! We now knew that our judgment had been correct, and we hastened down to the stream and quenched our thirst in the rippling waters.

Two of the men wanted to go back at once, but Albert and I were determined to proceed, and leaving them behind, we kept on down the river. We had not gone far, however, when we were overtaken by our companions.

They had heard some mysterious sound in the bushes

behind them, and the experiences of the day had made them nervous. They were only too pleased to join us again, and so we went along the river together, until we came to the first island above the Forks, when they once more insisted on returning. I then told them that if they would only go round the next point with me, I would go back at once, if nothing particular came in view which demanded our attention, and to this they consented.

I have often thought since how the curtain of fate may be likened to the thinnest fabric of gauze, as it severs us from circumstances or conditions, with which we are united the moment it rises. Had those men refused to listen to me that day, and prevailed upon me to turn back before rounding that point, who can tell what would have been my lot in after life? It was the traversing of those few hundred yards which decided so much that afterwards became of interest to me, and gave me for many years to come, friends, influence, even renown, and to-day, notwithstanding bitter experiences, many cherished memories.

As we rounded the point we beheld the Forks, the place of which we were in search, and which afterwards received the name of Downieville, while it became one of the most prominent points in the history of the Golden Age of California.

The scene that burst upon us was one of marvelous beauty, and after these many years it still lies before me like a lovely panorama, in my recollection of the moment when I first saw it. The silence of the woods was broken only by the rushing of the meeting currents below and the soughing of the breeze through the foliage. The sun was in the western sky, causing a variation of light and shadow to fall upon the landscape, which was exceedingly pleasing. The hillsides were covered with oaks, bending their crooked branches in phantastic forms, while here and there a mighty pine towered above them, and tall willows waved their slender branches, as it were, nodding us a welcome. They grew along the branch of the North Fork, where now stands the Craycroft building, and on the present site of the St. Charles Hotel stood a cluster of pines. Down on the very brink of the river grew a beautiful grove of Fir trees, and as we approached, a frightened deer ran from the thicket and made for the woods. Near a little spring, which bubbled up and made the surroundings look fresh and verdant, stood a few pieces of bark on end— the only sign that human foot had ever trod this region, and further indicating that here at some previous time the Indians had camped.

Add to this the waters leaping over rock and bowlders, and the clear azure sky stretching like a canopy over the whole landscape, and you have the picture, as far as I can describe it, that I first beheld, when I approached the Forks.

When we came to the Junction of the two streams and made our observations, Albert pointed out to me the fact that the water in the North Fork was not so clear as that in its sister branch. There could be but one explanation of this phenomenon—that men were at work somewhere above, "Hunting For Gold." None were now inclined to return. Curiosity and suspense got the better of reluctance and we started up the stream to explore.

After tramping a considerable distance we found that our conclusions had been right. We heard voices and the clanging of tools, and presently came upon a company of three men, who were at work on a little bar, just below the Bluebanks. The men seemed considerably surprised to see us, and as it were, at once, instinctively tried to hide what gold they had in their pan, but one of our boys caught sight of it nevertheless, and thus we were assured, not only that there was gold in that location, but also that it was quite different looking from what we had seen at Bullard's Bar.

I tried to get into conversation with the three men, but it was of no avail. When I asked them about the diggings, they would answer me, "yes;" "no;" "dunno;" "can't say," or pretend not to understand me at all, and after a quarter of an hour, spent in interrogations, I was no wiser than when I first started. I took a drink of water, and lighting my pipe, tried them on a different lay.

" What chance is there to get a claim here ? " I asked. It seemed that I had struck the keynote of conversation with them, for they at once became more communicative. "The chances are slim, " they said, but they had a claim they would sell, and they went on using their best powers of oratory in order to induce us to strike a bargain, there and then, something which, however, none of us would think of doing. These three men were working there in one crevice, one digging, another carrying dirt and the third working the rocker, and, from their manner of speech, there was every indication that they verily believed that when that crevice was worked out, there was no more gold to be found in California.

But their sullenness and reticence did not discourage us in the least. We knew that if there was anything to be had in these quarters, we had the right kind of company for locating it, and we determined before many days to make our new neighbors aware of the fact. So we left them to themselves and returned to our camp to report progress, and there was much rejoicing that evening.

WORKING THE ROCKER

The next morning we were up bright and early, and struck camp to remove to the Forks. The trail was bad, and every now and then a mule would slide down the declivity, sometimes a hundred feet or more. In order to keep them from going clear to the bottom we had to use the long ropes, used for tying them up with at night. We carried the one end coiled up in our hands, the mule being at the other end, and when the animal seemed likely to go too far down the hill, we slewed him head up, or, in sailor parlance, headed him to the wind. We had quite a hard time of it getting along in this fashion, moreover as it took us two days and one night to travel from McNair's Island to the Forks, and all the time without water. How different now, when the same journey can be made in one brief hour, but such are the changes wrought by time.

As soon as the thirsty mules saw the water in the river below, there was no more necessity for driving them. They scampered off on their own account, and never stopped till they stood in the water, drinking it in long, refreshing draughts. We unpacked on Jersey Flat, and I spent my first night at the Forks of the Yuba.

In the following pages I shall have considerable to say about this spot and its surroundings, but, as I write of my arrival there, I am put in mind of one of the very first men I met in this locality, whom I have known in after life as a friend and a gentlemen. This man is Mr. Philo Haven.

Mr. Haven was round those quarters in the early part of '51. Many years after he reminded me of the Indian shelter, referred to, and agreed with me that when I came on the ground, there was no other camp at the Forks. He told me that when he arrived at the South Fork he came upon a man skinning a deer, and being hungry, offered him any price for a few pounds of the meat; but the fellow would not sell any, not even when he was offered pound for pound--gold for venison. Mr. Haven did not know that I was at the Forks and had provisions, and when he made up his mind to go up that way, he paid a fellow $160 for a lot of half-decayed goods, which had been brought to Goodyear's Bar from a deserted mining store. The price was four dollars per pound all round, including hams, flour, nails, tobacco and other necessaries, but the edibles were hardly fit for eating. When he came to my camp, we were already well settled and kept a sort of open house for all travelers, who were welcome to share anything with us, which we had to eat. Charley Wilkins and Albert Callis, the two colored men, would cook for them and make them feel at home, and as far back as those early days I had become known as Major Downie, and travelers in search of shelter or relief were often told to go to Major Downie's cabin.

One thing I feel called upon to discuss here to some extent—the first discovery of gold at the Forks. I am aware that in one history of California, it is claimed that Frank Anderson was the original discoverer, whereas I claim that the precious metal was first unearthed by our company, and in this, Mr. Haven agrees with me, in as much as he considers it a mistake to give the honor to Anderson. It is at all events a fact that this man did not arrive at the flat till after we had been there for some time. He, and another man named Jack Culton, came along with Mr. Haven and were engaged by him to work a small, rich bar, for which they were paid fifty dollars per day, but the party did not leave Bullard's Bar for the Forks, till the 9th of January, '51. The bar that Mr. Haven was working, panned out well, for after a comparatively short stay, the company—four in number—left with 130 pounds of Gold. For my own part, I merely claim that we were the first white men who took out gold at the Forks, and I firmly believe that the Indians were aware of its presence there long, before our arrival.

CHAPTER V.

Down to Business—A Fish Story—Lead Weights and Brass Weights—Crevicing—Breyfogle Flat—A Mule in a Hornet's Nest—Mamoo the Egyptian—A Negro from Virginia—Rich Finds—Treacherous Friends—Mr. John Potter—Flour Worth More Than Gold—A Very Sick Man—On the Site of Downieville.

I have remarked in the previous chapter that I relied upon my company for finding gold in these environments, if gold were to be found. I knew that as prospectors we had the right kind of men in our crowd, and as will be seen, we soon had an opportunity to astonish our sulky neighbors.

First of all we arranged matters so as to operate systematically. One man was to keep camp, another to look after the mules, and the rest went in twos or threes up and down the river in search of patches, which would be worth working. We made it a provision that everyone should have whatever he happened to get into his pan. Anyone, who chose to do so, might go alone, but everybody had to report his day's doings in camp at night. It was also made a rule that whoever discovered any rich bar should have the first choice of the ground, and I may say that these regulations were strictly adhered to and found to be of great common advantage. They prevented a good deal of underhand work and gave us all a fair chance in the undertaking, for without them, two men, for instance, might go out together, and if they made a find, divide up between them, and report no progress.

In speaking of our start at the Forks, I am reminded of what my reader will no doubt call a fish story It is; but it is nevertheless a true one, and let this be said with all due deference to any narrator of piscatorial adventure. While we were camped on Jersey Flat, Jim Crow caught a monster salmon, weighing nearly fourteen pounds. We boiled the fish in the camp kettle, and afterwards, when we examined the water, we found gold at the bottom of it. Truly those have been appropriately called:

"The days of old—
The days of Gold."

We had a somewhat varied experience for some time after our arrival in these parts. We discovered a small bar at the lower end of Zumwalt Flat, which showed a good prospect, and therefore moved our camp up that way. It should be born in mind that I am calling many of these places by the names they received after my first stay there in '49. On Zumwalt Flat we went to work with a rocker, and the first day washed out about twelve ounces. As this looked very encouraging, we stayed here, till we considered the bar worked out.

While in this vicinity I dug a hole near a small bar that was afterwards named Tin-cup Diggings, and found it would pay about one dollar to the pan. For some time I worked by myself, but as I could get nobody to help me, I abandoned it.

We had some difficulty in weighing our gold. Some claimed to be making from thirteen to fourteen ounces a day, crevicing in the banks, but this measure was obtained by means of a lead weight, of which Jack Smith used to say with much indignation, that it was fit only for killing dogs with. We then started regulating our weights and did that by means of a half-ounce brass weight. We ultimately succeeded in getting, what we took to be a correct eight-ounce weight, and this was brought into requisition almost every day, for quite a while.

We returned to the Forks above, and worked on a bar there, until we thought that it was worked out, but afterwards found gold all along the banks, sometimes several hundred dollars within the short space of a few hours, very seldom using even a shovel. Our principal mining implements consisted of a butcher's knife, a tin pan and a crowbar. Whenever we saw a place that looked promising, we would cross the river on the rocks, if it happened to be on the opposite side, and delving into the crevice, dig out what there was in it, so quickly that we fairly astonished our sulky neighbors, who a few days before had taken us for innocents in the wilderness.

Our principal grievance when crevicing, was the scarcity of dirt, which often caused us great disappointments, for just as our hopes had been raised to the highest pitch of anticipation, the rich spot would give out, and after spooning and scraping for a while, we would realize that we were hunting a phantom treasure.

The season was now far advanced, and it became a matter of serious consideration whether we should face the winter in the mountains, or return to less exposed quarters. So we held a consultation and ultimately concluded to stay, provided we could find a bar to work on, and at the same time continue to lay in a sufficient supply of provisions. We gave up the crevices and went in search of a bar where plenty of dirt could be easily obtained.

Four of our company went up the South Fork to the place which was afterwards known as Breyfogle Flat, and there found a prospect in the south bank, which they thought would do us for the winter. We then determined to move up there, and got ready. I paid a visit to our inhospitable neighbors, and bought from them a dug-out or burnt-out rocker, for which I gave one ounce, and then we set out for our new camping ground. We had the same trouble getting our mules along the hillside as described in a previous chapter, and adopted the same tactics for keeping them from sliding down to the bottom, as has already been mentioned. My mule met with an accident which caused the party both surprise and merriment in our little crowd. The poor brute got foul of a hornets' nest. Under normal conditions that mule was as sedate, sober-minded, and quiet a mule as ever carried a pack, and as long as I had known him he had never attempted any pace outside a walk. Our surprise may, therefore, be easily imagined, when all of a sudden, without any perceptible reason, he kicked up his heels cloudwards, then stood on his tail-end, and then for a moment left the alluvial soil altogether and hung between heaven and earth, and ultimately, on reaching the latter once more, made off at the pace of Tam 'o Shanter's famous mare. I saw everything that I had strapped on his back, fly off. Frying-pan, blankets, rocker, everything he was carrying was strewn along the course he took, and for every time anything came off the pack, he seemed to quicken his pace. Only one fortnate circumstance occurred during the whole affair—he chanced to run in the right direction, and when we at last caught up with him, we were still on the right track, but my rocker was smashed to atoms. When we arrived at the bar, we found that another party had reached it ahead of us, and therefore had the first choice of ground. I went to work with

Mamoo on a portion of the bar, facing the river for about ten feet. This Mamoo was an Egyptian and a follower of Mahomet, the Prophet of "the only God." He was born in Alexandria, and was a sailor by occupation. He came to San Francisco in '49, and hearing of the discoveries made by John Marshall and Captain Sutter, left the ship for the mines, as did nearly every sailor in those days. I first met him at Bullard's Bar, where he was in company with the Kanakas and Jim Crow, and as he appeared to be an apparently good fellow, I had willingly admitted him to our company.

It was on a Sunday evening when we pitched our camp on the new ground, and bright and early Monday morning we were ready for work. The piece that had been allotted to Albert Callis, proved particularly rich, and gold could be seen in considerable quaintity by simply removing the dirt with the foot. As I have said, we arrived at our camp on a Sunday, but although Albert kicked the dirt off in sundry places, and saw the yellow gold, he conscientiously covered the metal up again, as he would not remove it on the Sabbath. He came originally from Mathews County, Virginia, and I believe, was a runaway slave.

He afterwards settled in Downieville, married and had quite a family, which he supported partly by working at his trade as a barber. I may state here that none of the darkies belonging to my company (I mean those of African blood), could have been induced to work Sunday, the effect, no doubt, of early training. But by and by Jim Crow came along. His religious and moral sentiments were both far below zero, and it did not take him long to remove the "taboo" from all the gold he could get sight of.

On the Monday two of us took out seventeen ounces,

on Tuesday, twenty-four, on Wednesday, twenty-nine, and early on Thursday, we had taken out forty ounces— as much as fourteen in one pan. Mamoo, who was cooking breakfast for us when we brought the gold into camp, looked with amazement at the treasure, and it seems to me I can yet hear him ejaculate : "Dam place worked out now! No more gold! No good!"

It was now high time for us to send below for provisions, and eight started out, taking with them all the mules. Jim Crow went with the rest, and they all intended to return in a few days. When I reflect upon the day when these men left camp, and the days that followed, it seems evident to me that every human being must have a mission to fulfill in this life, and until that is fulfilled, death would not dare overtake him. The four of us left in camp were, Albert Callis, Charles Wilkins, Michael Duvarney and myself, and as we bade good-bye, to the departing ones, we expected that they would speedily return, and little anticipated treachery. It became our lot to wait in vain. For many days we looked in expectation towards the direction from which they should return, but no one appeared, and but for providential circumstances and individual determination on our own part, our bones would have bleached in the wilderness, where we had been left to starve.

Many months had elapsed, when I again saw Jim Crow. Our next meeting was in the following spring, at Crow City, at the head of Jim Crow Canyon ,as these places are now called. He was in company with a number of Kanakas, and when I first caught sight of him, he was sitting face to face with little Mike, who was asking him all sorts of questions, as to why he did not return to our camp with the mules and provisions,

VIEW IN SACRAMENTO IN THE FIFTIES.

and what he had been doing all the time. The truth of the matter was, that Jim had never expected to see us alive again. He was making his way back with a company to the place where he had left us, to get some more of the gold, taking it for granted that we had starved to death long ago, and they had lost the trail.

Our meeting was accidental and more will be said of this later on. The rest of the boys, who went with him had gone on a spree and drank or gambled their dust away. In those days it was a common thing for miners, to come down to any settlement to change their dust for silver, often at any price, just to get coin enough with which to play poker, and my late companions had forgotten all about us over cards and whisky. Let me say here that I was never a heavy drinker. My favorite liquor, when disposed to indulge at all, was whisky, but I never drank to excess, and I never learned to play at cards during all the years I spent in the mines.

The four of us went to work with a will, but soon the rain set in, and our prospects began to look rather gloomy. The flour sack began to get more precious than the gold bag, and nobody came to our rescue, while Albert was lying sick in the camp. In this dilemma I made a trip down to the Forks, to see if I could fall in with anybody from the bars below, or perhaps hear something of my company. On this excursion I met John Potter, and told him of the fix we were in. Mr. Potter said that he had a partner down at Goodyear's Bar, and that they would like to winter up here, if there was any way of getting provisions up, and we discussed the situation together, and both returned to our camp, where we found Albert so bad that he had lost the use of his legs, while we could now make an over-hand knot in the flour bag. I have often, afterwards, in the crowded city, seen people begging for a small pittance, with which to buy bread, and it has then occurred to me how strange the reverse of that picture looks. There we were with a bag full of gold, anxious to pay dearly for anything that would sustain life, with no chance of purchasing even the poorest meal. The situation was becoming desperate, and something had to be done.

We then decided to take Potter and his partner, William Griffith, into our company, and as we had given up all hopes of the return of our men, it was decided that Potter should go down to Goodyear's Bar, to make arrangements for provisions, while we moved to the Forks. After he had left us, we started on our journey, but no one can imagine what difficulties we had to fight with. I had found a poor, half-starved mule in the woods. It had evidently strayed from some departed company, and I brought it into camp. On the back of this wretched animal we seated our sick comrade, and packing our traps on our own shoulders, we made the best of it, while the cold November rain continued to fall. We crossed the river, where Craycoft's mill was afterwards built, and thus entering the Forks from the branch, we made a roaring fire and settled on the site, which was later on called Downieville. Our tent was the only one at that time, as nobody else was then camping in the solitude of these wild surroundings, and here we now anxiously awaited the arrival of John Potter.

During my absence at Goodyear's Bar, which will be discussed in the following chapter, one of our party started building a cabin. The next party to arrive was a man named Kelly with a company, and soon after came Mr. S. Wood and his company. From these latter, who settled on Jersey Flat, I tried in vain to obtain some rations. Mr. Wood had gone back and left a man in charge of his stores, and he would not be persuaded to part with any of them, even at exhorbitant prices, which we offered. I must state here in justification of Mr. Wood, that he afterwards expressed his great regret at this, and assured us that had he, or his partner, been on the ground, we would certainly have obtained relief. As it was, there was nothing left for us but "chewing the rag" and await the return of the absent John Potter.

CHAPTER VI.

Death of a Friend—Andrew Goodyear—Bone Soup—At Simmons' Camp—Cooking Under Arms—Four Dead Mules—"Cut-Eye" Out of Temper—The Ax On The Ledge—Back at the Forks—The First Dwelling in Downieville—Christmas—The Stars and Stripes in the Sierras—Magnificent Scenery.

When John Potter arrived, he brought the somewhat discouraging news that provisions were on the way, but not in sufficient quantity to last us through the winter. Miles Goodyear was very ill and not expected to live, and he advised me to go down at once and secure more supplies, as Andrew, the younger brother of the sick man, had intimated that in case Miles died, he would leave the mountains. I hesitated for a few days, and meanwhile received news of Mr. Goodyear's death, which occurred, as far as I can place the date, on the 12th of November, 1849. His remains were buried in a rocker, but were afterwards removed by his brother Andrew, and interred in consecrated ground, in more civilized surroundings.

As soon as I heard of Mr. Goodyear's death, I set out for the bar to procure provisions, taking with me Billy Griffith and Mike Duvarney. We passed the place, on our road, where they had buried Goodyear, and soon reached the camp. We were doomed to disappointment and hardships, for expecting a supply of provisions, and being unwilling to stay in the locality, Andrew had already made an agreement to sell them to Sexton, Russell, and Dr. Vaughn, the physician who had attended his brother during his illness. At the time when we struck the bar, they were having rather hard luck. Rations were very scarce, and men were ekeing out an existence by subsisting upon a beef they had found lying upon the bar. By the time we arrived the meat was all gone, but they continued making soup of the bones, and the kettle containing this, to our palates, savory mess, was kept boiling for all it was worth. It is wonderful what one can relish when hunger drives him.

Six head of cattle were expected up at this time, and Andrew agreed to let us have two of them, Woods and his partner having contracted for the rest. On this occasion Andrew Goodyear showed himself a generous, large-hearted man. He charged us only one hundred dollars a head, although he knew that starving and in distress as we were, we would gladly have given him four or five times that amount. He also gave me a little rice and some dried apples, which I sent up to the Forks. Kindness under such circumstances, makes an indelible impression upon one's mind, and in the hour of distress it has the same soothing effect as has the light from the cottage window, that shines through the dark and stormy night, and shows the wayfarer that he is near his friends. In the years that have since passed, I have often thought of this incident, and realized how few there were—and I may say, are—who would have acted in the same spirit as did Andrew Goodyear.

I now made arrangements with Messrs. Sexton, Russell and Dr. Vaughn, to purchase the expected provisions from them for the sum of $3,900. The price amounted to two dollars per pound all around, including the sacks, which were wet with snow.

I was anxious to get over the river so as to go

down to meet the men who were bringing up the goods, but the water had risen—it was rushing past, and I could neither wade nor swim across. Griffith was camped on the opposite shore in a small blanket tent, and I indicated to him that I desired him to fell a tree which was bending over the river, so as to form a bridge for me to cross upon. He understood me, and at once set to work. For two days he labored hard, but when at last the tree fell, and I was ready to go over, the swift current swept it down the stream, and I was still on the wrong side of the river. So there was nothing to do but to await further developments. But it was very tedious waiting. The bones were getting scarce, and our larder was at a minimum, when, just as we were wondering how the hide would do, if properly cooked, we were saved such culinary experiment, for the water fell, and we were enabled to cross the river and join Bill Griffith.

As it happened, it did not seem to make much difference on which side of the river we were. We had only got into another starvation camp, and we concluded that we would have to take to the hills to find something with which to keep us alive, and once more Mike, Bill and myself set out, accompanied by a man named Morrison. Having succeeded in climbing the hill, then we went up the divide hoping to get to Simmons' camp, where the firm of Hawley, Simmons & Co., kept a store. We had all we could do to make any headway on this journey. A man's heart depends upon his stomach, to a great extent, but if the latter is as empty as a vacuum, and has been so for some time, the former is inclined to go below par. We had our misgivings as to the result of the tramp, lest some of us should give out before reaching our destination, and little Mike was the first to yield to the hardships we had to endure. After all, he was only a child, and the little fellow bore himself most bravely until he was fairly worn out. We tried to carry him on our backs, but found that our strength did not allow us to proceed in this way, and we ultimately decided to leave Morrison behind with the boy, while Bill and I pushed on towards the camp.

Our difficulties increased. The November day soon came to a close, and night, cold and dark, fell upon us. Still we went on through the woods. There was a trail, which in the daytime we could have easily found, but in the dark we often found ourselves wandering from it, and one of us would then stand still, while the other would go in search of the trail.

A LONELY MOUNTAINEER

Every now and then we would call out to one another, and thus, in this manner, we moved onward, until a welcome light, shining towards us from a distance, denoted that we were approaching the end of our journey.

Simmons' store was at the time poorly stocked, but he was a good, generous-hearted fellow, and gladly shared his scanty supply with us. He gave us a bottle of brandy and a few slap-jacks, and after resting awhile, Bill went back to Morrison and Mike to bring them relief, and the next morning they all arrived in camp.

I spent quite a pleasant evening at Simmons' camp, and after these many years I still remember the company that was there, some of whom were particularly good fellows. Among the rest was Tim Harris, who was full of fun and a most amiable companion. He was waiting for Sexton to come up with his provisions and did much to entertain the company. We had a joke the next morning, as to who tumbled out of the bunk during the night, Harris or I; and to this day the question has never been settled. I am certain however that Tim was the man that had the "sugar in his pocket." Simmons treated us very well indeed, and when the rest came up he shared his flour with us, and we were now in clover, I must admit with every due respect to the temperance cause and its advocates, that our brandy proved, "the staff of life" to us, notwithstanding all that has been said to the contrary. It is true, no doubt, that there are circumstances and conditions of life, when liquor is not absolutely necessary, but let every honest temperance preacher try a little starving in the mountains with nothing to drink but snow water, and it is just possible that the whole fraternity will feel called upon to change opinion.

We stayed at Simmons' camp for several days,

expecting that the provisions, which were on the way, would arrive, but the party bringing them up had been delayed by the floods, caused by the incessant rain, and could not get across the river. I became impatient and set out to look for them, expecting to meet them, and if I should fail in this, I intended to go as far as Nye's crossing and buy rations. But they had succeeded after great difficulties, in crossing at Foster's Bar, and I fell in with them between this place and Slate Range, and then turned back with them. When we got to Goodyear's Bar, everybody there seemed delighted at seeing such a quantity of provisions at once, a sight that had not been presented to them for some time. We had the greatest difficulty in cooking our meals, for Andrew Goodyear's men were all Indians, and there were fifteen or sixteen of them. It was a hungry, thieving lot, and the first panful we cooked, went out of sight in the twinkling of an eye. We were determined to have a good, square meal at once, when we came into camp, and this was our first experience, but we changed our tactics. I did the cooking after this, and Mike and Bill watched the pan, knife and pistol in hand, and gave out that the first man, who put his hand into that pan, would go home minus his fingers. We then enjoyed our meal and suspended any further cooking operations, until we got away from them. As previously stated we had already bargained for the provisions, and we now secured, in addition to what we had already bought, two gallons of vinegar for fifty dollars. Our goods consisted of 450 pounds of flour. a very small quantity indeed to winter on, and the rest was canned goods—meats, vegetables, fish, etc. I was offered half an ounce a pound for two of my hams, but declined the offer, as we had enough to do to get back home without packing gold. It seems strange now to think of the days, when in traveling, Mike and I sometimes used to quarrel about who should carry the gold bag, for although gold was what we suffered and toiled for, it often became very wearisome to carry it about, when we were tired and exhausted.

The next thing to be done was to get our stores packed up to our camp, and I made an arrangement with "Cut-Eye" to do the transportation, as he had plenty of horses and mules. He was to have thirty ounces for delivering them at Cox's Bar, as that was then the end of mule possibilities in those quarters, and I agreed to pay him for all horses or mules that might die on the road. I believe that those belonging to our company were the only 'forty niners, who remained in the mountains all winter, as the general thing was to go down below in the fall and return in the spring.

We had plenty of snow and rain on our trip up to the Forks, and we had to watch Cut-Eye very closely, as he was not altogether to be relied upon. When I reflect upon this trip, I am reminded of many scenes that happened, characteristic of the happy-go-lucky nature, of which most miners were possessed. I can see the boys yet scraping away the snow to make room alongside of some log that might be used as a table. Then the cards would be produced, the pipes lighted and the brandy bottle passed around, and in the midst of the wilds men would enjoy themselves with a most enviable disregard for the next difficulty that might arise. And as these scenes recur to me I am put in mind of the beautiful lines that begin with the question:

"Where is now the merry party—
I remember long ago?"

At Goodyear's Spring we halted. Bill was behind bringing a hundred weight of flour on a big horse belonging to "Cut-Eye." The sack had slipped forward and was right on the neck of the poor animal, which was thus considerably impeded in its progress and very nearly done for. When I saw them coming into camp, I began to think that it was a case, and that I would have to pay for one dead horse at all events, but fortune favored me, for the poor brute picked up again, when relieved of its load. As soon as we began descending Goodyear's hill, Mick and Bill went ahead to let the boys know at the Forks that we were coming, and it was indeed the best tidings they could hear. Old "Cut-Eye" was doing his utmost all along to string the trip out as much as possible. He had hoped that some of the mules would die on the road, so that he might make more money on the transaction. But with me it was a case of diamond cut diamond. I was up to his tricks and foresaw that the half starved mules could not last long. So I pressed on, and we arrived at Cox's Bar without losing any of them. I then paid Foster and advised him to hurry back, as the weather was getting dirty, and there was absolutely nothing for the mules to eat. He stayed with us that night however, and the next morning returned, some of the boys helping him to get over the hill. Before they left him four of the mules gave out, and he declared that the Major had got the start of him this time, but he would get even yet.

It was no easy matter to carry our stores on our shoulders from Cox's bar to the Forks, but we persevered, until we had it all in camp. The beef was stowed away in a snowdrift, and when packed in this manner and kept from the air, it will keep good for two or three months. We happened to get quite an addition to our supply in a somewhat singular manner. We met a party that had lost an ox. It had strayed from them, and they told us that if we could find it, we might keep it. After a diligent search, John Potter found the animal perched on the ledge of a rock above Cox's Bar on the south side of the river. How it got there is to this day inexplicable to me, but there it stood, unable to turn or get down, starving in the solitude, looking down upon the river in a sort of mute despair and beyond the reach of the lowing of its fellows. When we climbed up towards it, it turned its big sad eyes upon us with an expression, as if it hoped for relief, even from the race that bowed its head under the yoke and lashed its back, when its strength failed. It seemed a cruel thing to do, but there was no alternative, so we shot the poor brute, and it fell over the precipice, and as it rolled down the rocks, everyone turned his head away with a shudder.

Let it not appear to the reader that such tenderheartedness on the part of rough miners is improbable. Indeed, everybody who has lived in the wilds is well aware that even when a little squirrel ventures up to the tent and shows signs of confidence, no one will hurt it and it soon becomes a pet.

After we had done all the hard work, the snow ceased and we got a spell of pleasant weather. Just then some of our boys brought another mule load of provisions from Nye's Crossing and we were now prepared to meet the winter.

Meanwhile the building of our cabin had advanced, and when our provisions had been stored, we all lent a hand to finish it. The roof was covered with shingles, which were tied on with rawhide. The structure was crude as is all early backwood architecture, but it promised to answer its purpose well. It was strong, warm and watertight and would withstand the winter's storms. It became indeed well known to many, and there may be some, who read this, who will still remember the day when they were first welcomed in that cabin. It was moreover the first of its kind built at the Forks, and thus it virtually became the foundation of Downieville.

Since then I have dwelt in many houses, far more richly furnished in every respect, with modern conveniences and the latest improvements, but I must question whether I have been more comfortable in any of them, than I was in the cabin at the Forks. We were followed by Jack Smith and Gorman, afterwards came Kelly and Berry and several others, while Sam Woods, Jim Kearns and Murray settled on Jersey Flat.

It was on the 10th of December, 1849, that we moved into our new quarters, and then came Christmas. We were determined to make the best of the festive season, even though we were in the midst of the wilds, far away from friends and relations. Our greatest trouble was, that we had but one bottle of brandy in camp, and it took us some time before we could decide whether we would drink it on Christmas or New Years day. The discussion, pro and con, was very animated and resulted in the drawing of the cork on Christmas morning. It was quite early, when this important event took place, and we made punch with the liquor, using hot water and nutmeg. We drank to absent friends, to wives and sweethearts and to the great American Nation. Gradually as the sun rose higher in the heavens and the brandy got lower in the bottle, we became more enthusiastic. I had a small representation of the stars and stripes in my possession, and we determined that on this day it should adorn our house. So I climbed upon the roof with the flag in one hand, a pistol in the other. I made a short speech, waved the flag and fired a few shots and finished up by giving three cheers for the

DONNER LAKE, SUMMIT OF THE SIERRAS.

American Constitution. Then I fixed the flag on the gable point, and we all shouted for joy when we saw it unfurled to the breeze for the first time in the fastnesses of the Sierras.

I cannot conclude this chapter without drawing attention to the magnificent scenery that surrounded us. Summer and winter, the grandeur of nature in the Sierras is so wonderful, that it becomes sublime. The towering mountains, the snow clad peaks, the lakes, the mountain streams and the variety of vegetation—all blend harmoniously and form pictures, which my pen is too feeble to describe. In the midst of such surroundings we laid the foundation of a community, which passed through all the weird phases of border life, into the more settled condition of advanced civilization.

The following pages will contain many strange tales of happenings in that community, adventures of men, and sometimes of women. They will relate the disappointments they suffered or the triumphs they achieved; show how confusion brought about self-made laws, if not always absolute justice, and explain to some extent the conditions that caused many men to remain poor, who might to-day have been worth millions.

CHAPTER VII.

Life in the Cabin—The Bill of Fare—A Prospecting Fever—The Dangers of Traveling—Arrival of Mrs. James Galloway—A Poor Gin Mill— Jack Smith and His Jokes—Up a Tree After Gold—Expensive Rations—William Slater—A Rush of Miners—Taking up Claims—The Necessity for Laws—

As I now proceed with my narrative, I will endeavor as far as possible to bring the incidents and occurrences out in the order in which they happened. The region I had adopted as my home, remained so for over eight years, and although I traveled about a good deal, I still made the Forks my headquarters. During that period I met with many vicissitudes, and many strange scenes were enacted, and such of them will be related, as will give the reader an adequate idea of life in the Califoria mines in the early days.

After we had done justice to Christmas, we went prospecting in different directions and met with very good success. Just then a Mr. Lord, who was camped on Jersey Flat, came over to see us. He made a long face, spoke of his hard luck, said he had a family back in the States, and that he was anxious to return. He wanted to make a small raise and would pay anything to anybody, who would put him on to a good claim. I took pity on the man and gave him part of my claim, and he soon proved himself a mean, ungrateful wretch. He at once set to work with his partner and made from one to two hundred dollars a day, taking out as much as $1460 worth in one day, while I had to be satisfied with a few ounces. As soon as he found out that his end of the claim was so much better than mine, he became very reserved and silent, and even went so far as to draw a dividing line with stakes, so as to separate his portion from the Major's. I had many experiences of such ingratitude but learned to understand that this is nothing more than might be expected; for nature, in making up, from motives of economy, sometimes uses the odds and ends and sends the poorer work into the world, thus making her more creditable productions appear to greater advantage.

We did not expect to be able to get any more provisions up till about the month of May, and we made our bill of fare accordingly. One man always stayed in camp to look after it and do the cooking, while the others were at work. Our greatest scarcity was flour, and so it was only used once a day. The dough being made, it was divided into six equal parts and put into the oven, and each man knew exactly what to expect. Our every day dinner consisted of beans and rice, but on Sundays, we generally had something extra. At this time I was working by myself and making out very well. I seldom took out less than a pound a day, and it happened several times that I was rewarded with a find of from twenty to thirty ounces. Potter and I afterwards worked together, and on rainy days, when we did not care about going very far away to work, we would work at intervals on the site where now stands Craycroft's mill, and often make three or four ounces in a few hours. Indeed, these were the palmy days of gold digging, when one for obvious reason saved all he found. We dried our gold in a shovel and weighed it in a pair of scales. big enough to weigh "grub" in, using lead weights. But if our weights were not quite exact, what of it! We had plenty of gold, and a few ounces, more or less was neither here nor there.

Some time during February, Wood and his partners sold us a quantity of provisions which had been left at Negro Tent, then known as Hollow Log, and on the 25th of February, 1850, we started out to bring them in. On this trip we fell in with "Cut-Eye" Foster, and another man, who were the first to come up to the mountains that spring.

It may seem strange that men who were doing as well as we were, should not feel settled. There we were, making plenty of gold, and yet we wanted to go somewhere else, where we could make more, and get ahead of the many miners the approaching spring would bring up that way, and when we learned that a great many men were at that time at Sleighville, waiting for a favorable opportunity to get to the Forks, we made up our minds that it was time for us to look for richer fields, lest we should be elbowed out of fairer chance in the general scramble of the spring rush.

Potter went up to Twist's Flat, as it is now called, and in prospecting struck a very rich patch opposite Negro Point. On his return we talked matters over, and he advised that we go up at once, but I had that day taken thirty ounces out during his absence, and this fact partly unsettled us. The following day Potter returned and took out thirty-two ounces, and this two ounces over and above what I had taken out, decided us in favor of going. But there were other circumstances to take into consideration. It would have been easy enough for us to leave the Forks with our blankets, but the transportation of our gold would cause more trouble. We soon came to the conclusion that if we attempted to take the gold with us, we should certainly be killed or at least robbed on the road, and as we could not leave it behind, we had no alternative but to stay where we were, which we determined to do.

Jack Smith and two or three others went prospecting, They a built a brush shanty somewhere about the head of Kanaka Creek, which was then called Indian Creek, and there were many who afterwards thought that Jim Crow and his Kanakas had wintered there. I had tried to take up a claim on the North Fork, but a dispute arising about it, I went back to the old place on the South Fork.

My narrative is now taking me into the month of March in the year 1850. But, before proceeding any further, I must mention one of the most memorable events that took place in the solitudes of the Sierras—the arrival there of the first white woman. It was just about the first of March, 1850, that Mr. James Galloway and his most estimable wife arrived at the Forks. For a woman to brave the difficulties, not to say dangers, of traveling up the mountains in those days, was enough to arouse the admiration of us all, and the arrival in our midst, of Mrs. Galloway, was hailed with much enthusiasm.

Cut-eye Foster had arrived at Cox's Bar with provisions and liquors, and later opened a grocery and groggery on the hillside above our cabin. Jack Smith came with him from Goodyear's Hill, and brought with him a five-gallon keg of gin, packing it on his back all the way from Sleighville. It seems that before they started from this latter place, a good many drams leaked out of the keg, and Jack and Foster did not spare it on the road, but notwithstanding this fact they succeeded in bringing the keg full into camp The process by which this was achieved, remained a secret between Jack and Fos-

VIEW OF LAKE TAHOE.

ter, and was no doubt due to the latter's ingenuity. Foster was neither sentimental nor sensitive, in any sense of the word, and he never allowed conscience to prick him. When he opened his store at the Forks, he sold a quantity of gin to the men. They did not say much, but they doubted that it was the real article, they paid so dearly for, and people who came up from Sleighville, declared that there the liquor would certainly not have passed for gin. Jack had a hard time of it bringing the precious fluid, and spent one night seated at the roots of a tree, holding on to the keg all the time, with only a blanket over him, and no other fire than that contained in the liquor. However, when he arrived at the Forks, he found it impossible to keep the keg filled as fast as it was drawn, and the gin soon gave out.

The same Jack Smith was a character, and repeatedly got himself or others into some ludicrous position. I remember one time, when he was working below the Bluebanks, that I went across to see him. I found him engaged in a soliloquy, in which he poured particularly strong language upon all Missourians, and Pike County HOMBRES in particular. He was at the time panning dirt on a claim above his own, and at first he refused to tell me what all his trouble was about. At last it came out. He had taken up this claim for the purpose of selling out to the first "greenhorn" who might chance to come along, and to make it sell well, he had put two or three ounces in the hole, all ready for prospecting.

In a little while a Pike County HOMBRE came along with pick and pan, looking for a claim, and Jack put him onto the place, saying he was willing to sell. The stranger set to work, but instead of starting at the bottom he pulled down the sides, thus filling up the hole, and completely burying Jack's gold, and as he could scarcely raise the color, he left without buying. And there was Jack minus his sale, and left to find his gold for the second time, which the Missourian had failed to find. No wonder he was mad.

Strange to say, that very claim proved afterwards to be one of the richest at the Forks, and I have known Jack to take out as much as six pounds in one day from it. It was one of the crevicing claims that I have spoken of, which we used to work on wet days, and it was a common thing among as to trade our claims for a piece of tobacco, or other trifling exchange, if we had not had a successful day. In this manner Jack and I had several times traded this same claim backward and forward, but he was the one who owned it, when it began to pan out well.

Another story about Jack comes to my mind, as I write this, which shows that the joke he wished to perpetrate, did not always turn upon himself and he was full of practical jokes. It was altogether an age of tricks and trickery. Men had little to think about, outside the routine of their every day vocation, and the stories brought from home or travels, would become stale. So the miners entertained themselves and their friends at the expense of strangers or oftentimes of their own companions. It was a common thing for gold-seekers to keep in their pockets, several slugs of gold, varying in value. They were lumps worth, sometimes, as much as forty or fifty dollars, and often more. Jack was sitting under a tree, one day, wondering where he would try his luck next. In his pocket were the regulation slugs—four or five of them—and they were beauties. As his glance wandered across the open glade before him, he saw a man coming along, evidently a greenhorn in search of gold, and an idea struck Jack to have some fun at the prospector's expense. He pretended to be digging in the bark of the tree with his knife, and as the stranger came up to him, he apparently took a lump of gold out and put it in his pocket. The stranger halted, put down his blankets, and was about to use his own knife on the tree, when Jack stopped him. "No you don't!" said Jack, "This is my tree. There is one over there that looks pretty good, you may try that." The stranger took his knife and went for the other tree, while Jack pretended to find another lump. "Any luck?" queried Jack, after awhile.

"Can't raise the color," said the stranger.

"Hello!" shouted Jack, "one more. That makes three," and he held three big lumps out in his hand.

"That's queer," said the other, plunging his knife deep into the tough bark of the tree, and making a long slit as he drew it out with a twist, "It's mighty queer that there shouldn't be any here!"

"Maybe you are too near the ground," suggested Jack, "some of them are 'top-reefers' as we call them here; try about twenty feet higher up. Whew! here's another!"

The stranger began to think that it was time he also found something, and so, without any further ado, he began to climb up.

"How's this?" he shouted.

"Higher up, I think," suggested Jack.

"Here?" from the stranger.

"A little higher!" yelled Jack, in delight, not even being able to see the man, by this time. "Up as far as that fork above you, and I think you will strike it."

The stranger made a desperate effort, reached the fork and dug into the bark for gold. By this time Jack could no longer restrain his merriment, and bursting into a roar of laughter that raised the echo of the woods, he hurried to the camp to tell his adventure. But up in the top of the tree sat the gold-seeker, prospecting in the bark and wondering what had taken that crazy man below. Such practical joking formed one of the features, characteristic of mining life in those days. Generally the jokes were taken in good part, and, when opportunity allowed, practiced on somebody else.

"Cut-eye" Foster made a success at store-keeping, but his prices were absolutely ruinous to his customers. He charged three dollars per pound for potatoes and butter, two dollars for flour, and so on in proportion, making everybody recognize that, if life was worth living, we certainly had to pay dearly to sustain it. Foster got a man to attend his store by the name of William Slater, who afterwards proved to be an out-and-out swindler, preying on the confidence of his fellow men. As a business man Slater could not be surpassed. When a customer came into the store with money in his pocket and wanted four pounds of potatoes, Slater would invariably say: "You might as well take five pounds, for I have no change." But if another came in and asked for the same quantity with a request to have it booked, he would say in his suavest manner: "Would two pounds do you to-day? You know I am nearly run out of potatoes and want all to have an equal show." No wonder "Cut-Eye" made money, with such a commercial genius in his employ.

But later he took sick. His tent afforded but a poor shelter, and he was really very low. He sent for me to come over and see him, and when I realized the precarious condition in which he was, I had him moved over to my cabin, gave him my bunk and slept on the floor. My partner poked fun at me, and said I was too tenderhearted, but I felt that it would have been inhuman to leave him where he was, and I put up with it all. I merely mention this matter in order to show Slater off in bold relief later on, when he distinguished himself in a somewhat unexpected manner. At all events we nursed him and pulled him through his sickness, and when he began to recover he made himself quite popular with our company. There was some talk about going prospecting, and Slater heard us discuss the chances of sending our gold down below. He then gave us the startling information that to anybody, who knew his way about, it was perfectly easy to get as much as twenty-two dollars per ounce. This very much excited the boys, who had never dreampt of any more than sixteen dollars, and from that day Slater was looked upon with much admiration by the whole crowd, who thought that he was inside the ring and knew the ropes and how to pull them.

The miners now began to come up to the mountains. They came in flocks, so to speak, like migrating birds, that only wanted to stay for a season and then return to the home-nest, to feather and fix it. Our cabin was a happy one, and no one was ever turned away, who asked for shelter or a meal. When strangers came in so thick that space began to get scarce, we would crawl into our bunks so as to allow them room enough to get in and warm themselves and get their clothes dried, before proceeding any further. Many of them, more especially married men, would state that they merely wanted to accumulate two or three thousand dollars, and then they would go back home. Such talk generally elicited a smile on our part, and we told them that five or six thousand dollars would not satisfy them, and that when they had accumulated that much, they would think less about going home than they did before.

Those who were camped down the river about Cox's and Goodyear's Bar began staking off claims all the way up to the Forks. When they got that far, they would begin to explore the North and South Forks, and thinking that they had found something better still, they would drive in more stakes, until they got clear out of sight. Then, when they returned to their first claims, they would find that these had been occupied by other parties, and thus innumerable disputes would arise.

This state of affair was an unmistakable sign that the hour had arrived when it became necessary to establish certain laws by which to regulate operations in these parts, and thus it was, that out of chaos and confusion grew the first code that guided the dwellers at the Forks, and which it proved very hard to upset or alter, when later on attempts were made to do so.

CHAPTER VIII.

Adopting a Code—Remarkable Observations—The Oh-be-joyful—Changing a Name—A Bit of Early History—Samuel Langton—A Bag of Gold—Etiquette in the Bar-room—Corn Meal Fixings—Reading the First Newspaper—Meeting Jim Crow—Phantom Treasures.

For the purpose of settling the matter of laws, a meeting was called at Mr. Kelly's cabin, a series of resolutions was passed, establishing a code which was afterwards adhered to, and things went smoothly until the advent of the legal fraternity. It would have been better by far, for the miners, if the lawyers had never reached the gold-fields of the Yubas. They came there for the sake of "filthy lucre," and too easily they wrung from the miners what they had made through sheer hard work. In the following is presented an exact copy of the minutes of the meeting referred to, with Major Briggs in the Chair, and C. A. Russell acting as Secretary.

Forks of the Yuba, March 3d, 1850.

"Met, according to agreement, at Mr. Kelly's cabin. Meeting was organized by the appointment of Major Briggs, as Chairman, and C. A. Russell, as Secretary. Messrs. T. Sexton, N. Kelly and H. A. Russell, committee.

Moved and seconded that the report of the committee be accepted.

RESOLVED, First.—That ten yards be the amount of each claim, extending to the middle of the river.

Second.—That each claim be staked, and a tool, or tools left upon it.

Third.—That five days be allowed to prepare and occupy each claim.

Fourth.—That none but native and naturalized citizens of the United States shall be allowed to hold claims.

Fifth.—That the word "native" shall not include the Indians of this country.

Sixth —That companies damming the river, shall hold, each individual, a claim, and have a right to the bed of the river (below low-water mark) as far as it lies dry.

Seventh.—That claims be in conjunction with their dams.

Eighth.—That all matters of dispute be settled by referees.

Ninth.—That in case of trial for crime of any kind, there shall be ten present, besides the jury and witnesses.

Tenth.—That sea-faring men in possession of American protection, shall be allowed claims.

Eleventh.—That whoever shall not be able to show his papers, shall have a fair trial.

Twelfth.—That this code of laws be in force on and after the fourth of March.

Thirteenth.—That the upper Yuba District consist of Goodyear's Bar and all above.

Moved that this meeting adjourn to the first Sunday of next month.

MAJOR BRIGGS, President.
C. A. RUSSELL, Secretary.

O. S. SEXTON,
N. KELLY,   } Committee.
H. A. RUSSELL,

I made a very remarkable observation, which for some time puzzled my imagination and to this day remains unexplained. I was working a claim opposite Craycroft's sawmill, and it was quite a common occurrence to find heavy gold high upon the bank amongst loose, black dirt, or sticks and leaves. I saw the same thing afterwards below Breyfogle Flat, where I would find loose gold as far as thirty feet above the river. Without asserting that gold will float, I am at a loss to account for its presence in these places, if it had not been carried there by the water when the river was swolen. It was not heavy gold, but found in large, thin scales, and I saw one piece that measured about an inch and a half square, weighing half an ounce. This flaky gold would frequently average from two to five dollars to the pan, while the clay in the same location would not go one dollar to the pan.

Owing to some severe weather we were laying off for a spell, and it was decided to celebrate this occasion with an attack upon the "Oh-be-joyful," and sending out a general invitation, we opened proceedings. For some time we kept it up pretty well; life took on a rosy hue; we felt satisfied with ourselves and everybody else, and we drank our grog in the Sierras with the same relish that some of us might to-day drink champagne at Delmonico's. But after awhile it was advisable to stop the spree. It had to be done effectually and with a finishing touch worthy of the occasion, and it was suggested that we should drink all the liquor to be had at the Forks. We sent down to Slater to negotiate for the purchase of the balance of his grog supply, but he replied that he would not sell wholesale, as he had only part of one keg left, but to oblige us he was willing to let us have what he could spare. Unawares we were the victims of one of our friend Jack's tricks. He had already bought the lot from Slater, had it bottled, and had hidden the bottles in the snow behind the cabin. By and by the boys began to get dry, and one of them suggested that he would pay an ounce for a bottle, and Jack said he would go for it. On his return he remarked that it would be possible to get another bottle or two for the same price, after which he was quickly dispatched, and as a matter of course, treated, on his return, to a drink of the precious liquid. In this manner Jack made quite a good speculation, and for every time he came into the cabin with a couple of bottles, he would expatiate upon the depth of the snow and the numerous difficulties encountered on the way, while as a matter of fact, he had been only a few yards away from the cabin, taking the bottles out of the snow.

It was during this spring that the name of the Forks was changed to that of "Downieville." By this time people had begun to accumulate and to build small houses, cabins or shanties, and it became evident that the foundation of a town was being laid. Men began to organize matters; to build only in certain positions, and to leave space for future streets, which, however, so far had not been established. A man called Vineyard came up from Goodyear's Bar and staked off a lot above Craycroft's place and just in front of some land belonging to James Galloway. He left only seventeen feet for the width of the street, and this so much annoyed the people in the neighborhood, that they called a meeting, and it was finally decided that no street should be less than twenty-six feet wide. Mr. Galloway was in the chair, and there was quite a lengthy discussion as to the width to be decided upon. When it was all settled, Mr. Galloway took the floor and made a speech. He reminded those present that they had been arguing about the width of the streets, and yet they had not even named the town they were about to found. He then moved that it be called "Downieville," after Major Downie. Vineyard, who was annoyed at his defeat in regard to the width of the streets, objected. He proposed to call the place "Foster," but upon a vote being taken, he was the only one who opposed the name of "Downieville," which was then adopted with acclamation. I had just returned from a trip down the river, and happened to enter the room as they were all shouting themselves hoarse for "Downieville," and my appearance lent new impetus to the enthusiasm, which culminated when I called all hands out to drink to the success of the new town.

However, for some time after, the place continued to be called the "Forks," and it was not until Mr. Galloway was made Justice of the Peace, and dated his writs from "Downieville," that the little town became officially known by that name. The first territorial election under the constitution, outside the cities, took place on the 1st of June, 1850. Galloway and Vineyard were both running for the Justiceship, and as Downieville was entitled to two Justices, they were both elected. They had made an agreement that the one who received the most votes, should qualify. It proved a very close race for the office. Galloway received 496 votes, and qualified, his opponent receiving 492. The Justice's jurisdiction extended all over the present county of Sierra, and took in some outside territory, besides, and the nearest Court to this, was at Foster's Bar. During the first year Mr. Galloway tried three hundred and twenty-five cases, ranging in cost from half an ounce to six ounces, and embracing crimes and offenses of all kinds.

Frank Cook and John Capion were Constables at the same time. Cook afterwards joined the police force in Marysville, and later became Chief of Police there.

But I must go back a little in my account. One of the results of our gradual development was the appearance, at our camps, of expressmen, or mail-carriers as they should more properly have been called. These men speculated upon our isolation by bringing us mail from Sacramento at such prices as they might contract for with the miners, individually. In most cases the matter never went beyond a "proposition," and the advancement of certain money to men who had no intention of returning. It was, doubtless, the memory of this dishonesty that afterwords caused many to distrust a most worthy man, who came up to fulfill the obligations for which he had contracted. This man was Mr. Samuel Langton, and the accompanying picture gives a life-like representation of him and myself as we appeared in those days. I am represented as showing him some gold, on the occasion, and he as bending forward to examine it. Many a time have we sat outside that cabin, giving one another an account of happenings which had taken place since our last meeting. And to few men do the miners of the early days on the Yuba, owe a greater debt of gratitude, than to Sam. While the halls of Congress resounded with long-winded speeches about the admission of California to the Union; while we were being victimized by crafty adventurers, Sam was climbing the hills with his little budget of letters, to make the miner, in his brush shanty, glad with news from home. Summer and winter he toiled away, ever faithful to the discharge of his self-assumed duties. In the scorching sun, across swolen rivers, or through mighty snowdrifts, Sam Langton made his way to our

THE OLD CABIN AT DOWNIEVILLE.

camps, bringing tidings and messages that were looked for with impatience.

It had become a matter of ambition with a great many to act as expressmen, and among those who thought themselves particularly fitted for the position, was William Slater. He gave out, all along, that he was going to outshine the rest, and when he once got started in business, he certainly succeeded in doing so, in one sense. Mr. Langton became the agent for the great Express firm of Adams & Co., and opened an office at Downieville, but it took him quite a while to establish the desired confidence in the concern. I remember, on one occasion, meeting a miner in his office, who was asking innumerable questions as to the mode of sending money home. Sam explained the whole matter to him, showed him a draft on Adams & Co., which he would receive on depositing the gold, but the miner hesitated to let his dust go. He could, evidently, not understand that such a flimsy-looking paper could be good security for solid gold. He objected on the ground that the draft looked like "shinplaster," and that the bank might "bust up." He finally left with his gold. When he got outside, he called the boys up to have a drink, then he dived into the chances of the monte bank, and by night the pile was gone, which might have rewarded him for honest toil, and brought relief and joy to those left at home. I have heard many useless regrets expressed by the miserable victims of the gambling-table, who had staked their money on the wrong card, instead of leaving it in Sams strong-box. I never gambled, myself, but nevertheless, truth compels me to say that I also have suffered, though somewhat differently, for refusing the services of an honest and worthy man

During the spring flour went down in price, at the

Forks, and I bought one thousand pounds and had it taken to my camp on the South Fork. I paid a dollar a pound for it, and while it lasted, it was common property, and whosoever wanted a sack was welcome to it. On the day when it arrived, and after paying the packer, and on my way home, I was overtaken by a stranger, who held a bag of gold in his hand. He insisted that I lost it while paying the packer. I knew he was mistaken, and told him so, but he continued to insist until at last I stuck it in my belt, until I should find an owner. The bag was a heavy one, containing some five or six pounds, but I thought I knew who had lost it, and kept it by me. A few days after some of us went as far as the store kept by Messrs. Wagoner & Chase, who at the time had a keg of brandy going. Several people came in, and among them was my man, and to him I restored his lost property. Then came the question of reward. It was not an individual matter, by any means; it merely amounted to spending one ounce out of six pounds, to treat all hands, so as to celebrate the recovery of the lost gold in the orthodox manner. At that time, and with those surroundings, a "treat" meant the expenditure of one ounce, or sixteen dollars, and he was, indeed, looked upon as a very mean man who would refuse to follow the rule. But it so happened that the stranger, belonged to this penurious class, which, it must be admitted, was exceptionally rare in the diggings. He positively refused to spend more than half an ounce on the celebration, and as we had a reputation to sustain, we advised him accordingly. We told him that the kind of company to which we belonged could not be treated in this manner,—his offer was an insult to us, and he could not do better than quit the premises in double-quick time, which he did. In fact, no man ever went out of

Wagoner & Chase's store more quickly than did this fellow. This will show how the ideas of etiquette, of usage and established custom, force themselves upon all commuities, even at early stages, and how aristocratic or plebeian distinctions find a place there. I may remark here, that the rule of spending one ounce on a treat, was so strictly adhered to that, when there happened to be fewer men in the company than could get away with the liquor, one of them would go outside and drum up assistance from the passers-by, or neighbors.

One of these, who came up to engage in store-keeping during that spring, was a Mr. McGhee. In addition to the usual stock of provisions and liquors, Mac also brought a quantity of corn meal, and as this was something we had not known for many months, it was appreciated. McGhee was a very good fellow, and he invited us to come over to his store and see him. He was located about where the St. Charles hotel now stands, and he proved himself a most excellent host. He treated us to a drink which he called "corn-meal-fixings," and I think he was the inventor of it. It consisted of about a half a pint of brandy and water with a little corn meal stirred up in it, and when the cup was passed around, the unanimous verdict was that it was a most excellent drink. He had to go some distance for water, and not infrequently, when he left us for that purpose, we would help ourselves to the brandy, and drinking it without either corn meal or water, and agreed that, barring the water, it made just as good a drink when partaken of neat.

At one time during this spring, I was taking it easy for a few days. I had received a number of books and papers and spent all my time in perusing them Some men came up to my cabin and told me that the Kanakas had struck it rich at the head of Indian Creek, and urged me to come with them. I must admit that I was not eager to go. My newspapers, which by the way were the first ever read at the Forks, engrossed all my attention, and I was somewhat doubtful as to the truth of the report. However, I ultimately consented to go with them, and packing up a few New York Heralds and provisions for three or four days, I got ready to start. Of course it would not do to leave 'till after dark, for fear of others following us. There were about a dozen of us, and we presented an appearance very much like a number of jail-breakers, as we made our way in the dark, "cooning the log," and creeping through the brush as silently as possible. We supposed, for sometime, that we were the only ones in the secret, and were therefore surprised, when, after beginning to climb the hill on the other side of Breyfoyle Flat, we overtook a party of five, who were making for the mysterious diggings. They were waiting for one of their number, who had gone back to fetch a few bottles so as to get up sufficient steam for the ascent. We pushed on, and just as day was beginning to peep over the hills, we came upon another party, bound for the same diggings. They were melting snow for breakfast and we certainly thought that they would be the last competitors, we should fall in with on the road, but just as we came to the summit of the hill, we overtook another party, traveling for dear life to get in first.

At last we arrived at the place of our destination, and we all made for the ravine where the gold was said to be. But great was my surprise, when on my way to that place, I met Jim Crow. He was at the head of the Kanakas and held full sway over them. The place had already been named Crow City, and the canyon is to this day known as Jim Crow Canyon. The whole affair was well got up, and they had already a very perfect organization, with laws and regulations to guide them, and over forty white men had pledged themselves to extend to the Kanakas the same rights that they enjoyed.

In regard to Jim Crow, he seemed even more surprised than I, at our meeting, and told me a pack of lies to explain his singular conduct in leaving us in the lurch last fall, but the fact remained that he really intended to make his way back to our old camp, expecting to find us all starved to death and probably our gold left, ready to be taken away; at all events, a rich field to work in. I never could understand how Jim raised money for the outfit he was bossing on this occasion, after having spent all he took away from our camp, but it is possible that the "Blue Tent" people could tell a tale in this respect.

The diggings here did not by far answer to the great anticipations entertained of them. I for my own part took it easy. I read my papers, and at once saw through the game, and made up my mind not to excite myself. We camped against a huge log, the slope being so steep that this was the only way in which we could obtain any comfort, and when I had finished reading my papers I returned to my own camp.

Many of those who had come there, enticed by the rumors of great riches, were loth to leave. They had an idea that the Kanakas were only waiting for the white people to vacate, and then they would plunge into the very richest places. Altogether there prevailed, at that time, a singular superstition in regard to black or colored men. They were looked upon as "mascots," and it was a common belief that they had luck in seeking for gold. While in their company, Dutch, English, French, or any other nationality, alike felt sure of the "dead wood." But my experience with Jim Crow was such as to shake my faith in the race, and I made my way back, perfectly satisfied to leave them behind.

OFF TO THE DIGGINGS.

CHAPTER IX.

An Unfortunate Family—A Company of Sailors—After "Old Downie"—Single Men and Married Men—William Slater's Exit—A Note Due Over Forty Years—Law and Lawyers—"Uncle Jimmie"—A Discourse About Drinking—My Claim was Gone—The Eighth Commandment.

I cannot proceed without saying a few more words about Sam Langton and his family. They came from Washington City and met with a fate in California which was absolutely tragic. They were rich and influential at one time, but the heavy failure of the Adams Express Company practically ruined them financially, and the family is now almost extinct. Sam Langton was killed in Virginia City by a fall from his carriage; a younger brother died in poverty in San Francisco some years ago; and another brother—Tom Langton—was sent to the insane asylum at Stockton, but has since so far recovered as to hold, at present, an official position at that institution. One of the sisters pined to death grieving for the loss of her husband, a noted Mountain express rider, who lost his life in the execution of his duty; and the widow and daughter of Sam Langton, perished a few years ago in an avalanche at the Sierra Buttes.

Although I continued to keep my headquarters at, what I will hereafter call Downieville, I spent the greater part of my time prospecting in various parts of the surrounding country. I must admit, that as I now remember, I am surprised at the haste we often exhibited in leaving claims that paid us well, for strange locations and uncertain chances. It was a common occurrence for us to leave claims paying from three to four ounces per day, or even as much as a pound, and packing our blankets over the mountains, with the sun beating on our backs and snow blinding our eyes, in search of—we hardly knew what ourselves. But there are circumstances over which men seem to have no control, although they are created by themselves, and so in those days the life of the miner was a restless one; the alluring hope of greater treasures led him on and on, and in too many cases he became like the rolling stone that gathers no moss. Hope too often appeared like the will-o-the-wisp—a mere phantom that led us astray.

My company usually consisted of Scotch or English sailors. They would come to San Francisco, generally from Australia, and desert their ships to make for the mines. When they arrived there, they would, for some reason, frequently cast their lot with me, and after a time, the "Major's" company became pretty well known. It seems strange that, although I was a sailor, like the rest, and at all times moderate in partaking of liquor, the boys who followed me were nearly always a hard-drinking lot. On Saturday nights we would return to Downieville to celebrate our success, or try to forget our disappointments. On such occasions, the flowing bowl would not be left on the shelf, and as a rule, the "boys" would divide their attention between it and the gambling table, and often spend as much as three or four thousand dollars before Monday morning.

Roving about the country as much as I did, and meeting with a good deal of success at prospecting, I gradually became known throughout the gold-fields of the Yuba. It was no uncommon thing for men to attempt to watch my movements, or even plan some means of robbing me of my wealth, and I have had several strange adventures in this way. I was prospecting at one time with John Bell, and we were cooking our dinner, when I saw three men coming along in our direction. They were covered with dust, and their clothes had been torn in the thick chapparal through which

AFTER OLD DOWNIE

they had made their way. The perspiration stood in large beads on their foreheads, and they could hardly speak for want of breath.

"What's your hurry?" I inquired.

One of the men threw down his pack, and winked his

eye as he said in a half whisper: "We are after old Downie."

"The devil!" I ejaculated. "What's the matter with him?"

The stranger became more mysterious. At first he did not wish to speak, but I finally got out of him that "old Downie" had just made his way down the mountain with a mule carrying a sack of gold.

"When was he last seen?" I asked, greatly amused at the whole affair.

But to this I could get no other reply than a vague allusion to the "Bald Mountain" and the "Lone Tree," which, together with the "Gold Lake," formed parts of the myth of those regions. They were supposed to be places where fabulous treasures might be found, but their various locations were not generally known. When a miner had struck it rich, and his companions did not know where he had got it, it was put down as one of the places referred to. There was nothing very singular in this, when it is borne in mind that every move was made with the utmost secrecy, and miners themselves, as a rule, refused to speak of their finds. In regard to the men in pursuit of myself, I will simply remark that had their story been true, and they had met "Old Downie" on a mule carrying a sack of gold, I have no doubt, judging from their somewhat uncouth appearance, that they would have forced me to surrender all, or part of it, or, at all events, to reveal the location whence it came.

In selecting my men for prospecting purposes, I always preferred single men. Benedicts had too often proved themselves a nuisance to me, and I had no use for them. They would whine about their wives; wonder how their children were getting along; speculate upon the possibilities of a speedy return ; and at night, when we bachelors rolled ourselves in our blankets and slept the sleep of the just, they would grunt and groan, and pray and weep, and gaze at the stars, and make themselves unfit for the work on hand. A *pater familias* is a noble being in his right sphere, but in the gold diggings, in nine cases out of ten, he appeared to me entirely out of his element, and I religiously evaded him whenever 1 could.

Trade was flourishing at Downieville as the season advanced. "Judge" Paxton opened a store on Jersey Flat, and William Slater was doing a rushing business in whisky. He contemplated a trip to Sacramento for a large supply of goods. In our camp we had not forgotten Slater's statement in regard to the value of gold-dust, and we all agreed that now was the chance to make money. So we dug up our bags and gave them to Slater to take down with him. We considered that it was somewhat difficult to count with twenty-two, which was the number of dollars promised us per ounce, and so agreed to allow the two dollars on each ounce, to Slater. In addition to this, I made up a bag of specimens, all fine nuggets, weighing over two pounds, and told him to send it as a present to his wife in the States, and so we bade Slater "Farewell" and "God speed." This was Slater's debut as an express messenger, and he took with him about $25,000 worth of gold. We have never since seen the man we had nursed through his sickness ; whose store we had patronized ; and upon whose honesty we had implicitly relied. Slater never stopped until he reached San Francisco, and from there he shipped directly for his eastern home. Sometime after a man came up to the Yuba to try his luck. He had met Slater on the Isthmus, and had been advised by him to go up our way. Slater had spoken kindly of us all, and in particular urged him to look up the "Major," whom he had described as one of the best fellows in the world, ready to do all in his power to assist a stranger. And this splendid recommendation we got for our hospitality, our confidence and our gold, and it took us quite a while to persuade the newcomer that a man who had spoken so warmly of us all, could have treated us so badly as did Slater.

There were many who thought that "Cut-Eye" Foster had combined with Slater to rob us of our money, but I believe, on the contrary, that he was one of Slater's victims. Foster was not so bad as they made him out to be. I have, already, to some extent, dwelt upon his character. I am well aware that he was not overtroubled with conscience, and that he did not hesitate to drive strange stock to his ranch, if it chanced to mix with his own, but such irregularities were not regarded as serious offenses in those days, and the men who committed them did not consider themselves thieves, whatever the sufferers may have thought. He had a propensity for borrowing money, and I believe owes more to his friends than any other man I have known. I have held his note for over forty years, for a sum which, with the accumulated interest, would now amount to something over a million dollars. Some years ago I met him up north, where he was farming, and he offered me his ranch and several horses, but I was on my way to the Idaho diggings, and making a "raise" there, I refused his offer. One of Foster's good points was his native generosity. If a miner in needy circumstances applied to him, he received what he asked for, and if he happened to be unable to pay the debt, Foster did not worry him about it. Foster was also very kind toward strangers who were taken sick, and more than once kept men in his camp who, without his assistance, would have died from hunger, exposure and disease. Surely, charity should cover a multitude of sins, and with all his faults, "Cut-Eye" was by no means a bad man.

I have touched upon the advent of the legal talent, and the influence it had on the community. As a matter of course, the lawyers came as soon as the election had given a Justice of the Peace to Downieville, and the number of suits brought during the first year, will show that there was no fear of them starving. One of the earliest suits brought was caused by a dispute over a claim, belonging to "Uncle Jimmie." "Uncle" played a conspicuous part in the early days of Downieville. He was a shrewd, sharp business man, who never let an opportunity escape, when a gain could be made. He ran the Gem saloon; and it was a gem! He had a monte table going day and night and treated all strangers who came in, and he had a very clear idea of the persuasive powers of grog. With him the adage was, "one drink of brandy makes the whole world akin," and he used it as a maxim, by which he greatly profited. The claim in dispute was located on the upper end of Jersey Flat and extended into the river to low-water mark. The river was flumed, and for this reason the line of demarkation was not very distinctly defined, and on the day of the trial the jury and witnesses were called upon to closely examine into the situation. Uncle was up to the occasion. His proverbial liberality came to the front, and he put up a free bottle at the Gem. Jury, witnesses and everybody else, took advantage of the opportunity to get free drink, and by the time the examination was over, the tramping of feet in the sand, and the effect of the grog on their visual organs had made it an impossibility to discern the line of so much legal importance, and the verdict was given in favor of "Uncle Jimmie." That night there was a big time at Downieville, and a general "jamboree" took place. There was nothing mean about the landlord of the Gem. He had won the suit, and he was willing to express his satisfaction, according to the rules of the community. The drawing of the corks was a thing unknown in those quarters, the necks of the bottles being simply knocked off, and uncle was an expert in that line.

And what a scene to behold!

"Brandy or Champagne?" called "Uncle," and the desired drink was forthcoming.

"Fall back all you, who have just had a drink and let the "boys" have a chance."

"Get out on the street somebody, and tell all hands to come in, Uncle is just going to stand another basket."

Such was the talk, and the liquor flowed in an endless stream, and men drank till they reeled, and even then went on drinking. And yet, there must be something in drinking, which is sublime, for I find in the ancient mythologies that even the Gods of the Greeks and Norsemen held high carnival with mead and wine, and they were not ashamed to let drink master them at times. And yet both these races were brave, bold and intelligent, and they have both had a great deal of healthful influence on the further development of the world. Be this as it may, the miners of the early days were a sturdy lot. They indulged in drinking at times, it is true, but they bore hardships and endured privations at other times, with a fortitude which made them heroes, and at the sacrifice of comforts, often of health or even life, they helped to make the world richer, if not happier.

Naturally a great many lawsuits were brought about through disputed claims, but the losers never seemed to take their defeat much to heart. "Let her rip!" was the usual exclamation when a man was told that he had lost his claim. The revel went on all the same, and the man without a claim would soon get another. There was plenty of gold up and down the Yuba, in those days, and yet I met men, right in the hey-day of the gold discoveries there, who were making for the American river, asserting that the gold was all dug up on the Yuba.

I had a lawsuit, myself, at one time, with some fellows who came from the South Yuba, attempting to take possession of Downieville by jumping claims, and they ultimately called a public meeting for the purpose of introducing new laws. But in this they failed. Our code had proved entirely satisfactory, so far, and we did not propose to let these strangers run our affairs. They then changed their tactics and jumped all the claims of the "foreigners," and among others, mine. But I soon vindicated my rights as an American citizen, notwithstanding the fact that I was born in Scotland and "proud of the land that gave me birth." My accusers were fined fifty dollars and costs, but what ever became of that money, I never could learn, and suspect that it was sunk in ale. This beverage had been introduced in Downieville during the summer of fifty. It came in bottles, and soon became a very popular drink, and I remember being in court when, during the sitting, several adjournments were had for the purpose of of indulging in bottled ale. In those days attorneys could not speak as fluently as they can to-day, without a draught, and a bottle of ale seemed to have a magic effect upon them. The Judge, himself, enjoyed the amber fluid as much as any, and the only reason it was not

VARIOUS METHODS OF MINING IN THE EARLY DAYS.

partaken of in the court room, so as to save going out, was the fact that his Honor objected to the slops on his table, and so preferred adjourning court.

The claim I had recovered by law, I sold shortly afterwards to a young married man called "Bonney." His wife lived in the States, and he was anxious to return as soon as possible, with some kind of a fortune. As he did not have much money, I sold him the claim on easy terms. He was to give me two-thirds of the proceeds, as they came out, until he had paid for it. I do not recommend this as a good way of disposing of a claim, and on the present occasion I certainly became the loser.

My customer had every reason to be satisfied. For two or three days he paid my share conscientiously, and this amount ran over a thousand dollars per day, but then I had to leave, on a prospecting tour. I was away for about two weeks, and when I returned the bird had flown. My eastern friend was making for home with a pocket full of money, and had disposed of my claim to somebody else. I lost not only a splendid claim but two tents that were on it, a supply of cooking utensils, two gold-scales and a number of other things, which I had left there with full confidence in the honesty of the man, to whom I had sold. I made up my mind that henceforth I would have no dealings with married men, and I trust my reader does not blame me.

In these days we had neither locks, bars nor bolts on our doors, and sometimes indeed, we were duly prevented from indulging in such luxuries through the entire absence of the door itself. The burglar alarm, as we understood that term, to use a legal phrase came "after the the fact." It was a process without the expenditure of county money, it chiefly concerned the robbers individually, and the sequence was in nearly all instances certain death. There were no extenuating circumstances to be advanced, when the crime was theft. I remember one day coming past a rock upon which lay a buckskin purse, stuffed, and to all appearance, containing probably a thousand dollars in dust. There was nobody in sight, but I doubted not that the rightful owner was in hiding somewhere near, and I passed by on the opposite side of the road, feeling sure that anyone attempting to touch that purse, would be immediately introduced to Judge Lynch. It is true that we were not altogether a pious settlement, but for obvious reasons we kept the eighth commandment for all it was worth, and it may be that if matters were dealt with in the same manner to-day, there would be less thieving than there is. The penal code of the early days in the mining camps, was undoubtedly severe, but it was wonderfully effective.

CHAPTER X.

A Spree for a Tip—Our Social Conditions—The Glorious Fourth—A Dinner at Galloway's—A Fight for Blood—A Speedy Trial—Thirty-nine Lashes—Big Logan—A Singular Suicide—Prospecting with Kanakas—A Rough Journey—Verdant Pastures.

As a matter of course our prospecting tours could not always be attended with succees, but we took care to appear, on our return, as if we had achieved satisfactory results. I remember once being away for some time and bringing up at Charlie Simmons' on my return, while the "boys" went down to Downieville. We had not been very lucky, but we did not propose to make that anybody else's business. The "boys," as usual, wanted a spree after their hardships, but not having made it, they did not feel inclined to spend their money, and Joe, one of the crowd, cast about for some cheap manner in which to celebrate their return The opportunity soon presented itself. The *hombres*,* who were naturally a curious lot, were in the habit of inviting returning prospectors to their cabins, treating them to drink and then would attempt to pump them. It was of this custom that our friend Joe took advantage for the benefit of himself and his mates.

Being invited into a cabin, they were first offered a few drinks, and then the questioning began. Joe pretended to be getting confidential. He gave a knowing

---

* A Spanish word meaning companion, here used as meaning certain classes of the miners.

wink, and intimated that by and by he would tell them something worth knowing. More grog was passed out, and such of the "boys" as had not yet been asked to come in, were called up, and it was suggested that Joe should reveal his secret; but he told them not to be in a hurry. Brandy flowed fast and freely, and everyone went to bed half-seas over, to get up and resume the spree next morning. Their entertainers thought that, no doubt, Joe would tell them if his speaking organs were properly lubricated, and their faith in the "Major's" luck was great. In the course of the day the question was again put to Joe. "Keep dark, and I will tell you," he said. "Not a word about this! Do you understand? Nobody must know where you get it from."

"You need not fear," came back the answer. "Do you think I would be such a fool as to mention it?"

"I don't know when the 'Major' is going out again, but I am going with him, when he does go. It is rich; you bet it is rich!"

"Well," said the expectant host, "how much?"

Joe had a way of speaking, which inspired confidence. He put both hands on the shoulders of his interrogator, looked him straight in the eyes and said, in an undertone:

"Just $500 to the pan."

The eyes, cheeks and mouth of the listener expanded into an expression of supreme satisfaction. "And where is it?" he stammered, trying to fill his lungs, from which the breath had almost escaped. Joe put his mouth to the fellow's ear and whispered the direction, an entirely imaginary one, as the location only existed in Joe's inventive brain; but the information was well worth more drink, and a protracted spree followed, after which the *hombres* stole out of camp in the dead of night and made for the newly-discovered diggings "over the hills and far away."

My narrative now takes me up to the time when, for the second time in the far West, I should celebrate that greatest of American festivals, the Fourth of July. My reader will, no doubt, remember my brief mention of this celebration when, as a new-comer, I had only been in San Francisco one week. Strange, indeed, did the scenes appear to me then, as they unfolded themselves before my wondering gaze, but as I remembered the past year, what scenes far stranger still, lay before me, in many of which I had played a most important part. I had imagined, when I left San Francisco, that I should spend my near future in the quietude of isolated places, but I had found, as time passed by, that one of the main arteries of the world's great heart throbbed with quick pulsation in the very surroundings where I had lived and toiled in suffering, or in the enjoyment of life. I had seen the most varied phases of life—men, with many thousands of dollars within easy reach, starving for the want of food, and others living on the charity of their fellow-men for want of means; and I had seen men's passions rise until they carried away reason and made human brutes of those who felt their sway. There were many well-known scenes that greeted me in the retrospective view of that one year, and while some of them were terrible to behold, there were many others pleasing enough, reminding me of happy moments spent in congenial company or among men whose motto was: "Begone, dull care!"

There can be no doubt that men are moulded by circumstances. They assume characteristics according to the circumstances that surround them. The lawyer, the soldier, the scientist, are all different in their modes of

VIEW OF THE SIERRA BUTTES.

thinking and their ways of acting. The sailor is blunt; the tradesman suave and respectful. The California pioneer miner was a being entirely distinct from any of his fellow beings. He was rough, daring, indefatigable The nature in which he lived, and the object for which he toiled, made him so. But he was also generous, often to lavishness. He knew what it meant to suffer want, and he did not wish anyone else to experience it. He often made a fortune in the course of a few hours, and the value he placed upon it was small and in proportion to the brief space of time it took him to accumulate it. His associates were drawn from all classes, but on the gold-field in the early days, everybody was on the same level. Class distinctions crept in later on, it is true, but they were not known among the earliest pioneers, and when they came, they appeared in the same garb as they do to-day under our present conditions—the garb of "one man-richer-than-the other."

Early in the history of California mining, various elements crept in which tended to degrade and demoralize the community to some extent. The grog-vendor and the monte-banker became responsible for much trouble. Men who counted money of so little value, as did many of these miners, were not calculated to resist temptation, when thrown in their way as the only recreation obtainable, and as a result, irregularities followed. But the reckless spirit of that period prompted the community to make short work of the offenders. I have shown already how we made our own laws, but sometimes the court was spared any trouble in the matter through immediate action on the part of the crowd or offended parties; and if a criminal went into court, the jury understood the desire of the public and gave a verdict accordingly. In all such cases the severest punishment was meted out, and lynch-law often resorted to. It was the natural outcome of conditions which called for strict and decisive measure as the only means of subduing a spirit of lawlessness and a tendency to crime, and above all, theft and murder were vigorously prosecuted, and in either case, death was almost the inevitable sequence. I have made the above remarks with a view to explain, and to some extent excuse some of the more striking occurences that took place at Downieville in the early days.

Everything looked festive when the sun appeared over the lofty Sierras on that 4th of July morning. On Jersey Flat and up and down the Yuba, all around the Forks wherever tent or cabin served as habitation, the Stars and Stripes had been exhibited, denoting enthusiasm—not only on the part of native Americans, but on the part of the many who had sworn allegiance to the flag, and under its protection were seeking to make themselves and the world richer. As a matter of course, the store-keepers were kept busy, as the day wore on. Wherever there was a keg containing strong drink, clusters were gathered within or without, as space would allow, and men took turns to get to the counter and drink to the glorious Fourth. Where one year ago the timid deer gazed on the verdant meadow, undisturbed, save for the casual appearance of some Indian hunter, echoed on this day hundreds of jubilant shouts, while the miner forgot his toil and his tools lay idle on the deserted claims. The Downieville of to-day, presents a very different appearance from what it did then, and I doubt if, with all the national enthusiasm that fires its present loyal inhabitants, it would be possible to get up as much steam for a Fourth of July celebration, as we did on this, our first observance of the national holiday in those quarters.

At Galloway's an elaborate dinner was prepared. It was not served a *la Russe* or in the so-called, French style, there were no gilt-edged *menu* cards to tell us what the next course would be; neither were we waited upon by men in swallow-tails and white shirt fronts; nor did we drink wine from crystal goblets but we had the best that could be procured where money was no object, and where the only impediments were the distance from the market and the difficulties of getting there. Mrs. Galloway had prepared the dinner, and it was pronounced "fit for a prince." Bottled ale played an important part on that occasion, and it was varied with something stronger of different kinds. The company became animated and toast followed toast. We drank to the Star Spangled Banner, to George Washington and the galaxy of states—men and soldiers who had shared the laurels with him, to the American nation in general and the constitution in particular; to absent friends and to everything and anything else that it was possible to toast.

Meanwhile the carousing had been going on in other parts of the settlement, and in the afternoon men began to get hilarious. Shots were fired from guns and pistols, and the racket increased until the general tumult and excitement assumed dimensions which could hardly be exceeded by a modern celebration, when fire crackers, brass bands and processions are brought into action. Then occurred the first incident of which I am about to speak.

Two men, who had been indulging in the fiery liquid until their brains became giddy, had a quarrel. It passed from words to blows, and the fight became furious. In the heat of passion one of them drew a knife, and before his adversary could ward off the thrust, or by-standers interfere, he sunk it deep into his opponent's body. The blood spurted out, as the wounded man sank to the ground. The wound did not prove a dangerous one, but at the time no one knew the extent of the injury done, and the sight of blood inflamed the crowd with anger towards the man who did the stabbing. He was seized and bound, and while a few attended to the wounded man, the miscreant was at once brought to justice. He was comparatively a stranger and no doubt thought that in these rough surroundings the use of a knife was in order. But the jury saw no extenuating circumstances which could excuse him, and he was sentenced to thirty-nine lashes on the bare back.

There was no reason to postpone the execution of justice, and while the slanting rays of the midsummer sun fell upon the scene, and the hot air filled the valley with an almost stifling atmosphere, the wretched man was brought out to receive his punishment. He was tied hand and foot to a slender tree, and the flogging inflicted with a stout strip of rawhide. It was a sickening sight to behold. "Big" Logan, who wielded the instrument of torture, was a large, muscular man, whose sinewy arms denoted enormous strength. He was a sailor by occupation, but had lately driven an ox team across the plains, and was well practiced in the use of a whip, and moreover he was a cousin of the injured man. It may, therefore, be easily understood that he performed his task in a manner which would have done credit to any Siberian executioner, of whom Kenna or Paradyce has written. The unfortunate culprit writhed in agony, as the heavy strokes fell upon his body, which became more and more lacerated by each blow that tapped the blood from his veins, and at last, Logan seemed the only man in the crowd who was entirely unmoved by the horrible spectacle.

This same Logan was an extraordinary man. He will be mentioned later on, as playing a prominent part in another dramatic occurrence which took place one year later, but I cannot here refrain from saying a few words concerning his own remarkable career and end.

He was seemingly a man entirely void of any nobler sentiments. Sympathy seemed strange to him, and fear he did not know. He was cool, indifferent to circumstances, strong in the knowledge of his own physical power, and a giant in proportions, yet he was not vicious, except his passions were aroused, when he became ferocious. What other men shrunk from, he could do in cold blood without flinching, and therefore he was repeatedly called upon to act as executioner when the sentence of the law demanded one. He performed his task with neither hesitation nor pleasure; he simply seemed to do it because he was asked to do it, just as he would have lent a man a tool, or otherwise accommodated him, if requested to do so.

Still, for some reasons, I think that Logan had a liking for revolting scenes, and concealed his satisfaction under a cloak of assumed indifference. When afterwards Walker got ready for his famous Nicaragua expedition, Logan enlisted in his battalion and went with him. It was while fighting a savage foe in those regions, that Logan volunteered to pass in his checks rather than to allow himself to be taken prisoner, and perhaps be subjected to some such tortures as he had inflicted upon others without flinching. It is hard to say whether he was prompted by courage or cowardice, but when he saw himself surrounded by the enemy, instead of surrendering, he disengaged the bayonet from his rifle, and piercing his own heart with it, fell dead at the feet of his captors.

CATCHING BREAKFAST ON THE YUBA.

This was the strange end of a remarkable man. He was repulsive rather than otherwise, but the singular manner of his death threw a halo over his memory, which in the eyes of many raised him to a hero.

But I return to my story of the 4th of July. The excitement continued till far into the night. The flogging scene was soon forgotten by everybody except the culprit, and "Big" Logan, who was treated by all his admirers who appreciated his nerve and herculean strength. The miners drank in bumpers, while the gold flew over the counters in the stores where grog was dispensed. The keeper of the monte table called for attention, and fickle fortune was tempted while the night passed on, and the day of liberty had been spent in a manner worthy of its cause, proving that morally and physically, the celebrants, with one exception, knew neither shackles nor fetters.

It may be remarked in connection with this, that the flogging of that day had a remarkably healthy influence on our community. The miners had established a precedent, and whenever anybody flourished a knife in an angry moment, it was merely necessary to remind him of what happened on the Fourth of July, and for a long time the effect of such a reminder, was simply magical.

About this time I had opened a store on Kanaka Flat, in partnership with a man named H. B. Cossitt. He was to run the store, while I went prospecting, for the in-door life of store-keeping was not according to my taste. I was nearly always traveling about, looking for new diggings, and was, as a rule, very fortunate in prospecting. Among the men who belonged to my company, was a Kanaka who went by the name of John Wilson. He spoke but imperfect English, but he was fond of telling, us in his best lingo, that in his own country he was a Prince and looked upon with much reverence. When addressing us, he would strike his breast and say:

"Me prince in my own country; me great man; me very big man at home." It would seem that this dark-hued miner was really a member of the illustrious Kamehameha family, and I have been told that he was afterwards made King of the Sandwich Islands. I do not know how far this statement is true, but he is by no means the only man with whom I have worked in the mines, whether white or colored, who claimed close relationship with famous men, and at times succeeded to prominent positions in the world. He was one out of many of this class who came to the gold-fields to find out that birth and associations did not help a man to discover gold, and who, after spending many weary months in blasting rocks or damming rivers, without finding the color, have at last come to the conclusion that Dame Fortune chooses her favorites independently of their rank.

It was getting on towards the Fall, and I thought I would make one more prospecting tour, before the season closed. I took four Kanakas with me, and left Kanaka Flat with a donkey packed with provisions sufficient to last us for a few weeks. My ambition was to get to one particular mountain, situated near the pass at the head waters of the South Fork, as I expected to find plenty of gold there. The mountain was shaped like the roof of a house, and summer and winter its summit was covered with snow. I did not think that it was very far distant, but discovered, 'ere long, that my judgment was considerably at fault. It is altogether remarkable how the chapparal will deceive in the matter of distances. One may think himself fast approaching a towering mountain, and suddenly discover that he has miles to travel before reaching it, and I have often in this manner been reminded of the journey of life, where we are always looking ahead to some sunny spot before us, which seems continually to recede, as we advance. Our journey proved full of difficulties. We crossed the North Yuba and kept up the divide, until we came to the meadows, about where Jackson's ranch now stands, but after that our troubles increased. The Chapparal was in some places impenetrable, and our donkey got stuck, pack and all, and we had to cut him out with hatchets and make a way for him, and this operation was not unlike the cutting through the ice to get a ship out of the floes. At other times, in descending mountains, the declivity would be so steep that the poor brute could not walk down. Then we had to unpack its burden and lower it over the shelving rock, and afterwards rope the donkey down; and this same operation we reversed, when ascending a similar steep incline. One night we camped on one of these shelves. Darkness had come upon us, and we could not safely proceed. We had no water, but far below our feet we heard the rushing of the mountain stream, babbling its lullaby to us in a tantalizing manner, while we had nothing with which to quench our thirst. But privations in those days had become a matter of usage, and they were soon forgotten. Camped in such places, the "boys" generally invented some kind of sport as a divertisement, and it was a common thing to see them setting fire to the moss on the bark of the trees and watch the blaze run up to the top of the mighty trunk. Or, if it were daylight, they would loosen rocks and bowlders and send them crashing down the mountain side. I have seen them prying, four or five at a time, at some huge bowlder, and when it rolled down with ever-increasing force, they would watch it with the same interest as the sports watch a horse-race.

At last we reached our mountain, and as we traveled round it, it assumed all sorts of shapes, but the gold which we expected to find lying loose on the surface was not there, although there was plenty of slate and black sand and quartz, and I still believe that there is gold there, although we did not find it.

Our provisions were now getting scarce, and we were affraid of being overtaken by the winter storms, so we made for home. We kept on the outskirts of the chapparel and passed through meadows and the most luxurious pastures. On Wolf creek we found gold, and there fell in with Mr. Fugent and my old friend, Jack Smith, who were prospecting. From there I went down to Downieville, more particularly to report the discovery of pastural land, and then returned to my store on Kanaka Flat.

CHAPTER XI.

Another Winter in the Mountains—Captain Thomas R. Stoddard—Two Well-known Millionaires—Fifteen-Hundred Dollars a Day—Gold on the Wagon Tires—Sleeping on a Fortune—Fluming a River—Poorman's Creek—Back to Downieville—Ten Bits to the Pan—Rantedodler Bar—Sunday Reminiscences.

Let me briefly take my readers through the winter of '50 '51. It was during that period that some of the richest treasures hidden in California soil were unearthed, and our company was undoubtedly instrumental in creating that tremendous excitement which in the following spring, swept over the diggings in our part of the world, and caused many miners to abandon their claims to go in search of other and better chances.

The Yuba began to look bare, as the fall advanced. At Kanaka Flat the sable hunters became more scarce, as they went below for the winter, and I regret to say, most of them without settling their bills at our store.

I had been in a similar position before, and when I desired to move away, had simply settled all accounts by burning my books and giving the balance of my stock away, as I never allowed myself to cry over spilt milk. On the present occasion, my partner went down to Marysville to see about a fresh supply of stores, and I got ready to look for other diggings.

I had in my company at that time, a few old standbys—men on whom I could rely, and who had been with me all along, with one exception. They were Charlie Thompson, "Dutch" Harry, little Mike Duvarney and Captain Thomas R. Stoddard. The latter was comparatively a new-comer amongst us. He was a remarkable man, and played a peculiar part in the early history of California mining. More than any other, he contributed towards the sensation caused by the rumors of the "Gold Lake" diggings, to which reference has already been made. He insisted that he had been there, and he told some romantic tales of encounters with Indians, and showed a scar below his knee, where the Redskins had wounded him with an arrow. He also told how, on his flight from them, he had made his way across the mountains and the middle Yuba, but his accounts were incoherent, and in some respects appeared improbable. He was possessed of a gentlemanly bearing, and of more than ordinary education, and undoubtedly belonged to a good family. But my impression is that he was not mentally well balanced. Be this as it may, the miners had a dislike for him because of his singular stories, which had disappointed the hopes of a good many of them, and I had taken him into my company partly for the purpose of protecting him. He would often say, when we struck anything particularly rich, "At Gold Lake we would not consider this worth picking up." But the location of this wonderful place remained forever a mystery.

I was determined to try my luck in Plumas county, and got everything ready for a start, and with my company and a couple of horses made my way across the mountains to the north of Downieville. We met with the usual hardships, and found Sear's Diggings abandoned, the miners having left after the first storm. There were only two cabins on the field at that time, and in one of these deserted habitations we found a quantity of flour which had been left in the hurry of departure.

THE DESERTED CABINS.

We took the trail for Poorman's Creek, and found that nearly everybody had left for the winter. But we decided to make our camp here, so we located a claim on the left-hand side of the creek, below the first fall, and were soon taking out plenty of gold. We found the precious metal in big lumps, weighing from one pound to twenty-five ounces, and set to work to build a cabin in this El Dorado. Not long after we were settled, Messrs. Flood and O'Brien called at our camp. They had been prospecting in the locality, but had not found any of the lumps, and were surprised when we showed them our find. They remained for a few days with us, and then left for parts unknown, but their phenomonal success in later years, makes up for their disappointment on Poorman's creek, when they made a "ten-strike" in the silver mines of Nevada, the celebrated Comstock lode, as did also several old-timers of the Yuba diggings. A train of fifty-three pack mules came up about this time with provisions, and I was glad to give some of our lumpy gold in exchange for the whole stock, after which we built a cabin and made ourselves comfortable for the winter.

We had every reason to be satisfied, as we were taking out from ten to fifteen hundred dollars a day, but yet, we often discussed the next move to be made with the return of spring. The wonderful tales that Captain Stoddard used to tell, made some of us wish to try and find Gold Lake, or at all events, some other spot, richer still than where we were located; but our prospecting fever reached its climax long before we expected.

One day two men found their way down the creek, and like all stragglers, made a bee-line for Major Downie's cabin. We found them there on our return that evening. They were making themselves comfortable by the fire, and soon proved very agreeable fellows. They stayed with us for several days, and saw the rich gold we took out, and when they became familiar enough to impart a secret, they told us of a wonderful "strike" they had made in coming over the mountains. They described the location fully, and told us that they had found surface gold in lumps so large that they had hammered them on the wagon tires. They stated that as they did not know much about gold, they were not sure whether they had really struck it or not, but their description left no doubt in our minds that they had found the genuine article.

We all listened eagerly to their accounts, and even Captain Stoddard began to think that the fabulous riches of Gold Lake had been surpassed. As to myself, I admit that I was staggered by their accounts. I gave them a good deal of consideration, and it seemed to me that these strangers must have discovered the fountain-head of all the lumpy gold in these parts. I imagined, and with some reason, that our late finds were merely the tail-end of an auriferous comet, so to speak—the nucleus of which might be found somewhere, and probably existed exactly where our visitors indicated; and building up up such a theory in my own mind, I determined to find the place. It was arranged that my partner, Mr. Cossitt should open a store on the creek as a stand-by, while I went in search of the treasure.

At Downeiville I made up a company of six, among whom were Dr. Young and Henry Cosair. We went north, crossing Little Canyon Creek, but when we got to Big Canyon Creek, there was no way of getting over but by wading. It was very cold. The snow lay upon the mountains, and the water that came down was chilled with it; but we had no alternative, and so we stripped and waded in up to our armpits in snow-water, carrying our packs on our heads. Truly the magnetic pole has no greater power over the needle of the compass, than has gold over the desire of man, and in those days the pioneer miners would dare and do anything for the lust of it. On the opposite shore we had to make our way over frozen snow. The incline was steep, and we were often obliged to cut our foot-holds in the snow, but we braved the difficulties, and at last reached the Red Mountains.

We soon arrived at the conclusion that we were on a wild-goose chase. All our prospecting failed to reveal the expected treasures, and the chisel, which one of our party had brought for the purpose of breaking the large lumps with, proved superfluous. The gold quarry, of which we were in search, could not be found, and we turned our steps towards the North Yuba, this time crossing Canyon Creek without trouble. None of us had any fault to find. We had become used to disappointments of this kind, and when, that night, we camped at the Buttes, we were perfectly resigned to our fate, and took our disappointment in good part.

Our camping ground was on the site where now stands the Buttes Mill, and when we awoke in the morning, and looked about to examine the location, we were agreeably surprised to discover that we had been sleeping on a particularly rich spot. The place was a small Flat at the mouth of a small ravine, and all around we found large pieces of quartz mixed with gold, which appeared in considerable quantities. As soon as we had ascertained our good luck, I got out pencil and paper to write out a notice, when I was stayed by Henry Cosair, who drew my attention to the fact that a number of men were making their way down the ravine. Sure enough, there was a party of miners, headed by a man named Leonard. As usual, they had followed the "Major's" track, trusting that they might share in some of the proverbial good fortune which was supposed to always attend him. We then decided to withdraw for the time-being, and moved our camp higher up the ravine.

Our stratagem however, proved in vain. We took it easy, and the men settled down to play at bean poker, but the other company took possession of our rich find. They picked up the gold that we had found, and, to make a long story short, although we were the first white men to ascend the Sierra Buttes, we did not get anything for our trouble. The news of the discovery traveled quickly abroad, and for days kept the miners on the neighboring fields in a fever of excitement, but personally I did not get one single lump of all this gold.

I was not disheartened, but somewhat disgusted. I turned my steps down the South Fork, and set about putting in a flume in the river above Kanaka Flat. I paid ten dollars a day for whip-sawyers to cut my lumber. When the flume was finished, it had cost me ten thousand dollars. But worst of all—the current of the river had washed away all the gold, and I got nothing for my trouble but a poor experience. The experiment had proved a hard-cash failure, and I returned to Poorman's Creek.

It will be remembered that I had instructed my partner to establish a store here. He had accordingly gone down below, bought what he thought would be a good speculation, and on his return opened an establishment which did not at all suit my taste. There was plenty of whisky, brandy and champagne, and in front of the store a round tent, where the monte cards were being dealt, while several young fellows of the "Fancy

Class" appeared in the crowd—so-called "dead beats," whose only duty was to keep the game going. Provisions were scarce on the Creek, notwithstanding the demand for them, and somebody kept packing whisky kegs down the hill to the miners below, until they swore that the next keg that arrived, before flour was brought down, would be knocked to pieces, and the contents allowed to run to waste. I now went back to my claim, but to my great surprise, my partner had sold it to a stranger for one ounce. I did not feel inclined to dispute the possession of it, and so left him alone, but I learned afterwards that he had taken $80,000 out of it, and meanwhile, I had swum the cold rivers, slept in the snow, been within finger-touch of an enormous fortune, and missed it—sunk $10,000 cash in a futile effort to find gold in a river bed, and here I stood, minus a claim that was yielding me as much as $1,500 per day when I left it, and all I had received in return, was a succession of brilliant hopes which had exploded like sky-rockets in the night, leaving no trace of their radiant paths. I began to think that I would try the Yuba once more, and went back to Downieville, hoping for better luck next time.

It is astonishing how implicitly all kinds of stories of big strikes were believed. My own case was by no means a singular one, as everyone seemed ready to give up what he had, however good it might be, should he happen to hear even the vaguest rumor of something better. I remember an instance where a few greenhorns set the whole town in a fever of excitement through their own ignorance of what they were doing. They were camping on the river bank, about one mile away, and as they stayed there for sometime, it was concluded, by the knowing ones, that they were making it. A fellow called Steve, made up his mind to find out, and one day, when some of them were in town for provisions, he approached them and began quizzing them. He was told in reply that they had found what they called "a right smart chance of gold."

"How much does it prospect?" inquired Steve.

"Sometimes more, and sometimes less;" said the man questioned, evasively.

"But on an average—?" Suggested Steve, determined to learn something.

"Well, never less than eight or ten bits to the pan," said the other.

Steve was delighted. He made straight for his camp and communicated the fact to his companions. It was decided to keep the matter dark until they had located their own claims, and that night, under cover of darkness, the company and about a dozen friends, stole out of camp, and the next morning the sun rose upon a number of miners who had put up their tents on new claims, and were busily engaged staking them off according to mining regulations. After breakfast, the pick and pan were brought into requisition, and the men examined the bank up and down the creek, but none could find more than just a few specks. Steve was deputed to interview the discoverer of the supposed gold, and ask him for further directions. He was told that there was plenty of gold "right down there". Steve asked him to be kind enough to go down and wash a pan or two, and the man readily complied. The stranger set to work, dug a pan of dirt, washed it down pretty close, and began turning it round and round, so that a little black sand could be seen.

Then he began counting: "One, two, three, four, five, six, seven, eight, nine! Yes there are nine bits in that pan."

"Where?" asked Steve, thinking for a moment that he had suddenly become color-blind.

"There!" Ejaculated the other, impatiently, "can't you see?" And he pointed to a few specks in the sand.

Steve straightened himself up, turned his back upon the stranger, and ran back to his mates. He could hadly speak for laughter, and besides, he stammered considerably; but when he had composed himself a little, he burst out; "The da-da-damned greenhorns call a sp-sp-speck a bit, and t-t-ten sp-sp-specks, they call t-t-ten b-b-bits. And this was the end of the mining on Greenhorn Creek, where the gold ran ten bits to the pan.

Towards spring our company began work in Secret Canyon, just below Jim Crow Canyon. We were doing well, and filling our sacks, but one night one of the party got up and left with all our gold. He made for Canada, where he stayed for a while, but afterwards had the audacity to come back to Downieville. Here he met with a reception somewhat cooler than he had anticipated, and left for Australia, where he is reported to have made a large fortune; but on his return with it to America the ship foundered and he was never heard of after.

I next tried my luck below Goodyear's Bar, and located on Rantedodler Bar, where I found good diggings, and put up a cabin. Somehow I always got the hardest drinking men in my company, and often had considerable trouble on that account. I have seen two of my men meeting in the cabin door, each carrying a pail of whisky.

"Where were you?" Asked the one.

"Down for the bitters," said the other; and they would call their mates and drink the contents as an appetizer before breakfast. It got to be so bad, that

VIEW OF GOLD LAKE.

when a man was found lying dead-drunk, with the sun beating down upon him, and a bottle sticking out of his pocket, people would say. "Oh he is all right; he knows how to take care of himself; he belongs to the Major's crowd," and whether he really did or not, made no difference, he got the credit anyhow. I had two married men with me here, whose drinking propensities severely tried my patience. Several times I determined to discharge them, but they always found some excuse. They would generally begin to cry, and between their tears and draughts of whisky, tell me that they had just had letters from home.

"The wife has just had a baby," one would say, and the other would follow with a story about "The old woman wanting him to come home, but he had not made enough to go." Indeed, it was hard to see how some of those fellows could ever expect to make enough, at the rate they threw their gold away for whisky. One of these fell head foremost down a shaft thirty feet deep. The other, who had seen him go up to the shaft and suddenly missed him, went down to the mouth of it and called out: "Are you down there, Scotty?"

"Aye aye!" cried Scotty, "Send down the rope Charlie." The man was not injured at all, save for a shaking, which a draught of whisky soon made him forget.

One of this drunken crowd got into a scrape with a Dutchman, and nothing would do to vindicate honor, but to fight a duel with pistols. So he went down to Goodyear's Bar to buy paper and ink, intending to ask me to write out a challenge. On the way home, in some manner the cork came out of the bottle, and the black fluid got all over his hands and face. His appearance in camp created much amusement, and he looked like a monkey coming out of a tar barrel. Nothing more was heard of his intentions to fight a duel, and he was kept busy for several days, trying to scour the black patches off his face.

The water in the river rose and we had to leave off working for a while. Dust became scarce and some of the boys involuntarily sobered up. There was a Mr. Briggs, who kept a store at Goodyear's Bar, and also owned a claim adjoining mine at Rantedodler. One day some of my men, hanging round his place without a cent in their pockets, contrived a scheme for getting free drinks, which shows, both the knowledge they possessed of human nature, and also the spirit of the age. Seated in the bar-room they began to talk of the "Major's latest strike,"

"And sure," says one, "that is pretty nice gold right against Mr. Brigg's claim."

"Yes," joined in another, "The Major says he is going to lose the best of it; it is all in Mr. Briggs' claim."

"What's that," inquired the store-keeper, pricking up his ears.

Then followed an account of a wonderful discovery of a rich lead that lost itself into Mr. Briggs' claim, and all the Major had said about it.

"And did the Major really say so?" shouted the delighted storekeeper.

"Sure!"

"Come up boys and have a drink," called the man who now saw thousands of bright dollars shining in his imagination.

"Oh no thank you," said one of the crowd modestly, "We left the dust in the camp."

"Dust or no dust! What matter? Money is no object, come up boys, can Downie's men no longer drink?"

That settled it. Determined not to lose their reputation, they sailed in and never let go till the store-keeper had filled them up to their utmost capacity. But what did he care? He saw before him a large fortune in his splendid claim. He lived for the hour in the sunshine of brilliant hopes, as so many of us have done both before and since, and after all a man generally enjoys himself as well if not better, while looking into the future with hopeful eyes, than he does when the reality is reached, which is too often attended by bitter disappointments.

CHAPTER XII.

A Severe Winter—Alexander McDonald—Close to a Fortune—A Lawsuit—Organizing a Mining District—Sluicing and Tunneling—The Summer of '58—Reports From the Fraser—A Wind-up—Now and Then—Quoting a Forty-niner.

I should, indeed, weary my reader, were I to continue my every-day experience as time passed, during my stay in the California mines, and will, therefore, bring this portion of my account to a close, briefly passing over the remainder of the time before I left for other fields.

The winter of '51-52 was an unusually severe one, and I and my companions suffered a good deal of hardship. It was during this period that I met Alexander McDonald, and a very warm friendship sprang up between us, which lasted for many years. We became mates, both on the California gold-fields, and later on in British Columbia; and I shall have more to say in a future chapter, of the tragic fate which befell this man, who was, indeed, one of the best of friends, and one of the most generous of men. Towards the close of the winter, McDonald and I went to Indian Creek, where we met with unexpected success, and notwithstanding the severity of the season took out a large quantity of gold. From this place I afterward moved to Grizzly Hill, but had no luck there, and determined again to turn my attention to sluicing, for which purpose I went to Indian Hill.

I stayed at Indian Hill for quite a while and took out some gold. Later on I removed to Ramshorn Creek near St. Joe Bar. Never were prospects brighter and my heart was full of hope, but I was doomed to suffer the humiliation of succumbing in a contest where the most money carried the greatest weight.

Right ahead of me on the creek was a company, known as the St. Louis Boy. They were rich and influential, and had come there with the fixed purpose of increasing their fortune, even if they had to go to some expense. It did not take them long to find out that the locality was a first-class one, but, unfortunately for me, they wanted all within reach, and I became a thorn in their side. At first they attempted to persuade me to give up my claim, but I was fully aware of the great chances I had in this place, and would not be bluffed. Then they cast about for some tangible reason to bring a lawsuit, and indeed succeded in finding a pretext, to my great surprise. I saw at once, that it was a matter of feeding the lawyers, and realized that I could not compete with my opponents. For a while I held out, but found it wiser to yield and withdraw rather than spend my money in vain. But in letting go my claim, I gave up one of the best chances I ever had of making a fortune.

I then tried Clark's Canyon, where I struck it rich, but for want of water I did not succeed in making a raise, and went into Plumas County, prospecting. On my return to my old location I found that my claim had gone. Mr. G. Hughes had been working higher up in the canyon and had met with some success, taking away several bags of gold.

I next went to Slate Creek House, with Dr. Jump, for the purpose of making laws and organizing a new mining district. We also formed a company which undertook to run a tunnel on the west branch of Canyon Creek, and for sometime we pushed ahead with

GROUND SLUICING IN THE EARLY DAYS.

this work, but ultimately gave it up, and I formed another company, which drove a tunnel in the Fir Cap ridge, known as the Alma tunnel. Here we spent twenty-two months in a very rough country. Our only shelter was a "dug out" in the mountain side, and any stranger, wishing to find it, had no other land-mark to go by than the smoke coming out of the flue.

After sinking $14,000 in a vain attempt to find anything worth working, we gave up the Alma, and I bought into the Keystone Tunnel Company, and afterwards mined below Forest City, but with no success.

I next tried in succession, Poorman's Creek, South, Scotchman Creek and Washington, where I bought a share from Charlie Stymer in the Hagler Tunnel on Brandy Flat. There was plenty of hard work here, with but small returns, and then the reports of the Fraser River excitement reached the mining camps of California.

I have now briefly taken my reader as far as the Spring of '58, the year when the great exodus to British Columbia was inaugurated. California miners were ready to listen to the call that came from these northern fields. Ever reckless; ever on the move for some better chance, they would at all times have followed promptings which bade them go in search of possible treasures, but on this occasion they went partly for other reasons. The fact of the matter was, that gold-seeking on the old lines was gradually decreasing. When the stream of adventurers first flooded California, after Marshall's discovery had been proclaimed, gold was readily found. My reader will remember how often I have mentioned it as lying on the very surface of the earth, over which we traveled. It is true that such accounts as were spread in regard to the Gold Lake and other places, were mere fables, but it is nevertheless a fact that in many localities the gold was found, as if it had been strewn over the soil like so much grain. Not only was it found on the very surface, but also in the crevices of the mountain side. In all these places it was easily gathered. The bare hand, a pick and a pan, or a blunt knife, would secure all there was, with no expense to the finder, and the fortune-seeker might arrive on the gold-fields as poor as the proverbial church mouse, and leave—a second Croesus.

But there were many thousands of these fortune-hunters, and the persistency with which they carried on their search, caused a rapid decrease in the surface gold. A few years had considerably altered the aspect of California mining. When the precious metal disappeared from view, the gold-hunter had to unearth it somehow. It was, as yet, to be found in the mountains and in the river beds, and tunneling and sluicing were inaugurated as the next modes of operation. But these undertakings cost money. The man who, a few years before, could start in poor and go home as a peer, was not "in it" any longer as his own master. If he wished to turn miner, he must go to work for the man who had the money. But it was the independence and the absolute equality in the world of chance, which Dame Fortune bestows upon all her worshipers, that had been the chief attraction of mining life, and had given to it its chief characteristics, and when this equality and independence disappeared, the inspiration of mining life became extinct.

For the purpose of gradually surviving the change which was creeping upon them, many of the most courageous miners ran heavily into debt. Many of them had worked hard with but little success in gaining the expected fortunes. When it became apparent that the gold must be sought for in the rivers and rocks, they borrowed money, generally from the store-keepers, to whose enormous revenues they had for years contributed, and sunk the capital in mining engineering, which unfortunately, often in addition to poverty, heaped upon them the burden of debt. Oftentimes the river bed did not reveal any treasures, and the dark, cold tunnels did not lead to any mines, while the debt increased, and the creditors became troublesome. This kind of mining was vastly different from the old style, and required an amount of perseverence and tenacity, which but few possessed, but it must be said, in justice to the California miner of those days, that a braver, pluckier class of men never engaged in the hazards of mining.

By degrees, machinery was brought into the fields; and the expense still further increased, and where formerly individual lines opened the possibility for an enormous fortune, now-a-days syndicates, corporations, companies, operate on a scale which makes mining a question of capital, from start to finish.

Such were the conditions in '58, when the news of the Fraser River excitement reached California, and found its way to the mining camps in the mountain regions. Everything was ripe for a change. Some anxious to get away from the cold, damp tunnels; others from the importunities of creditors whose demands they could not meet; and many sighed for the relief that independence would bring them once more. As to myself, I was pleased with the prospect of a change. I was heartily sick of boring into the bleak, hard mountains, which seemed to swallow up all the capital we could rake and scrape together, without yielding us any return.

DOWNIEVILLE IN THE EARLY FIFTIES.

Just at that time a favorable opportunity presented itself to me to sell out, and I eagerly took advantage of it. I then made for San Francisco, for the purpose of shipping for British Columbia, and I was not surprised at finding the city of the bay filled with miners, who had flocked from the diggings in all parts of California, anxious to try their luck on the far-away river, of which rumor had painted such glowing pictures.

I cannot sum up this portion of my account any better than by quoting here a short article, published in the year 1877, in a Sierra paper, by an old miner, who, taking a retrospective glance, writes as follows:

"Twenty-nine years seeking for gold! But how changed are the same class of miners in twenty-nine years. Then all was bright and rosy to him; no matter what obstacles he met with, he would face them, and if defeated, try again. If a tunnel had to be run in hard bedrock, and numbers of them may be found in the highest ranges, from two hundred to two thousand feet long, abandoned years ago, without a sign of gold or even gravel in the prospective; yet after expending thousands of dollars, they gave them up, but to try again. If they flumed the river, and every timber and board were carried away by the mountain floods, still he would go into the next operation with the same hope and energy, possibly to be wrecked once more; but what matters? Somebody was taking out big piles, and his turn would come by-and-by. And thus he worked and hoped until time began to lay his fingers on him, and "Silver threads amongst the gold," began to show themselves, yet the prize seemed to be in the near future. Had he not spent the best years of his life searching from the river beds to the mountain's crown for the big strike that was to make him happy the rest of his days, and realize his brightest dreams.

Disappointments have often changed his whole nature, but he cannot see it; he has long ago ceased to write to friends and relatives; no doubt they think he is dead, and generally it is his wish that they think so. His plea is, he has no good news to send, and he has not the heart to write discouraging letters now, when life seems to him a blank and a failure. His energy has about died out; he is content to work in the primitive way of mining, living from hand to mouth, still hoping, as it were, against fate. His house, now a rough cabin, he can call his own, and it generally contains all his worldly possessions. He has the walls of his cabin papered with cuts from illustrated newspapers, one bunk, a sack of flour, some few other provisions, a cat or two, often a small garden patch, a few drooping chickens, the inevitable smoking pipe and the home-made arm-chair. Solitude has soured his temper, and made him morose in the society of his fellow men, and often he shuns that of the opposite sex. Of course there are exceptions, and one will occasionally come across the countenance of some of the early miners, whose face may show the lines that time has made, but whose laugh rings as merry as ever, and whose heart is ever fresh. But they are silent and reserved at first, and will ever remain so. You will find them in their solitary claims, from the foot-hills to the highest Sierras. Talk with them of early times; then you break through their reserve, the eye will sparkle and the countenance light up, as they tell of rich bars, benches and river claims that they have worked or known of. How such and such a company went home with piles of gold, and where the largest chunks were found; they can tell you where the Blue

Lead crosses on every range; where it enters and where it breaks out; and yet, you will mostly find them the worst dead-broke class in the mine, and they—well, they had had luck; this and that was a failure—nothing seemed to prosper with them; the very elements were against them. They made quite a stake in such a place, and sank it in prospecting another. But while some miners were taking out gold on river bars and benches, others were depositing it into bars of another, and to them less profitable kind, thus anchoring themselves down for a lifetime. A few more years and the old '49, '50-1-2 men, will belong to the history of the past, and they may treasure up the sentiment of Moore, the Irish poet:

> "When I remember all the friends linked together,
> I've seen around me fall, like leaves in wintry weather;
> I feel like one who treads alone,
> Some banquet hall, deserted,
> Whose lights are fled,
> Whose garlands dead,
> And all but he departed."

"Soon the claims, the traps they contain, together with the owners, will be swept away by the ruthless hand of time, and the gold seekers, who almost opened a new world, will sleep the sleep that knows no waking."

SKETCHES

FROM

THE YUBA

DOWNIEVILLE OF TO-DAY.

LYNCHING A BEAUTY.

It was the Fourth of July, 1851. The little town of Downieville was basking in the hot rays of the California midsummer sun; the atmosphere was oppressive, and the only feature in the landscape that brought any relief to the inhabitants of the beautiful valley of the Forks was the rippling of the waters of the river, as they met on their way from the cool Sierras.

The national holiday had risen for the second time on the little settlement, to witness a great change, brought about by the march of time. The community had become more settled in regard to general organization, and California had becone a state of the Union. But for many years, even after that important event, the social conditions in these parts partook of the characteristics of border life. The population had increased, and there were signs that many had come there to stay, but the place was isolated, far from the center of law, order and protection, and so the people took the law into their own hands, when occcasion demanded it.

On the Fourth of July, one year ago, a man had been flogged for wounding another with a knife. The offence, trial and punishment had followed in quick succession, and the result had been that for many months after the occurrence all such lawlessness and violence had been in check. It was therefore no wonder thal the incident had impressed itself upon the community as a precedent worthy of note. It was not a spirit of revenge nor a craving for extreme punishment that prompted the community to adopt rigid measures on all occasions, it was simply a desire to enforce order and subdue any attempt to violence, as the only means of protection in a community, where so many different elements had come together.

One year ago most of the habitations were merely canvas tents, a few cabins forming the exception. Now the latter had considerably multiplied, and in addition, a few adobe houses had been built. These latter were introduced by the Mexican element, which soon appeared upon the California gold field in all their different shades and mixtures of blood, by which they are known.

In one of these adobe houses lived a Mexican, whose name has long been forgotten, and who would personally never have been known save for his partner in the clay hut, a woman, known as Juanita. Whether she was his wife or not makes no difference in this story. She had come there with him, and with him she had shared the hardships of life in a mining camp. She cooked his meals, mended his clothes, and otherwise added to his comforts, when he had an opportunity to indulge in any, the rough and ready life in the mountains only rarely allowing such luxuries. But the most striking feature about Juanita was her personality. She was of the Spanish-Mexican mixture, and the blood of her fathers flowed fast and warmly in her veins. She was proud, and self-possessed, and her bearing was graceful, almost majestic.

She was in the miners parlance "well put up." Her figure was richly developed and in strict proportions; her features delicate, and her olive complexion lent them a pleasing softness. Her black hair was neatly done up on state occasions, and the lustre in her eyes shone in various degrees, from the soft dove-like expression of a love-sick maiden, to the fierce scowl of an infuriated lioness, according to her temper, which was the only thing not well balanced about her. Add to this, that when dressed up, Juanita wore the picturesque costume of her native soil, in which rich laces and bright colors blended harmoniously, and it may be well understood that this woman was known all through the settlement.

On this Fourth of July, of which I am about to speak, the usual celebration took place throughout the mining camps on the Yuba. The pick and pan lay idle, and the miners drank as usual on such occasions, until the air seemed hazy around them and numbers were hard to define. The row went on all day and far into the night, and it was towards midnight when the last stragglers made for home to take a few hours' sleep before the rising sun should call them to labor again.

Among those returning at that late hour was a man named Cannon, who with a couple of companions had left the dram shop to go back to camp. They were all more or less under the influence of liquor, but Cannon was the worst. He staggered along, every now and then stumbling over protruding rocks, or knocking against the side of a cabin, and just as he came in front of the house in which the Mexican and the handsome woman lived, he again stumbled, and before his friends could stay him, had rolled through the rickety door of the adobe hut, into the room. It was perfectly dark, and as one of his companions, who struck a light on the outside, perceived what had become of his friend, he went in and raised him from the ground.

"Come out!" he said, "there is a woman in this house: Come along man!"

Cannon rose to his feet, and in doing so brought with him a silk handkerchief, which he had picked up on the floor, but he was persuaded to throw it back by his companions, who hustled him out of the room, fixed the door as well as possible, and made for home. During the whole of the proceedings not a word had been spoken by the inmates, and it was supposed that they had either slept through it all, or that fear had silenced them.

It was late the following morning when Cannon awoke after a heavy sleep. He had almost forgotten the incident of the previous evening, and when some of his friends, in the course of conversation, related to him the occurrence in which he had taken such a prominent part, he felt much concerned at having occasioned the scene described to him, and at once resolved to offer a personal apology. Cannon could speak Spanish, and accompanied by one of his friends who had been with him on the previous evening, he went down to the adobe hut. The man came to the open door, and the two engaged in a conversation in Spanish, of which his companion could not understand much, but it seemed to him that the Mexican exhibited a good deal of anger. Presently Juanita appeared by his side, and the words grew louder and more excited. Seemingly Cannon was attempting to smooth matters over, and to pacify the two. The woman appeared more excited, even, than her male companion, and Cannon evidently increased his exertions to arrange matters satisfactorily, speaking in a conciliatory tone; but his words, whatever they were, proved of no avail, the woman giving vent to the most violent outburst of anger.

Suddenly she drew from the folds of her dress a knife, and quick as lightning buried the blade to the hilt in the body of Cannon. It was the work of a moment, and her victim fell, with one last groan, at the feet of the beautiful woman, who threw the knife, dripping with blood, on the ground, and withdrew with the Mexican, into the house.

For a moment Cannon's companion stood as if petrified. He had come for the purpose of witnessing a reconciliation, and instead of that, a hideous murder had been committed in his presence. The warm sunshine fell upon the prostrate body of his friend, whose blood was oozing out upon the sand, and it seemed, for one moment, as if everything danced before the gaze of the bewildered miner. Then, suddenly realizing the situation, he turned away and made for the nearest camp to tell what had happened.

A short time sufficed to spread the report through the camps and claims. It seemed as if the very air had breathed the word "murder," and soon the adobe house was surrounded by a mob of infuriated men. But, somehow, during that brief interval, Juanita had found time to dress herself fit for a reception. Clad in her picturesque costume—the very best she had—with her luxuriant hair artistically braided; adorned with rings and armlets and spangles of precious metals; and above all, with her own personal loveliness, she met the men who cried for vengeance, at the door, calm, deliberate, beautiful. Under any other circumstances, no man could have resisted her exceeding beauty. The fierceness of anger had melted from her eyes; there was nothing left but an expression of perfect resignation and that haughty pride which was natural to her.

But the miners' law was "Life for Life." She was at once seized with her companion, and the two were at once tried by a self-established court. One man only, had the courage to take Juanita's part, a Mr. Thayer. He pleaded for the woman and denounced the mode of procedure in dealing with her, but he was quickly silenced by threats of violence, and even death.

"Hang the greaser devils!"
"Give them a trial!"
"No; hang them now!"
"Give them a trial first and then hang them!"

Such were the shouts that filled the air, but the last suggestion of compromise was accepted, and the trial began, then and there. Cannon's friend testified that there had been no intent to insult the woman, or in any way annoy her, and that the whole affair had been perfectly accidental, and was merely the outcome of a drunken spree. He proved the regret the deceased had felt upon learning of the accident, as demonstrated by his immediate step to make reparition.

The Mexican was found innocent and at once acquitted and the unfortunate woman put up as her defense that there was an intention of gross insult, when Cannon broke into her house and that he used offensive language to her when he returned to the house, and that in the heat of passion she had committed an act for which, under the circumstances, she was not wholly responsible. But the jury was not to be convinced of innocence on her part. When the case closed, they found her guilty of murder in the first degree, and she was sentenced to death. Never were the terrible words of such a sentence pronounced on anyone more composed than Juanita. She was apparently perfectly unmoved, her cheeks neither flushed nor turned pallid, and she seemed quite satisfied to abide by the verdict.

Where now the suspension bridge crosses the river, an improvised scaffold was hastily erected, and thither Juanita was conducted, accompanied by a howling bloodthirsty mob, that cried for vengeance. She never broke

HANGING OF THE MEXICAN WOMAN.

down; nor even flinched. "Big" Logan's services had been called into requisition—it took a man like him to hang a woman—but Juanita was of a different mind. It was getting towards evening, and sunshine fell upon the landscape; the Yuba ran its rushing course as usual; a little bird whistled in the woods; otherwise there was no sound save the humming of insects and the soughing of the breeze. But on every claim the miners' tools lay idle, and the men had gone to feast upon the spectacle, the horrors of which they expected to surpass their own imaginations.

But Juanita seemed to be in perfect harmony with the surrounding nature. Calm and dignified she mounted the scaffold. Her hands were unbound, her loose, picturesque garments floating in the summer breeze, and her beautiful face looked into those of the vicious throng that surged around her. Then she spoke. Without a tremor, her soft, melodious voice told the story of the unfortunate incident that had brought her there, in the light she viewed it. She declared that if she should live to be again provoked in the same manner, she would repeat her act, and when she had finished she turned to "Big Logan" and took from his hands the fatal rope.

There was a death-like silence in the crowd, everybody wondering what she was about to do. Logan seemed involuntarily to surrender the rope he was supposed to place around her neck, and with her own soft hands she placed the noose in position.

"*Adios Senors!*" she said with a graceful wave of her hand, and ere the astonished spectators could realize what had happened, she had leaped from the scaffold into eternity. The sun set in Downieville. The men, careless of circumstances, assembled in the grog-stores, and spoke of the heroic woman, drank, and then drifted into mining talk. But there was a blot on the fair name of the Yuba which it took years to wash out. It was one of those blots that stained the early history of California, and especially of the mining camps, until men and women grew up who were born and raised here during the crude age of the early days.

Then the dross and the gold became separated; then intelligence, industry and ingenuity were allowed full sway; and this splendid generation, with the sterling qualities of their fathers running in their veins, and the ennobling effect of more domestic conditions and educational facilities, threw a veil over the past, and raised California to the level of Christian civilization.

THE BLOODY CODE.

During the year 1855 there came to the State of California a lady by the name of Miss Sarah Pellet. She was young, handsome, possessed of more than ordinary intelligence, and of a kindly disposition, which caused her to be loved by all who came in personal contact with her.

Miss Pellet had a mission to fulfill. She was a temperance lecturer and belonged to the same school of lady-reformers as did Lucy Stone Blackwell, Antoinette Brown and others of their contemporaries. In this connection the name of Sarah Pellet still lives. Whatever may be the individual opinion of the temperance reform movement, there can be no doubt that those who have engaged in it with honesty of purpose, have done much to advance the social condition of men at certain periods and under certain conditions. If this important question were held aloof from church and politics alike, it would, no doubt, as a purely social proposition, attract more attention, and awaken more sympathy, than it does under circumstances where it appears to act as a cloak, hiding either ecclesiastical propaganda or political schemes. It is this latter fact which has always contributed to the sense of suspicion with which the apostles have been viewed, and when Miss Pellet began her crusade in California, she was made the target for many scurrilous remarks from a large portion of the press, which mercilessly attacked her, imputing to her motives which, indeed, were far from her pure and generous mind.

At that time Calvin B. McDonald was conducting the "Sierra Citizen" at Downieville, and he took it upon himself to champion the fair lecturer through her difficulties with the opposing press. Mr. McDonald is now well known as a writer of force and brilliancy, and he was then laying the foundation for the fame which in after years made his name familiar to most newspaper readers in California. His articles not long remained unread by Miss Pellet, and she determined to pay Downieville a visit and take advantage of the friendship proffered her through the "Sierra Citizen."

The advent of Miss Pellet in the little mining town was fraught with remarkable results. The reader, who has followed me through the preceding pages, is aware that there was a vast field for labor in the cause of temperance, and certainly some need of a reform of this kind. The young lecturer lost no time in going to work, and, aided by her editor friend, soon succeeded in establishing a large and flourishing division of the Sons of Temperance. Nearly all the reputable young men joined the movement. As is often the case, people went from one extreme to the other, and for some time total abstinence was looked upon as the only correct thing in the very place where, shortly before, the man who could not drink with the rest, had been considered a crank or a suspicious character. The Fourth of July was drawing near, and a temperance demonstration was projected and a committee set to work to arrange the programme.

It seems strange that the most thrilling incidents that took place in the early days of Downieville, should, in some way, be connected with a Fourth of July celebration. I have already had occasion to mention two, in which drinking bouts were followed by sanguinary results, but it seems still more curious that this celebration, which was not attended by any indulgence in strong liquors, should be the cause of the tragedy I am now about to relate.

The committee on programme had quite a task to perform in arranging matters. It was the desire of many that Miss Pellet should be asked to deliver the oration, and again there were many others who were oppposed to women orators. The latter faction was principally influenced by a young gentleman named Robert Tevis, of whom I must say a few words before proceeding. Mr. Tevis was a brother of Lloyd Tevis, well known in California to-day. He was anxious to obtain a seat in Congress, and for that purpose had lately come to Downieville to make himself popular with the people in the district. He had joined the Sons of Temperance, and was doing his best to make friends, although

COMING OVER THE MOUNTAINS.

he lacked personal magnetism, and that power of making himself popular, which is of great advantage to all men entering the political arena.

Nevertheless, Tevis was well thought of. He came of a Kentucky family and exhibited all that polish of manner and speech, characteristic of southern gentlemen. He was of pleasing appearance, and his ideas of chivalry and honor were in strict accordance with the orthodox code of the community in which he was brought up. He was fond of sports; was an excellent marksman, and without being brilliant, possessed more than average intelligence. But his temperament was highly nervous and excitable, his feelings were easily provoked and, when wounded, he would take the offence deeply to heart.

Anxious to make a favorable impression upon the people, whose support he was soliciting, Mr. Tevis fought hard to be made orator of the day, and hence the difficulties of the committee. Ultimately a compromise was brought about. It was decided that Miss Pellet should be invited to deliver the oration, while Robert Tevis was appointed to read the Declaration of Independence, and was granted permission to make some appropriate remarks on the illustrious document.

There were probably 3,000 people in Downieville at that time and there was no lack of loyalty among them. The throng that gathered to listen to the oration was a large one and included nearly every one in town. The celebration began with a salute from all the rifles, shotguns, pistols, and everything else that would go off with a bang, after which the primitive brass band played a few patriotic airs as an introduction to the more serious features of the programme.

Then Mr. Tevis read the Declaration. As soon as he

had finished he took advantage of the privilege granted him by the committee, and addressed the meeting on the importance of the Constitution; on national issues and on anything and everything else that occurred to his mind as a means of making himself heard and impressing himself upon the public. He went on speaking, apparently without any consideration of the time he was occupying and annoyance he was causing, until at last the Sons of Temperance, who were at the head of the celebration, took offence at his persistency, and determined to silence him. Accordingly the order was given for more firing, and soon the hills around echoed with a thundering noise of exploding powder, which continued, until Mr. Tevis found it impossible to make himself heard any more, and sat down with evident signs of anger, while the fair orator of the day stepped to the front, and silence having now been restored, delivered her address, which was received with much enthusiasm. The event caused a great deal of comment unfavorable to the ambitious candidate for Congress and rather retarded than furthered his chances.

The Hon. Chas. Lippencott was at that time State Senator from Yuba County. He was the son of a clergyman in Illinois, and a gentleman of exemplary habits. He was an excellent writer, possessed of a highly cultivated mind and a keen sense of the humorous. There was no Democratic paper in Downieville then, but the Democrats had made an arrangement with the proprietor of the "Sierra Citizen" to run a few columns in that paper, and Lippencott had been appointed editor of them, and was solely responsible for their contents.

The ludicrous position in which young Tevis had placed himself at the Fourth of July celebration, had so much impressed the Senator that he could not resist the temptation to give him a roasting in his part of the paper, and when the "Citizen" made its appearance, the aspiring politician was hauled over coals in a manner far from complimentary to him.

The next day Tevis appeared in the editorial room of the "Citizen" and demanded the publication of a card, which pronounced the author of Lippencott's article "a liar and a slanderer." He was beside himself with rage; his cheeks were palid, his voice shook with emotion, and he would not listen to argument. Mr. McDonald, who knew Lippencott well and was aware of his wonderful skill with fire-arms, advised Tevis to let matters drop. He told him that the inevitable consequence of such publication would be a challenge, and that bloodshed would follow. The young Kentuckian said that he was anxious to fight; his honor had been assailed, and only a duel could satisfy him. If the card were not published, he would consider it an act of hostility to himself. He had been held up to public ridicule, and wanted revenge. He would fight in the streets or anywhere else, but there had to be a fight somewhere, as he was determined to satisfy honor. So the card was published, and immediately Lippencott sent a challenge, which was promptly accepted.

Both men were Democrats and Odd Fellows, and some of the leading Democrats at once took steps to settle the matter amicably, but soon realized that their endeavors were in vain. The Odd Fellows took more pains. Neither of the two antagonists belonged to the local lodge, but nevertheless, a meeting was called at once, and every effort made to settle the difficulty. The brethren remained in session all through the night, and until far into the following day, and several times it looked as if they might succeed, but whenever a settlement of the affair appeared probable, some of them who wanted the excitement of the duel, interfered in such a manner as to prevent any pacific arrangement, and about noon the following day, the meeting broke up without having attained the desired result.

Besides the mental attainments which Lippencott possessed, he was also an excellent woodsman. He had spent some time in bear hunting and killing other game, and was a dead-sure shot. He was a small, heavy-set man, with light hair, piercing black eyes, deliberate and resolute in his speech, and gave one the impression of steadiness and self-possession. But he was of a much gentler nature than his adversary. He declared, several times, that he had no wish to kill a man with whom he had never even spoken, and that he would rather avoid a fight, but the nature of the public insult compelled him to send the challenge.

Tevis was given the choice of weapons, and he selected double-barreled shotguns carrying ounce balls, unconscious of the fact, that with no weapon was his adversary more familiar. The distance agreed upon was forty yards, and each man in practicing, broke a bottle at the first shot.

While the Odd Fellows were yet deliberating and trying to use their influence in the cause of humanity, the two combatants and their seconds left town on the quiet. The public did not know whither they had gone, but the Sheriff went in pursuit to prevent the fight. The ground selected for the fatal encounter, was situated some six miles from town. It was a flat up in the Sierras, surrounded by tall firs that cast their sombre shadows over the place; but no sooner had the party reached it than the Sheriff's posse was seen on a distant eminence, and it was deemed advisable to move into an adjoining county, so as to bebeyond the jurisdiction of the pursuing officers. Consequently, they crossed the border and selected another place suitable for their purpose.

It was towards evening when they arrived there. The lofty fir trees reared their mighty stems around the place, looking like so many watchmen, placed there to guard the unbroken silence that prevailed. Not a bird sang its ditty in these woods; not a sound was heard outside the heavy breathing of the men, as they made their way up the hill to the place of meeting. The light of the waning day was still bright, although no sun ray lighted up the scene, which was, to say the least, sepulchral in its aspect. No spot could be found perfectly level, and in drawing for position, the higher ground fell to the lot of Tevis. The distance was measured and the two men took position ready for their deadly work. Both appeared perfectly composed, and each one kept his eyes steadily on his adversary, as he assumed his place. It was then that Lippencott noticed that Tevis' second, in parting with him, pointed to his own breast, as indicating where to aim, and he took the hint to himself. Had he not been persuaded already that Tevis was a master shot he might have satisfied himself with inflicting upon his antagonist a slight wound, but his experience and the motion he had just observed, persuaded him that this was to be a fight for life.

The combatants were ready and the signal given. Both guns cracked simultaneously, and while the echo repeated the tale of the deed again and again throughout the silent forest, Robert Tevis sank without a groan to the ground with a bullet through the heart, while a lock of hair flew from Lippencott's head like feathers from a wounded bird. The fallen man had not made the nec-

Duel Between Lippincott and Tevis.

(From a Sketch by a Yuba Miner.)

essary allowance for the incline of the ground, and his murderous lead had passed directly over his adversary's left shoulder, grazing his face.

The survivor and his friend took their departure, and the former fled to Nevada. In the gathering twilight the companions of the dead man buried the body of their friend in this lonely spot, and made their way to Downieville to report the tragedy. Next day the body was removed to town and interred in the hill-side cemetery. The funeral was large and demonstrative, and a great deal of sympathy was expressed for the deceased. Undoubtedly the whole affair had been properly conducted throughout with the utmost fairness, but there were still many who looked upon Tevis as the victim of that reckless spirit which characterized early life in California, and too often caused the unnecessary shedding of blood.

Thus ended another quarrel brought about through a Fourth of July celebration in Downieville, but I feel called upon, before closing this, to give a brief account of the two principal survivors of this episode, as far as I have been able to follow them afterwards.

After awhile Lippencott returned to Downieville, but he felt himself like another Ishmael. He was a sensitive man, and it seemed to him that old friends did not shake his hand with the wonted warmth, and acquaintances reluctantly recognized him. Miss Pellet, who regarded herself as the innocent cause of all the trouble, never forsook him during this trying period. She exerted all her personal influence to reconcile public opinion with the man who had merely defended himself when challenged, and the brave stand she took in the matter could not help exciting much admiration for her. When she ultimately left Downieville, her departure was much regretted, and the cold-water brigade dwindled down for want of a leader, and the Sons of Temperance became an order of the past.

There seemed to be a strange fatality hovering about this woman, which soon after once more brought destruction in her path. She went to Oregon, and while there a settler undertook to pilot her through the wilderness, but when the guide returned to his home he found that the Indians had taken advantage of his absence, murdered his wife and children, and burnt his home. Miss Pellet afterwards returned East across the plains, and the last I heard of her was that she was attending a woman suffrage convention at Syracuse, New York, somewhere about the year 1870.

Mr. Lippencott was a strong supporter and warm friend of the late Senator Broderick, who was shot down in the famous duel with Judge Terry, the latter's tragic end forming the closing chapter of an eventful life, in which the reckless spirit of a border community had been nurtured and developed. Senator Broderick regarded Lippencott as his ablest advocate and partisan, and indeed the two men were placed in the same position during their lifetime—that of having to accept the inevitable and submit to the code that the community, the age, and the custom prescribed for them. Senator Lippencott was an honorable man, and his career in California distinguished him as such. His unfortunate entanglement in the duel resulted simply from his position, and the prevailing spirit of border life, for at that time a politician who would suffer himself to be called "a liar and a slanderer," without prompt resentment, would have been considered disgraced by most of his fellow-citizens.

After Mr. Lippencott had finished his term in the State Senate, he returned to his home in Illinois, to find his aged father dying, and it has been said that the report of his son's connection with the fatal duel, broke the old man's heart.

When the war broke out, Lippencott's undaunted spirit led him into a new field of activity. He joined the Union Army, and distinguished himself in battle on various occasions. He ultimately became a Brigadier General, and after the war, rose to important civil offices, becoming Secretary of State of Illinois, which office he held for several terms, proving himself, throughout, a man of great physical and mental capacity—a true soldier and useful citizen.

RIVALRY AND DEATH.

One of the most exciting events, which took place in Downieville in the early days, occurred in the fall of '55, and is remembered by the encounter between Dave Butler and a miner named Moffatt.

Butler was a gambler and a bully, and Moffatt was a man whose uncontrolable temper had on many occasions led him to the verge of disaster. Only a few days before the occurence took place, which suddenly terminated his career, Moffatt had undertaken to move the stakes of a claim, belonging to, and worked by Philo Haven, and when the latter remonstrated with him, he had struck Haven violently between the eyes. On that occasion Haven said to him: "Moffatt, you wont live another ten days." There was no intent on Haven's part to take the life of Moffatt, but he was prompted to speak as he did, through his conviction that the man's violent temper would soon run him into serious trouble, and the following will show how singularly the phrophecy was fulfilled.

In those days a good many traveling shows, principally dramatic and operatic, visited Downieville. The prima donnas were Sarah Bernhardts or Mrs. Langtrys on a small scale—the glitter of gold had more to do with their soul's contentment, than the inspiration of the arts they professed to practice. They allowed the poor man to look at them from the auditorium and the rich men to court their favors, green room fashion, giving them a fair race in the competition, as the bids gradually rose.

The reward of the fortunate ones generally consisted of a recollection of bewitching smiles, and as many ounces of gold dust as they had been in a position to put up.

Among the stars which occasionally rose upon Downieville, was a Mrs. Robb, who had become quite famous for her beauty alike of face and voice, and who is probably better remembered by her maiden name as Marian Goodenow. Her presence was the signal for so many aspirations among a certain class of the miners, and everybody who had any gold to spare, was willing to sacrifice on the alter of worship in the race for this sweet singer's preference.

Among those who more in particular lay siege to the woman's good graces, were Butler and Moffat. What means the former adopted to gain this point, is not exactly known, but it appears that he left his rival under the impression that he had outshone him with the fair Marian.

Moffat, indeed, had not been idle. He had exhibited all the ingenuity of a Californian miner for "catching," and to that end had fired from the muzzle of his shotgun something like six hundred dollars worth of gold dust into one corner of his claim—"salting it," as it was called. Then he had conducted the object of his temporary worship to the claim, had told her to dig and helped her to pan, and in a very brief space of time the charming songstress had carried from the claim in a bag some thirty-six ounces of gold, believing it, or at least pretending to believe it, one of the richest mines on the field.

It was the recollection of these thirty-six ounces of gold, which did not come into harmony with an inward suspicion, that after all, he had been outdone by Butler.

A few days after the departure of the company

Moffat was standing in the bar-room of Craycroft's saloon, when Butler entered. "There comes that scroundrel Butler," said Moffat, accompanying his expression with a terrible oath. But these were his last words in this world, as a well man, for Butler hearing the expression, drew quickly from his belt a revolver, and sent the burly miner to the floor with a bullet in his breast. Moffat did not die instantly, but was carried into a room behind the bar, where he lay for several hours before he expired.

Meanwhile, the wildest excitement prevailed. Butler fled from the scene during the first confusion and made out of town under cover of darkness and aided by the gamblers who stood in with him. But as the news spread, angry miners massed at the corners and in the open plaza, and then a wild pursuit began. That night the hills, up and down the Forks, were scoured high and low, and had Butler been caught, he would not have lived to recognize his captors; but he succeeded in making his escape, and the sequel of the affair was not enacted until several years afterwards.

The miners, seeing that their efforts to capture the murderer had been frustrated, turned in anger upon those who had aided and abetted him in his escape, and the cry arose that the gamblers must go. And, indeed, so summarily were these men dealt with that within a few days the whole fraternity had quit the scene of activity in Downieville, with the exception of old "Uncle Jimmie," of whom I have previously spoken. Uncle Jimmie had, at one time, been a baptist preacher, and had merely changed his plane for administering to his fellow-men. I always regarded him as a villain of the blackest dye, but his previous connection with the cloth saved him on this occasion.

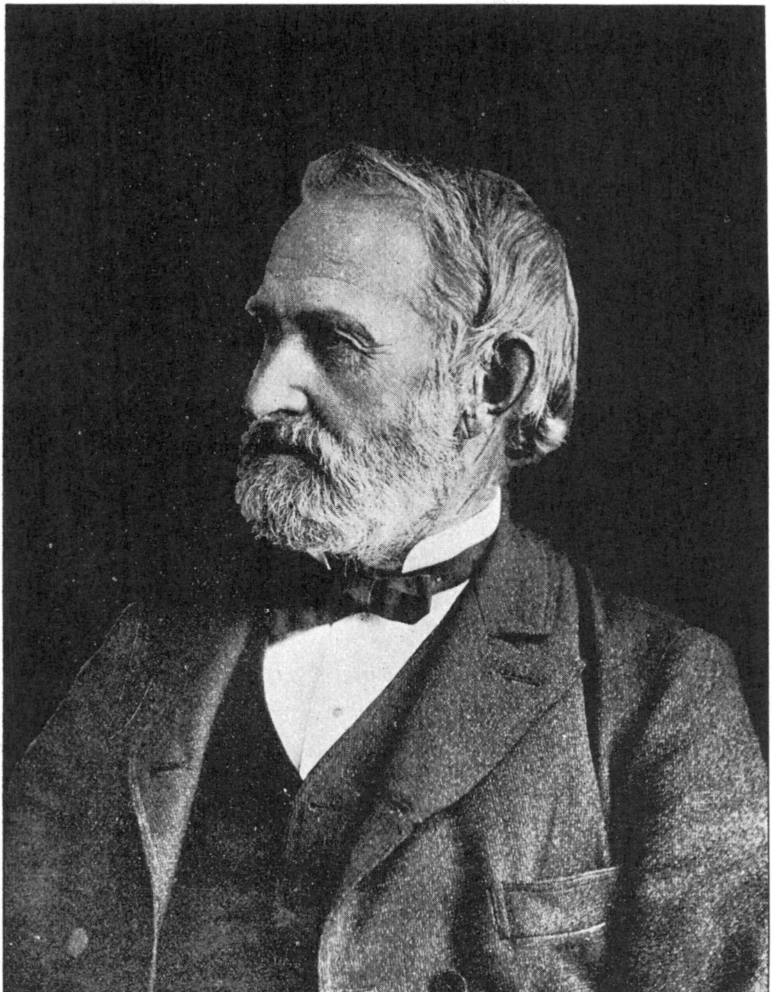

Philo A. Haven

Among those, who took the most active part in these proceedings, was Calvin B. McDonald, the editor of the "Sierra Citizen." It was he, who wrote an article which called the miners together in the Plaza, and in consequence of which it was determined to expel the gamblers from the town. McDonald was carried over the heads of the excited miners into the middle of the plaza, where he made a rousing speech, in the course of which he urged the expulsion of the gamblers. In recognition of his action the miners raised a subscription, gave him a champagne supper and presented him with a $300 watch. It was a great feast and many enthusiastic speeches were made on the occasion. The watch was afterwards deposited with Ladd and Reese, who ran a bank in Downieville, and one hundred dollars borrowed on it, but, when some years after the little mountain town was laid in ashes, the bank burnt up, and the watch disappeared in a process of cremation.

A strange thing happened in regard to Moffat lying mortally wounded on a lounge at the back of Craycroft's saloon; the dying man sent for Haven. When the latter walked in, Moffat disclosed the wound in his breast, and Haven merely said: "What have you got in there—lead?"

"That is what!" ejaculated the wounded man.

'You were right the other day, when you told me that I would not live another ten days; I know it—I am going,"

Dave Butler, the murderer, succeeded in getting out of the country, but the awful avenger followed him, and ultimately tracked him to his lair. His victim had been a Free Mason, and it was said that, with unceasing zeal, the Masons pursued him until they found him in Oregon, two years after, and brought him to justice. A constable was sent up for him, and the two came down on a small coasting schooner. One evening the officer took him on deck for an airing, and after that the officer was never seen. It is supposed that Butler threw him overboard, although he strenuously asserted that he did not know what had become of him. But Butler did not evade his punishment. He was taken to Downieville, tried and convicted, and expired at one end of a strong rope.

A FORTY-NINER'S YARNS.

I have previously referred to Mr. Philo Haven, and will now relate a few of the remembrances he recalls to my mind, as we converse together, of the long-ago, and conjure up old, familiar scenes. My friend, whom I met first in '49, is two years my senior, and is, mentally and physically, well preserved. He is tall, bony, spare, and has a facial expression varying from stern determination to genial kindliness, with intervening shades of temperament; on the whole, pretty well denoting the man as he is.

We were talking over old scences and incidents that we both remembered, when, suddenly, Philo says, with a laugh: "I never saw anything so absolutely ridiculous as one scene that recurs to my mind just now. It happened up in the mountains, about the Yuba, and made me laugh at the time, and often after, till my sides fairly ached. I was traveling a short distance behind a Yankee who was driving his mule before him. The animal was heavily laden, and carried, among other things, a long-handled shovel which was packed so as to project upward and outward considerably, on the right side.

"Gradually the trail became more difficult to travel. It wound around the mountain, and ultimately led us across a ledge for a short distance. The path was narrow. On the right the rocks rose almost perpendicularly, and on the left was a sheer precipice of some thirty or forty feet, before our gaze met the sloping side of the mountain which extended its rugged side to the river below. Of course we were used to traveling over such thoroughfares, and I would, probably, never have remembered this particular trip, had it not been for a sudden bend in the path, which occurred just as we were traveling across the overhanging ledge.

The mule, which led the procession, was the first to turn. It was just at the corner, when, owing to the general shaking of the pack, the top end of the long-handled shovel struck a protruding bowlder with an effect which fairly took us all by surprise. The force of the collision was so great as to send the poor animal off its feet, and over the verge of the ledge; and the Yankee saw his pack getting down hill at a rate entirely unexpected. But the funny feature of the occurence was the manner in which he acted when he saw the animal dashing like a bird through space. With both arms akimbo, and looking at the animal with an expression of utter amazement, he yelled with a few strong oaths interspersed: "Ho gray! Ho gray! Ho gray!" The idea of a man calling to a mule, which is turning sommersaults in mid-air, for the purpose of halting it in its mad career, appeared to me so ludicrous, that I smile whenever I think of it.

In regard to the Indians, knowing the value of gold long before Europeans began to look for it, Mr. Haven not only bears me out in my ideas, previously expressed, but relates that he has seen Indian squaws panning gold in baskets made of wicker work, and covered within with a layer of pitch. In connection with this Mr. Haven tells the following amusing story: "I was camped on the Yuba at one time with a small party, prospecting. We had been particularly fortunate, and our provisions were beginning to run short, but I hung on in hopes of striking something. We were living chiefly on jerked venison, but a good deal of it had gone bad and was unfit for eating. In those days a man who afterwards became well known in Downieville, was in the habit of following the camps and picking up such provisions as the miners had discarded, selling the same to the Indians for gold lumps or dust. This man was at our camp at the time, and I saw him several times dealing with an old Indian who came down with his son, and always brought some very fine specimens of lumpy gold.

"I decided to find out, from the redskin, where he obtained the lumps, and one day called him to me. 'See here,' I said, 'if you will point with your finger in the direction where you find that gold, I will give you and your boy all you can eat right now.' My men began to remonstrate. They knew that the limit of our supplies was a magnitude much more easily defined than the appetite of the two Indians, but I was determined, and I repeated my request.

"The Indian looked at me with a hungry expression. He pointed with one finger to the base of his stomach, then moved the same member of his anatomy slowly up the front of his body, until he came to his mouth, which he opened wide and laid his finger in it cross ways.

"'That much?' he queried.

"'Yes,' I said, 'I will fill you both right up to there.'

"'All right;' said the Indian, and the bargain was concluded. I started in the manner of a taxidermist to stuff them, and flap-jacks, venison, onions, hard biscuits, tea and whatever else was at hand, disappeared almost as quickly as it was placed before them. After having thoroughly gorged themselves, and considerably diminished our stores they both arose, evidently satisfied.

"'Are you all right?' I asked.

"'All right,' said the father.

"'Now,' I said, 'I have fulfilled my part of the bargain, it is your turn.'

"The old man looked at his son, to whom he spoke a few words, giving him, at the same time, a meaning glance, which I afterwards was able to translate, and then placed himself with his face towards a high bluff that arose just in front of us. He seized the index finger of his left hand between the index finger and thumb of his right hand, and holding it in the manner of a gun, pointed it towards the bluff, looking straight at it all the time.

"'You say, captain!' he said after a pause, meaning that he wanted me to repeat my request.

"'Now,' I said, 'you point with that finger, in the direction where you find those lumps of gold.'

"'All right!' said the indian, and without raising his eyes from his finger, or changing his position, he slowly turned around until he had resumed his former attitude —facing the bluff.

"I was so much impressed with the streak of humor in the cunning device on the part of the Indian, which left me a fool on my own proposition, that I laughed heartily as I realized how I had been sold, notwithstanding the fact that my men looked glum and angry. In fact, I laughed until the tears rolled down my cheeks, and the Indian, when I had recovered myself, turned to me and said: 'I like you; you good man. You no get mad. Good man no get mad; bad man get mad.'

He then told me that on the following morning he would send another son to me. I should give him some flour, and he would conduct me to the place where the gold was. In this respect he kept faith with me, but that expedition does not belong to the story I wanted to tell, which merely concerns the Indian and his interpretation of a contract, which would, no doubt, have puzzled a 'Philidelphia lawyer' in court.

"I have mentioned the so-called 'Gold Lake' excitement, which was caused by Captain Stoddard, who declared that he had been at the wonderful lake, and showed what he alleged to be a wound, on his leg, inflicted by the Indians. Captain Stoddard's report caused the wildest excitement for a while, and he ultimately undertook to guide a party of miners to the lake where the fabulous treasures were supposed to be. The small party that set out for the lake, gradually increased in numbers, until at last, several thousand men made towards the goal of their anticipations, with as fervent a desire to reach it as ever inspired the Jews of old, in looking for the promised land."

In regard to this expedition, Mr. Haven tells the following story, which throws some light upon the matter:

"I was traveling over the mountains with a companion, on a prospecting tour, when one evening we made our camp at the base of a high hill. I ascended the hill to take a look over the surrounding country, and to my utmost surprise, found the valley alive with at least three thousand people, who were, evidently, camped there temporarily. Calling my partner, we descended together, and joined the throng. I found there a man with whom I had crossed the plains, and he pointed out to me Captain Stoddard, a Philadelphia gentleman, who had offered to conduct this crowd to new diggings at "Gold Lake," where, he had assured them, wealth untold could be found.

"For several days we traveled along, Captain Stoddard guiding our course, and at last we came upon a lake nestled among lofty mountains.

DEATH OF MOFFATT.

(From a sketch by a Yuba miner.)

"'That is it!' said Stoddard. 'You see now the lake with the blue water, which I have described; the three peaks, and the log yonder, where I camped. There are tons of gold there.'

"About four hundred men at once started, on a run, for the supposed log, but it was found hard to get at, and when ultimately reached by a circuitous route, was found to be a bowlder shaped somewhat like a log, but not a sign of gold near it.

"Meanwhile, the rest were descending the slope, headed by Colonel X—— and Captain Stoddard. 'You say there are three peaks?' said the Colonel 'but I see five.'

'Stoddard looked in the direction, where in reality five peaks towered aloft, and then, glancing at the lake below, he turned deadly pale.

'What ails you?' asked his companion.

'When I get down there.' exclaimed Stoddard, evidently greatly distressed. 'I shall not be able to see the peaks—then how can I find the gold?'

"Within an hour it had become evident to several thousand men, that they represented as many fools. Not a trace of gold was found, and expectations, hopes, anticipations had suddenly turned to anger and a thirst for revenge of the most intense nature. 'Hang him!' 'I have a rope that will hold him!' 'Here's a branch that will carry him!' 'String him up!' Such were the exclamations mingled with imprecations that filled the air for a few moments, as hundreds of men made a rush in search of the Captain.

The strange conduct of the latter, and his incoherent talk, as we approached the place, had persuaded Colonel X——, myself and a few others that the man was crazy, or at least, not in his right senses. So, when the mob approached to seek vengeance on the unfortunate man, we drew our revolvers and told them that so long as we were able to defend him, no one in that crowd would be allowed to hurt a crazy man. That settled it, and although the poor fellow was made the target for a good deal of abuse, after this no further attempt was made to kill him.

While I was encamped with him I met a certain John F. ———, of Philadelphia, with whom I had had previous dealings. I told him of the Captain, who also claimed to hail from the Quaker City. "I know him," said John. "The man is crazy. He is the son of an English lord, and was sent to America to be kept out of the way. He stayed for some time at my father's house, and a certain sum of money was paid for his keeping."

After awhile Stoddard came in and apparently corroborated John in some of what he had been saying. After awhile the young Philadelphian said: "You say you were wounded by some of the Indians, show me the scar."

Stoddard uncovered that part of his leg where the mark was, which he alleged was the result of an arrow wound. "That," said John, pointing to the scar, "is the result of a wound received from a fall he received in Philadelphia city some years ago, at the same time breaking three ribs."

I cannot vouch for the correctness of John's statement but at all events it helped to shield the poor Captain against the revengeful spirit of many of the miners, whose anger it took sometime to cool down. After awhile Stoddard joined Major Downie's camp, where he found protection against any attempts to annoy him.

FROM OBSCURITY TO FAME.

There are two persons whom I remember from the early days of Downieville, whose separate lives afterwards took them out of the hum-drum, general routine of our ordinary existence, and led them into the paths of strange adventures and unexpected circumstances. I allude to Colonel Daniel E. Hungerford, and his daughter, Mrs. Louisa Mackey, wife of the California Bonanza King.

Daniel E. Hungerford was born in the State of New York, in the year 1812. During that year, his father fought against the British, and his grandfather, Daniel Hungerford, fought in the revolution. The family, which settled in America as early as 1628, is of old English extraction, and can trace its ancestors as far back as 1325, during the reign of Edward II, when Sir Robert Hungerford was Knight of Shire of Wilt. Farleigh castle, in Somersetshire, was for centuries, the seat of the Hungerfords, most of whom distinguished themselves as soldiers.

It was, then, an inherited military spirit which drove Daniel Hungerford to the field of battle when the Mexican war broke out, notwithstanding that he had a young wife and family to leave behind. The official reports of that war frequently mention the name of Hungerford in connection with "personal valor," and indeed, he proved himself a man of extraordinary metal.

After the war, he came to California. In July '49 he arrived in San Francisco, having made a most adventurous trip overland from San Jose del Cabo, and early in '50 the young adventurer appeared on the Yuba, In '51 he settled in Downieville, and went into partnership with Dr. C. D. Aiken, with whom he conducted a drug buisness for several years, meanwhile bringing his family out from the East. He organized the "Sierra Guards" and held the commission of Major, and was, in '55, presented with a magnificent sword, bearing the inscription:

"Major Daniel E. Hungerford, from the Sierra Guards, January 8 1855. Vera Cruz, Cerro Gordo, Contreras, Chapultepec, Gariten de Belen. Our volunteers were there."

But Major Hungerford also had an opportunity to distinguish himself as a soldier during that period. After the Ormsby massacre he led the troops, organized in Nevada, against the Indians in the Washoe war, operating in conjunction with Colonel Jack Hayes and Captain Creed Haymond, and to Hungerford is accorded the honor of the Indians' defeat. He also headed the first navigation of Pyramid Lake. With him was a party of thirteen, nearly all Downieville men, and on the island, at the north end of the lake, they buried a bottle, containing an account of the expedition.

The desire for adventure afterwards took Hungerford through part of the civil war, when he became a Colonel, and afterwards led him into a romantic expedition to Mexico, which was full of interesting details and at one time nearly brought him into serious trouble.

After having for some years engaged in railroad speculations in Texas, and other enterprises, he retired from active life and now resides at the Villa Ada, near Rome, with his son-in-law and daughter, the Count and Countess Telfener. He is a member of various scientific societies and spends his life's eventide in interesting researches and special studies.

I come now to the second character in my sketch, Maria Louise Antoinette, generally called by her second name, the eldest daughter of Colonel Hungerford. Mrs. Hungerford was a Mademoiselle Eveline de la Visera. Her parents were both French, but she was born in New York City, and had received a liberal education. As a wife and mother she set a brilliant example to most women; for, although devoted to her husband, she never stood in his way when his patriotic nature urged him to the front to defend his country's honor, or when his adventure-seeking instincts drove him into distant fields, where he expected that personal qualifications would warrant success. On all such occasions she submitted to her husband's desire and judgment, hoping for the best, and in her letters expressing her tender love and devoted prayers for the absent one.

The issue of their marriage was a son, who died as a mere child; the subject of this sketch, and Ada Elmira who married Count Geseppe Telfener. In '53 this family followed the husband and father, and became residents of Downieville. I remember the two girls well, and more especially the elder one, whom we used to call Louise. She was conspicuous, not merely for her beauty, but for her pleasing personality and manners. Her eyes were large and expressive; her features soft and round; her *teint* of a fair, delicate tint, and her hair fell in rich tresses, over her shoulders. But her winsome ways crowned all her attractions, and denoted, not only excellent breeding and a rare example, but also a warm and generous heart, which, indeed, she had. But for all that—who would have dreamed that the little Downieville girl would grow up to rule like a princess in a fairy tale. She was raised on the mines, and out of them, as by the magic wand of witchcraft, rose the pow-

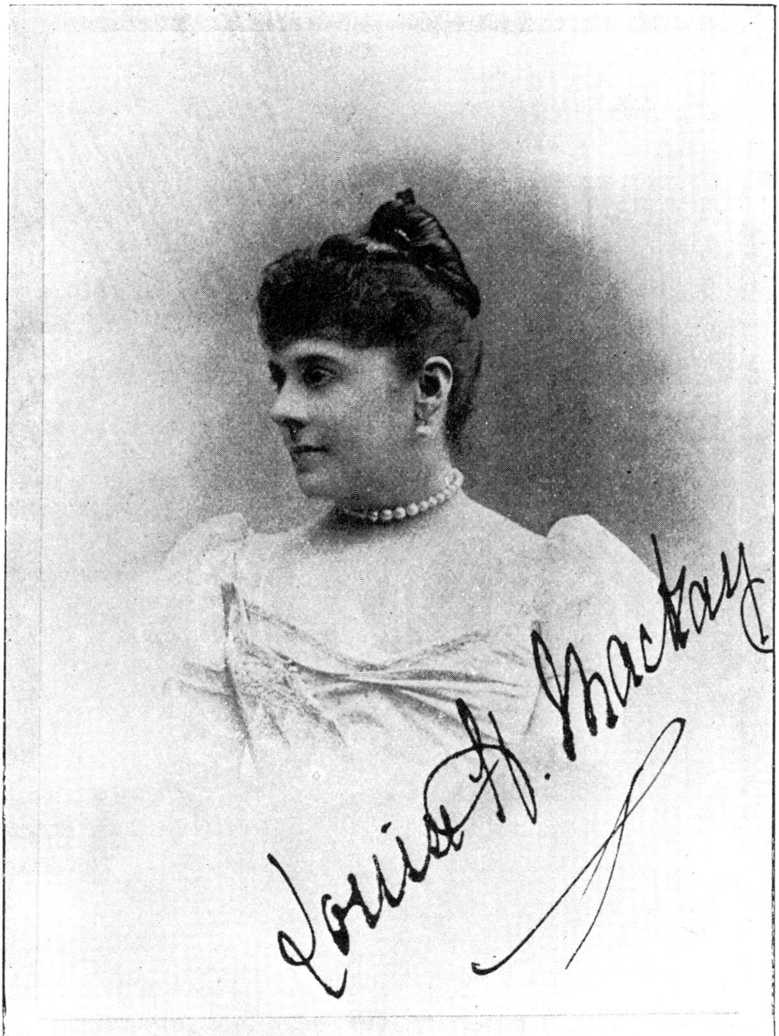

er that in after years, gave her the fame that she now enjoys,

At the age of seventeen she married Dr. E. Bryant. This prominent young gentlemen had become attached to her father's staff, but his career was cut short after two years and a half of wedded life, leaving her a widow with a baby girl, the present Princess Colonna. Rarely perhaps has a woman had to pass through an ordeal as trying as did the subject of this sketch during that period, but she bore up with a fortitude and buoyancy of temperament, characteristic of the soldier child, who had inherited her father's courage.

By this time Colonel Hungerford was fighting under General McClellan, and his wife had transferred her residence to Virginia City, Nevada. Thither the young widow went, and in order to help matters along during a period when their means were scarce, she established a school in which she taught English and French, most of her pupils being miners, and belonging to all grades of society. Among them was John W. Mackay, whose kindly and generous nature the most extravagant change of fortune has not to this day altered.

The fire that destroyed Virginia City in the early sixties is yet remembered by many. Among the havoc wrought was the total destruction of widow Bryant's residence, school-house, and all her worldly possessions. Immediately the sympathizing miners circulated a subscription for the benefit of the unfortunate woman and her mother; but when it was presented to Mackay, he looked it over, put it in his pocket, and remarking that he would attend to that business himself, disappeared down the shaft.

And he did. He had just then bought the controling share in the Hale and Norcross mine for $13,000 in solid gold, and he added to his fortune by making the handsome widow his wife shortly after.

The phenomenal success which attended Mackay in his later career, needs no historiographer here. The immense wealth which he amassed, enabled him to place his wife in a position in which she became world-famed; and in after years the little Downieville girl has exercised a spell, which could only be brought about, by the possession of extravagant means, combined with the personal attractions of Louise Mackay.

As I write this, I have before me a leading San Francisco paper, which announces that Mrs. Mackay, after an absence of sixteen years, spent chifley in Paris and London, has returned to San Francisco. In it I read one paragraph, which entirely endorses my own views, already expressed, and I quote it here:

"Undoubtedly the impressiveness of her great wealth and the enormous array of attractions it can buy, has had its part in her phenomenal social victories; but her natural endowments, her quick wit, and her great tact, have been the more important factors in making many of the first people of Europe her friends."

I will not finish this sketch without making one more allusion to her husband. He has often been judged harshly and hard things have been said of him. Phenomenal success is often followed by envy, and the green-eyed monster will plant its claws in a man's character, irrespective of truth. Personally speaking, California's bonanza king is the same plain-spoken, unpretentious man he was when, years ago, his hands were hard with wielding the miner's tool. He strove for success with integrity, foresight and judgment, and he is eminently deserving of it, yet it never turned his head or heart. I will close with an instance which came to my notice.

In the fall of 1876 Edwin Adams, the famous actor, returned to San Francisco, having completed a tour through Australia. His health was broken, his purse almost empty, and his friends in San Francisco either dead or gone away. The great impersonator of Enoch Arden was on the verge of dispair, and was daily sinking, physically and mentally. His misfortunes came to the ears of Mackay, and the next day a letter, containing a check for $2,000, was recieved by Adams to the following effect:

" My dear Mr. Adams:— Knowing you to be in some slight financial strait, may I beg your acceptance of enclosed accommodation, and thus permit me to discharge in part the vast obligation I feel in common with hundreds of others for your efforts in our behalf. I trust that we may long be honored with your presence, and that our stage may not soon be deprived of one of its brightest ornaments. With my best wishes for your success, and thanks for past favors, I have the honor to remain your obliged and obedient servant,

John W. Mackay."

When Mr. Mackay was afterwards told that Adams shed tears on receipt of the letter, he dryly remarked: "Poor fellow, I wish to God I had sent him ten thousand dollars."

Those who know the millionaire best say that his life has been full of such acts, but he is one of those who lets not his right hand know what his left hand doeth.

And such is the character of the man with whom the Downieville girl was destined to share a wonderful fortune and a life full of romantic events.

A SLAP-JACK FIEND

In the good old days, when "Wash" Hughes and Page were partners and ran the United States Hotel, the air in Downieville was full of fun, and practical jokes were the order of the day. This caravansary was then a big institution. It stood at the corner of the Upper plaza and the proprietors were doing a rousing business, having always a number of constant boarders and the trade of a large proportion of visitors who came to Downieville.

Among those who occasionally dropped into the hotel to get a meal, was one particular man whom the waiters called "Slaps" and as that is just as good as any other name and fitted him better than his own, I shall retain it here.

Mr. "Slaps," was not a regular boarder, either there or at any other place. He was one of those individuals whose erratic means do not always permit of a square meal, and who therefore, as a matter of course and self-defense, would upon more favorable opportunities counteract the evil effects of limited meals, by having a real good fill.

If there were a thing that culinary skill and a plea to the waiter could produce, which tickled the palet of Mr. "Slaps," that one thing was Slap-jacks, and the reader will now see the connection. Slap-Jacks were to his mind more palatable than *paties de fois gras* to the *gourmand* of more advanced civilization and taste, and fricassee of nightingales' tongues could not be sweeter relish to the oriental glutton, than were the hot cakes of the United States Hotel to the hero of this sketch.

Whenever he made his appearance at the hotel the waiters would give one another that silent sign, consisting of a "one and a half wink" with the left eye, which only waiters can give and understand, and which in ordinary parlance means "Here goes!" The visitor would take his seat and assume an air as if he ran the place and owned all the slap-jacks—past, present, and future conditional—and call out "hot cakes." Then the fun began. Our friend could eat a plate of slap-jacks in shorter time than it takes to tell, and no sooner disposed of, he would call again: "Another plate of hot cakes, waiter, if you please!"

It had been attempted several times to count the number of plates he ordered at any particular sitting, but waiters as a rule, are busy men, when at work, and the count had never been carried through so as to supply a true statistic. One morning there was a rush at the hotel. A number of people had come to town to be present at a land sale in the neighborhood, and the hostelry of Hughes & Page was crowded. In the dining room it was "waiter" here, and "waiter" there, and the obliging servants of hungry humanity ran to and fro in their endeavors to please everybody, racing against time, as they did their best.

In the midst of all this, our friend of Slap jack fame entered. The busy waiters blanched as they beheld him, they knew that he would give them additional work and impede progress—and he did! Three helpings followed in quick succession. Our friend yelled "hot cakes" till strangers dropped their knives and forks and looked about, curious to see the "other fellow," thinking they had got to a slap-jack contest. As "Slap" made the final lap in the third round and opened his mouth to call out "hot cakes" the waiter attending him, lost patience. He strode into the kitchen, where Mr. Hughes was busy at the time, and laying the case before him, asked the boss whether he could think of any way in which to satisfy the extraordinary demand on the part of "Slaps."

Mr. Hughes was a man of quick perception, and he at once saw his way clear to solve the problem. On the top of the stove a number of "slaps" were sizzling, getting ready for the table, but Mr. Hughes, with one brush, had them in a heap, and emptied the batter bucket over the top of the large stove, dumping about three quarts of the paste-like mixture upon it. In a moment the stove top looked like a geological map of California, but it did not take long to make it resemble what a witness described as a "cross between a horse-blanket and a door-mat," and when it was finished, it was put on the biggest dish in the establishment, and two men placed it before the slap-jack fiend, just as he was about to make another frantic demand for more "hot cakes."

Our friend looked at the slap-jack, at the men who brought it, and at the people around. The latter were taking it all in, when they dropped to the joke, a peal of laughter went up which scared the stranger and caused his hasty retreat. Since that day he never came to the United States Hotel, and where he ate his hot cakes afterwards, I know not.

YUBA POETS AND POETRY.

During the gold mining days on the Yuba a good deal of poetry has been written by local men of talent in that district, who wielded the pick and shovel during their working hours, and rode Pegassus during their leisure. It is true that the verses are often wanting in "feet" and therefore somewhat lame, but most of the authors do not claim to be more than songsters of the hour.

I have thought fit to mention a few of them here, as they in some degree express the sentiment of the mining camp and in their very simplicity and faultiness are often charming illustrations of the men who wrote them, as well as of those for whom they were written. Foremost among the Yuba poets stands W. K Weare. Mr. Weare had participated in the Mexican war and returned with honor. He was for many years mining on the Yuba in various parts, and was afterwards a guard at the State Prison, at San Quentin. Mr. Weare is now a very old man, and is living in Nevada City, remembered by all who knew him, as a genial, warm-hearted companion. His poetry embraced epics and lyrics as well as odes; heroic poems and sketches, and many of his productions are very good. His "Ode to the Pioneers" is remembered by many as a very impressive poem. It begins as follows:

"Magician! Memory! break the spell of intervening time,
  While we rehearse the deeds of all, wrought by a faith sublime,
Since when on the Sierra's crest a Pioneer first trod,
  When all was wild as when it sprang from chaos, or from God."

The end of this Ode is very touching in all its simplicity:

"How every day we hear of some, whose earthly bonds are riven;
　Whose hands their last deep shaft have sunk, their last long tunnel driven.
Let's hope that in the fatherland they're called on to explore,
　Are treasures richer, brighter far, than gold and silver ore,
For while the glorious West shall live, the pride of future years,
　Thousands of happy homes shall bless the grand old Pioneers."

Weare's real bend of mind and poetic perception comes out well in his poem entitled "San Quentin's Graves," in the following lines:

"Yonder, near St. Francis City, queenly—mistress of the Bay,
　Stands Lone Mountain, proud and stately, where the rich and honored lay.
There are tombs—proud mausoleums—spires and statues tow'ring high;
　Dainty in their sculptured beauty—which is but a sculptured lie,
Telling to the humble mourner who shall seek the lonely spot,
　Not the tenant's life relations, but precisely what was not.
Vain are all the towers and columns raised to conquerers by slaves;
　These are just as near their maker as San Quentin's outcast's graves."

Indeed, Weare expressed very many pretty thoughts in simple, but sympathetic language, and when, in 1879, he published a volume of his poetry, his old friends were glad of an opportunity to secure a collection they had long urged him to bring out.

Following is a poem entitled "Sierra Buttes," the author of which is unknown to me, although he was a Yuba miner.

"Through Time's dim vista looking down,
　Perhaps frowning o'er some ancient sea,
　Dark clouds then resting on thy crown,
　　And all around thee mystery.

"Thou watchest the fiery craters flow,
  And mountains heaving at their birth,
Amid the molten lava's glow;
  Before mankind had touched the earth.

"Still towering upward into space,
  A landmark when the morning breaks,
Yet men are delving at thy base,
  And heeding not thy darksome peaks.

"Time fades, yet ever rolling on,
  Men come and go and gaze on thee;
Like fleeting shadows they are gone,
  But thou art for eternity."

Fred Stone, I believe, is the author of the following poem, entitled "The Village Maiden." Fred was something of a singer and had a tune for the words, which I think was his own composition although it may not have been very original.

"Mother, dear, the bells are ringing,
  There's holly on the window pane;
I hear the distant voices singing,
  Christmas-tide has come again.
Winter's mantle, white, is lying—
  On the earth lies crystal snow,
Gleaming, as the day is dying,
  In the sunset's golden glow.

"Oh, it seems so hard to leave you;
  To the earth I fondly cling.
Do not let these moments grieve you,
  Yet I'd like to see the Spring,
With its sunshine, all its flowers,
  And its perfume-laden breeze;
Glistening raindrops, after showers,
  Like gems sparkling on the trees.

"I hear no more from absent Willie;
  He stays so long beyond the sea;
There's the faded rose and lily,
  Which at parting he gave me.

See, I press them, softly sighing,
  And bedew them with a tear;
They are dead, and I am dying,
  Dying with the waning year.

Do you think dear friends will miss me,
  When wild mirth will freely flow?
No more village youth will kiss me,
  Underneath the mistletoe?

Nor Old Christmas, ag'd and hoary,
  Bring its joys and hopes to me?
'Tis faded, gone; and in its glory,
  Vanished with our Christmas tree.

Hark! the bells so joyfully ringing;
  The holly's on the window-pane,
And soft voices, sweetly singing—
  "Kiss me, mother, once again."

Thus she sang; her heart o'erladen;
  Her parting breath she softly sighed;
Death had claimed the village maiden,
  Whils't yet 'twas Christmas-tide.

Old Sam Hartley took to rhyming, occasionally, and one of his productions is called:

MINING FOR GOLD.

I have traveled this world wearily o'er,
Sailed its wide seas, viewed many a shore,
Seeking to find, each path that I went,
For joys once found in a gold miner's tent,
That stood on the bank of Yuba's rich stream;
E'er life's fond illusions passed like a dream;
The songs that we sung, the stories we told,
Down by the river, when mining for gold.
All's changed; but my heart it feels the same glow,
For friends and old times in that long ago;
The hills are as grand, as stately the pines,
But where are the friends I knew in the mines.
I viewed the old spot where the log cabin stood,
It braved the stern winter storms, and the flood;
The roof has gone down, the logs scattered lay,

>   That the hand of old time has brought to decay.
>   These rafters will sing no more with wild glee,
>   Nor make the lone stranger welcome and free;
>   The place now is silent, unlike of old,
>   Down by the river when mining for gold.
>   Hearty the greeting of friends we would meet,
>   In town midst the throng and crowds on the street;
>   No brow was o'ercast, nor tinctured with gloom,
>   All was success in the flats or the flume,
>   Many are scattered to come not again,
>   Few are the faces we see that remain,
>   Hands that we clasped with warmth, now are cold,
>   Down by the river—laid under the mold.

Both the latter poems were sung by their respective authors, one Christmas Eve, a good many years ago, in a miner's cabin on the Yuba. The night was cold and wild. Outside the snow fell fast, and the wind howled round the corners; but within was good-cheer and merry company. In the midst of this scene of comfort and contentment, a knock came to the door, and upon opening, a stranger staggered in, nearly overcome with fatigue, cold and hunger. He carried a violin in a case and was at once made welcome by the miners. They did all to revive the traveler who was on the point of succumbing to the hardships he had been exposed to. He turned out to be Mr. Frank Littleton, the well-known musician, and soon recovering under the influence of an exceeding hospitality, he participated in the entertainment and played the accompaniment for the two miners mentioned above, as they sang their songs.

A frequent contributor to the poetic corner of Sierra papers, uses the pseudonym of "Miner." His productions are generally descriptive, and in the following poem, entitled "The Snow-shoe Races," he has given a good picture of a local sport which affords much amusement:

When snow lies deep on every hill,
Silence reigns—the birds are still;
Where gold is nestling in the mines,
And dark cliffs rest among the pines;
The earth is robed in purest white,
The sun gives out its dazzling light;
The snow-shoe racers each in place,
The given signal starts the race.

People in cities can never know,
How jolly it is to glide o'er the snow.

Down the mountain side, like birds in flight,
Or meteors on a starry night—
Bending low to miss the breeze,
Flying past the stately trees,
Rushing down to flat below,
Dancing o'er the "beautiful snow,"
Falling, rolling, seeing stars—
Then hear the laughing crowd's hurrah!

Away down the valley where oranges grow,
They miss all the fun we have in the snow.

The ladies, too, with modest grace,
Will take their chance to win the race;
Their hearts may beat with fear or hope,
But each has got her lightning "dope"—
The signal's given, off they go;
Pull wild at starting, scratching snow,
And if the dears are not experts,
The air seems filled with snow and skirts.

They try again, with face aglow,
Determined to win or die in the snow.

When darkness o'er the hills advance,
The sport ends with a social dance;
Chill winter thus his pleasures bring,
And water flows with early spring,
Then glittering gold that lay below,
Is brought to light by melting snow;
The track is gone, but beaming faces,
With glee recall the snow-shoe races.

People in cities and valleys may know,
When it is falling there's gold in the snow.

"Miner" is also the author of a poem which he calls "The hanging of the Mexican woman," wherein he describes a scene with which my readers are already familiar. I append "Miner's" version and verses relative to the incident which I have more fully described in the preceding pages:

'Twas long ago—a July morn—
   The stars paled in the early light;
A man lay stark and dead at dawn,
   His life ebbed with the shades of night.
A woman wronged by brawler's strife,
   Bravely took the avenger's part;
One swift-aimed blow her glist'ning knife,
   Plunged deep into a miner's heart.

Men gathered, then, from near and far,
   And left to silence many a mine,
On many a far-off creek and bar,
   Then shaded by the oak and pine,
And rushed to swell the surging throng,
   Like gath'ring streams in onward flood;
Men thus were wildly borne along,
   Who shrank from shedding human blood.

The hot sun shone above the scene,
   The river murmured in its bed,
The hills were clothed in summer green,
   And birds were fluttering overhead.
Friends tried to shield her—all in vain—
   They brought her forth with wildest jeers;
The die was cast, her blood must stain,
   The annals of the Pioneers.

BRITISH

COLUMBIA.

VICTORIA BEFORE THE BOOM.

CHAPTER I.

Arrival at Victoria—Sharp Practice—Indians Bring the First Gold—The Hudson Bay Company—An Energetic Governor—A Route to the Mines—Joining an Expedition—Natives Surprised—The Dame and the Bullets—Adventures on a Stream—Lilooet Lake—A Favorable Report—An Attempt that Failed.

During the month of July, 1858, I arrived for the first time in British Columbia, landing in Victoria.

At that time a tremendous excitement prevailed in this colony, caused by the discovery of gold, the news of which had spread all over the world. Rumors had sped like carrier pigeons to the remote mountain diggings of California, as well as to the more civilized portions of the globe, and the spirit for adventure and the lust for gold once more drew men toward a common center. In this throng that flocked northward along the Pacific Coast, were many of the pioneers of the Californian miners, early settlers on the Yuba and American Rivers, while other gold fields of Alta California were well represented.

For several years gold had been known to exist in British Columbia, but it may not have suited the first Caucasian discoverers of this fact to reveal the same. As early as '52 Mr. McLean, who then represented the Hudson Bay Company as chief trader at Kamloops, learned of the presence of gold, but not of its whereabouts. As in California, it was the native son of the soil who first brought the precious metal into notice, but as in the latter place, the priests, for reasons already given, suppressed the fact; thus the keen business men of the Hudson Bay Company may have also thought it wise to remain silent about the matter. The Indians were the first bearers of gold to his Caucasian lord, to whom he traded it, generally in the form of dust, for such trifles as his fellow-men—fairer in complexion only —saw fit to give for it. But by degrees the truth leaked out, and the fact was revealed. Adventurers came from the adjacent districts—Oregon and Washington in particular. They made their way up the rugged country on either side of the Thompson and other tributaries of the Fraser River, and it was soon apparent that gold was plentiful. Then the stream of immigration began. I have shown how at this period the Californian miner had become tired of home chances, which by degrees had become few and far between, and with his characteristic hopefulness he had left his old claim that paid moderately, or his sluice and tunnel that kept him in debt; had packed his pick and pan, rolled up his tent, and like the Arab, silently stolen away.

To one who had profited by the schooling which mining life imparts, as much as I had, the singular conditions which presented themselves in Victoria during those days did not seem very strange, but the youth who had just left his mother's apron strings to go in search of fortune, may, indeed, have felt some surprise at his first experience on the road to the new *El Dorado*. The crowd that gathered in Victoria was larger and more mixed than any I had seen before, and the number of "sharpers" who practiced their tricks upon strangers, and made the poor "greenhorns" their victims, was astonishing. I regret to say that in several of these unscrupulous speculations I recognized some of my old Californian acquaintances, even a former Downieville miner.

Provisions became scarce at one time and prices rose

accordingly. Some of the old miners, who knew from experience, what hungry men will pay for food, combined and offered the Hudson Bay Company to buy the balance of their flour. Thus they secured several hundred barrels, costing $10 per barrel at the one end, and a couple of dollars per pound at the other. Then the men became disheartened. They went to the Company to inquire whether all of their flour had been really disposed of, and were greatly relieved when told that the lot sold merely comprised their local stock on hand, but that in others of their stores they had plenty which they would be glad to sell at their ordinary rates. Thus the schemes to extort money from the miners were frustrated, and the speculators suddenly became wholesale dealers in flour, without any chance of realizing an expected enormous profit.

The man who at that time controlled the Hudson Bay Company, was James Douglas, who very shortly afterwards was appointed governor of British Columbia. Mr. Douglas became very popular with the strangers after this episode, and I may remark here that the officers of that Company, throughout, were able, clear-headed, and very accommodating men. I have had much to do with them and always found them particularly pleasant to deal with. Another corner was secured by a former Monte-Cristo miner, whose labor in California had been fraught with success. He bought up all the pans in the market, and for awhile pans were at a premium; but the mercenary vendor rendered himself so much detested through this deal that, no doubt, he had occasion to regret his nefarious speculation.

The gold mining of British Columbia proved somewhat different from that of California. In the first place the northern Indian was not as easily handled when the question was "digging for gold," as was his more southern brother. The reason for this may probably be found in the different manner, in which the value of gold was presented to him. In California the suave priest would not apparently place any value upon the gold. A meal, a piece of cloth, a little tobacco, and if the Indian professed Christianity, the absolution from his sins, would constitute the barter, in which a lump of gold or a quantity of dust represented his side of the bargain. In British Columbia the proposition was very different. The mercantile world had thought fit to establish proper business relations with the Indians. They had traded with them on a commercial basis, and when they discovered that gold was worth anything to the pale-face, they had accepted and received for it, if not an adequate value, at all events, a value which was measured by a business proposition. No wonder, therefore, that these savages objected to the sudden invasion of many thousands of men, who came to take away part of the material, for the finding of which they were, in their own estimation, handsomely rewarded.

But in addition to the hostility which the Indians exhibited in so many instances, the miners had to contend with the difficulties presented by the natural formation of the country. Probably no part of the world is more cut up by rugged mountains and rushing rivers, than British Columbia, and the road that naturally presented itself to the miner, as leading to the upper Fraser, was a dangerous one. No sooner had Douglas been made Governor of the possession, than he determined to send out a party for the purpose of finding, if possible, another route, and he commissioned Mr. J. G. McKay to head the expedition, which I was invited to join. The idea was to find a route to the upper Fraser, *via* Howe Sound and Lilooet Lake, and thus avoid ascending the river through the canyons, where the frequent rapids rendered the journey practically risky. This trip afforded me the first good opportunity of making myself acquainted with a new and interesting country.

We went first to Fort Langley, where we were equipped with all the necessaries for our expedition. The so-called forts were trading posts, established in various parts of the country by the Hudson Bay Company, and most of them were called by the name of some prominent officer of this famous organization, which at these centers carried on their traffic with the native tribes. The forts were all constructed on the same plan, although they differed in regard to the number of buildings they contained. The sites selected for the forts, was commonly a spot on the bank of a lake or river, elevated so as to form a point of vantage over the surrounding country, and the buildings of which the post consisted, were constructed of hewn timbers, and varied in number from a single block-house to fifteen or twenty. In the latter case they consisted of one or two large houses for the officers and clerks, and the quarters for the mechanics and laborers. In addition to these were spacious store-houses for the reception of goods, more particularly furs, shops for carpenters, coopers, blacksmiths and other trades, and a powder magazine, built of brick or stone. In some few cases the posts also had a school-house and chapel.

The whole of the little settlement was surrounded by a strongly-built stockade from fifteen to twenty feet high, on the inside of which, near the top, ran a gallery, provided with loop-holes for muskets, in the manner of mediæval fortifications. The picket-work or palisading, was flanked with bastions, of which there were generally two, placed diagonally at the corners of the fort, and mounted with small pieces of cannon, and provided with the necessary loop-holes for muskets. In founding these posts the principal items, taken into consideration, generally were the accessibility of the location, the number of Indians and the abundance of fur-producing animals in the neighborhood, as well as the soil in which grain and vegetables were raised for the supply of the place. At most of the posts gardening and farming were carried on quite extensively and successfully, and large numbers of fine cattle were raised; while at others, less favored, the brave representatives of the company had, as a rule, but a scanty supply of food, principally consisting of salmon and other fish, with such wild fruit as the Indians might bring, and occasional contributions of game. The latter was, however, already, in those days becoming a luxury, owing to the persistency with which the deer had been hunted for years for the sake of its meat and the antlers of the stag. I was much impressed by these forts, when I first saw them. It is true, that they offered but a poor protection against modern artillery, even as it was then; but they presented quite a formidable appearance, and have always been found to serve their purpose well by over-awing the Indians and successfully resisting their attacks.

Fort Langley is situated on the South side of the river Fraser, about twenty-five miles from its mouth. It was already then an old, extensive establishment, I believe at that time, under the supervision of Mr. Yale, who held a prominent position with the company The company had a large farm here with a considerable amount of stock. The land, which had been cleared of

SIR JAMES DOUGLASS, K. C. B.

heavy timber, produced excellent crops and vegetables and fruit grew in abundance, during their respective seasons. All through the district were small prairies, in which a luxuriant growth of grass afforded splendid pasture for the cattle, and yielded, in addition, an abundant supply of hay for the winter. On the opposite side of the river there was an Indian village, in which dwelt the remnant of a once numerous tribe. They had, however, in common with many of their sister tribes, who enjoyed the close association of the pale-face, become considerably reduced, both in numbers and morals, for it is a sad fact, that in the contest between civilization and savagedom, the latter is generally annihilated.

In later chapters I shall have more to say about these, our copper-colored fellow-beings, for I came much in contact with them and had ample opportunity to observe them. Meanwhile I return to our trip in search of a route, by which the miners might more easily reach the regions of the Upper Fraser. From Langley we took the trail to Howe Sound and then steered our course for Lilooet Lake, arriving there after several adventures. We got a right royal reception, when we approached the first Indian village. The whole population came out to meet us, but the welcome was sent per musket ball, and we did not care for it. Some of the braves mounted a pile of wood and continued pointing their guns at us, but I realized that the first exhibition of fear would mean death to us and told McKay so. Linked arm in arm, we marched bravely forward, and when we reached the base of the stack of wood, we held out our hands for them to help us up, which they did in a mechanical sort of way, apparently taken aback by our cool demeanor. My eye caught sight of one old dame, who carried a long bag, apparently containing lumps of something. My curiosity was aroused, and, thinking for certain that it was gold, I made up my mind to lay siege to the good will of the ancient beauty; but I entirely lost my ambition in that direction, when I saw her opening the bag a few minutes later and take from it a number of muskets balls, which she distributed among the young braves, that they might make holes in us. Such conduct would have put a damper on the good opinions of her most ardent admirer.

After awhile, we succeeded in making friends with the Indians, who were known as the "Unamish," and were considered a somewhat treacherous tribe. In return for a musket they gave us a canoe, and we now followed the stream thinking that we had improved our conditions somewhat; but we soon discovered that the canoe was too small to be of actual service to us. However, we made the best of it for several miles and then came across another canoe on a bar. We left a musket in payment for it and traveled on, after having divided our pack; but we had not gone far, when we were overtaken by the owner of our new craft, who came after us in another dug-out;standing up in the bow of it, he shouted to us to halt, and we thought best to obey. He had a long *wa wa* talk with Mr. McKay, who gave him some tobacco and made friends, and then we proceeded up the river.

I must admit I did not relish our navigation very much; and I suppose it was because, at that time, I was unused to the scenes that presented themselves. Every now and then we came upon Indian villages, and every time we had to halt and keep talking with the inhabitants, who came down to accost us. We also had to give them presents at every place, consisting of powder, musket balls, tobacco or other things, which they appreciated. They had a disagreeably, insinuating way of hanging over the gunwale of our canoe with big bowie knives in their hands. It is an old saying, and a true one, that familiarity breeds contempt, and I suppose, it did with me, for I soon became accustomed to their ways and took no notice of them afterwards, but on the occasion of my first introduction to these people, their manner of approaching strangers offended my sensibilities.

We were fortunate enough to be able to report the possibility of traveling by the route, proposed, and reach Lake Lilooet by it. This watershed possesses at least one remarkable feature—the turbid appearance of its waters, which are of a dirty green hue. This is quite an exception to the general rule, for in British Columbia the water of the lakes is noted for its remarkable purity and clearness, the lakes, as a rule, being exceedingly deep. The reason Lake Lilooet does not follow suit in this respect, may be found in the fact, that the feeders run over a species of argillacious earth, which, no doubt, imparts to the water the offensive color.

The importance of our successful endeavors to find this passage could be only fully realized by men who had traveled in these regions. It was not long before a proper route was established to the Fraser river by way of Lilooet Lake, the Lilooet and Harrison mines, the Lilooet Meadows, lakes Anderson and Seton, these points being interspersed with mule trails.

On our return we went to Nanaimo, where we were kindly received by Captain Stewart, Adam Howe and Dr. Benson, all of the Hudson Bay Company. Governor Douglas received our report with much satisfaction but desired us to find, if possible, another short route, which could be utilized at once without any further trouble in the making of trails, etc. The Governor had a theory that this could be realized by starting from a point higher up on the coast, and we made an attempt, starting from Jarvis Inlet, but after a very hazardous trip, on which we suffered numerous hardships, we had to abandon the idea, as wholly impracticable.

CHAPTER II.

Queen Charlotte Island—Gold Harbor—Scotch Guy—The Majesty of Nature—Captain Gold—Potlatch—Political Campaigns—Totems—Architecture and Art—An Interesting People—Vanity of Savagedom—Curious Customs—The Death-dance—Myth and Legend.

Early in the year 1859 I was one of a party, embarking for the Queen Charlotte Islands. We had chartered a schooner in command of Captain Robinson, and my intention was to prospect the islands for gold and afterwards explore the cost of the mainland, as Governor Douglas was anxious to know more about the numerous inlets there, as well as the possibility of locating an available pass for the building of the projected Great Canadian and Pacific Railway.

We were a band of twenty-seven miners, all old hands and well tried, and we steered our course for Gold Harbor on Moresby Island, but only to find it a second Gold Lake of California fame. We carefully examined a spot where a large quantity of gold had been taken out sometime before, but could not find anything worth working, although we saw quartz and did some blasting. The general nature of the rock was trap and hornblend, and, at the head of Douglas Inlet, we found granite, as well as slate, talcose rock and coal, but not gold; and I concluded, that the large amount of this metal, which had been found previously in those parts with so little difficulty, existed merely in what the miners call an off-shoot or blow-out, which can only be explained as one of those freaks of nature, so often found in a mining country.

In the Skidgate Channel we met with but little better success. We were wind-bound for some time near the Casswer Indian village, where we discovered traces of previous prospecting. Here the indications of gold were certainly more distinct. We met an Indian Chief, who to accommodate us gave his name as Scotch Guy. He wore a large piece of gold, weighing probably two ounces, but he could not be persuaded to tell us, where he found it. As to ourselves, we could not find any gold. There was plenty of sulphurate of iron, talcose slate, and red earth, and I received the impression, that the natives there are first-class prospectors, and know all about gold mining.

The coast from Casswer village to Skidgate Channel presents some of the wildest scenery, I have ever seen. The rocks rise like mighty giants, daring the approaching sailor to set foot on the island they guard. They stand bold and defiant with the scars of ages seaming their sides in the shape of rifts and fissures, and, at their feet, the waters roll with a strong underswell towards the uninviting shore. But here and there a narrow inlet will admit the traveler into a small natural harbor. Also this may be surrounded by towering mountains, rearing aloft with the same threatening appearance, while here and there a waterfall, like a thundering, splashing cascade, throws its contents into the otherwise quiet harbor and makes its waters turbulent.

An investigation of the northwest portion of the island revealed the fact that it consists chiefly of low, sandy or gravel flats with no indications of being a gold bearing country. We therefore gave up our search for gold in these quarters and set sail for the mainland, intending to explore the country from Fort Simpson to Fort St. James.

But while I have thus briefly taken my reader over what I may call the business portion of my first trip to Queen Charlotte Island, I propose to dwell a little longer on the natural conditions that came to my notice, whilst there. I consider this part of the world a highly interesting one and my observation of the Indians showed them to be a race, different in many respects to the ordinary redskin.

The large group of islands was originally discovered in the year 1774 by a Spanish navigator, named Juan Perez, who called them Cabo De St. Margarita, but as early as 1787 a Captain Dixon, in command of the ship "Queen Charlotte," gave them their present name, and during the following year Captain William Douglas of the ship "Iphigenia," with a portion of his crew, were the first white men who sat foot on the islands, landing in Parry Sound and establishing the first trade with the natives. However, up till the time when I first visited these Islands, no systematic attempt had been made to explore them, with the exception of one, made by the French adventurer, Captain Etienne Marchand, who in the year 1791 with the ship "Solide," visited the southern seas and explored a small portion of this archipelago. Since my first visit to these islands the Colonial government has done much to ascertain the nature of them and has made exact charts of the group, and I may mention the name of Newton H. Chittenden as a gentleman, who has spared no efforts to explore them, gaining, as a result, not only much knowledge as to their physical condition, but also learning many interesting facts about their inhabitants.

The whole group is said to consist of some 150 islands. They are separated from the mainland by Queen Charlotte Sound, which varies in width from thirty to eighty miles. Their most southern point, Cape St. James, is one hundred and fifty miles from the nearest point of Vancouver Island, and to the north they are separated from the Prince William group of Alaska by Dixon Entrance, having an average width of about thirty miles.

The general physical conditions of this archipelago would give the impression that it is merely the remnants of a *terra firma*, which, through some fearful revolution, has been reduced to a most bewildering labyrinth of islands and islets, separated by sounds, straits, passages, and fringed with inlets of the most phantastic shapes. Through the entire length of the islands runs a mountain chain, ranging in hight from six hundred to five thousand feet, covered with an evergreen forest of spruce, hemlock and cedar, which, with few exceptions, stretch from their summit to the coast. The exceptions occur where the coast in some places is rock-bound, and in others is found of sandy soil.

Many remarkable effects are produced, both in scenic and geological respect, where the coast is rocky. In some places the highest elevations on the immediate coast do not exceed four hundred feet, while in others bold, rocky bluffs rise to the highth of eight hundred feet, at times as high as twenty-five hundred feet, above the level of the sea, the mountains bordering on the inlets, presenting an almost perpendicular front.

There are, I suppose, an uncounted number of streams on these islands. They are naturally only short, but rush towards the ocean with swift currents, and fall into the larger waters with a thundering noise, as they leap down the steep rocks or make their way over the more gradual mountain slopes. They add considerably to the grandeur of this singular nature, which on the whole is exceedingly picturesque, forming wonderful scenes, in which blend the ocean blue and the forest verdure, with the silver spray of the rivers and the solemn rocks that rise where the breakers toss their white-capped heads at their feet.

If the theory be correct, that these islands at one time belonged to a *terra firma*, a portion of which is now buried beneath the rolling waters, there can be no doubt that this land was gold bearing and probably richly so. The gold found in '52 in Mitchell Harbor, better known as Gold Harbor, may have been a corner, broken away from a large and rich supply, which now lies many fathoms below. In parts of the island there are indications of gold, but I have not learned as yet, that any quantity has been found since the Hudson Bay Company took out the gold referred to, the presence of it being revealed by an Indian, known ever since as Captain Gold The whole of that quantity amounted to only $5,000, which after all was nothing. I have already mentioned the existence of coal in some places, and I think that copper might be found on the island, at least I saw indications of it on Moresby Island. But, notwithstanding the evident trace of gold, coal and copper, to this day neither of these minerals have been found in sufficient quantity to warrant the expense of working them. They are merely there as pointing to the existence of larger stores of their own kinds hidden somewhere in that wonderful architecture of that locality. But where ---- ? That is the great enigma, which remains unsolved. No feature of these islands, however, surpassed in interest the natives, who are called Hydah Indians. To me the study of man has always been more attractive than anything else I know of, and I have had great opportunities for practicing it under varied circum-

HYDAH INDIAN CHIEFS.

stances, applying my observations to human beings of different races and nationalities.

The Hydah Indian is probably the finest savage I have ever had the pleasure of meeting, and I shall, at all events, always feel kindly towards him, when I recollect, that he never showed any desire to scalp me or in any other way molest me, which is a good deal more than I can say for his brethren on the mainland. They are not a handsome-featured people, and their women lack graceful movements. Their hair and eyes are very black; their teeth shining white and their complexions of an olive hue. The average hight of the male is about five feet seven inches, and both men and women have finely developed chests and forearms, caused by their incessant handling of the oars; for they are the best boatmen I have ever met, and in saying this I refer to both sexes. They have, indeed, an amphibious-like nature, for they seem to be as much at home in the water as they are ashore, and for feats of diving and swimming their equals are not easily found.

Their political institutions seemed to me to have much in common with our own American ways. The man who wishes to become chief has to pay dearly for the honor. The payment consists of a feast, which often lasts for days. Everybody is then invited and handsomely entertained, and blankets are distributed in great numbers. It will be seen by this, that the idea of buying friends in a political campaign is by no means a result of progressive American civilization, but rather a return to savagedom. At all events, he who entertains the handsomest; who has the most money to spend and can make himself most popular through his means, wins the contest, which is often most bitterly fought. These feasts are called *potlatch,* a term which indicates the distinction of certain things, and they are celebrated on various occasions, such as the funeral of a deceased member of the tribe, the inauguration of a new house, etc.

Strangely enough, when I first knew these people, the missionaries did not seem to have had much to do with them, and what civilization they had appeared to me to have been carried to them principally through traders and more in particular through the Hudson Bay Company. They were very distinctly classified, not only in castes but also in different tribes, which had evidently been done for the purpose of preventing too close intermarriage. Each one of these tribes, or families, has its own crest, which is frequently engraved upon their belongings. They are called *totems* and the natives, belonging to the same *totem*, are forbidden to intermarry. They have a number of these *totems*, known in their own language as the eagle, the wolf, the crow and so on.

Their moral standard did not appear to be very high, and they were in absolute ignorance of the sentiments expressed in a good many of the ten commandments, or otherwise they utterly disregarded them. As I have said, they were not blood-thirsty, but they often forgot to distinguish between our belongings and their own, and were frequently persistent in insisting upon a potlatch, or distribution of our effects among themselves.

As mechanics they far surpassed what I had then seen of savage skill in this direction, and their villages were to me a most wonderful sight. They had learned from the traders to build proper houses and constructed some very comfortable habitations, which nearly always presented the gable, to what I should call the front. But their poles were the most singular feature about the villages. The proper meaning of these poles I have never learned, but they tower like huge columns from thirty to seventy feet in hight outside many of their houses. They are covered from the base to the apex with carvings of the most grotesque order. It must be said, that in the art of carving these savages stand very high, more especially considering the few and primitive implements with which they do their work. I have seen later in Alaska similar artistic work; but when for the first time I beheld it at the village of Gold Harbor on Maud Island, I was fairly taken aback. Not only are their columns decorated with such carvings, but every other conceivable thing belonging to them, such as their ax handles, oars, canoes, even spoons or drinking vessels, and they appear to think nothing worth having which has not been artistically carved. Their skill in building canoes is very wonderful, and it is a question to me, whether any other nation, savage or civilized, can produce better boats for speed than these people, whose principal boat building place is at Massett.

They have the same hankering for personal adornments as their Caucasian fellow-beings, and their women more particularly do not give their fairer sisters any odds, although, as a matter of course, they differ in style and fashion. When I first came among them, European fashions were not much in vogue, although later on, the blanket, breech cloth and leather coverings have been discarded for cloaks made from the skin of the sea otter, proper pants and dresses, and woven underwear, but in common with all savage races boots are the last portion of civilized dress they will adopt. By way of ornamentation, men and women tatooed themselves, often profusely so, and here again the *totems* frequently appear. The women were quite clever at braiding and manufactured a kind of hat, which they wore. They also prepared certain paints, with which they covered their faces, and for this purpose they used vermillion, common charcoal, deer tallow and other ingredients, which showed that the artist of the hare's foot and the inventors of beauty powder and face enamel are by no means original in their endeavors to hide nature's own gift. For additional ornament both perforated the septum of the nose and inserted a silver ring, and the women often decorated their fingers with a number of rings and used feathers, mother of pearl and a variety of shells for further decoration.

Their social enjoyments were mostly confined to dancing and masquerades and they exhibited great ingenuity in their make-up. Their object seemed generally to be to imitate the animals, which rove through the forests of their island home, but not only did they wear on their own heads the heads of bears, deer, goats and other animals, as well as masks, representing birds, but they were also adepts at imitating on reed whistles the shrill cry of many of the wild forest birds. They also wore other masks with moving eyes and lips and a most hideous expression. On festive occasions they wore a shawl of their own manufacture, which was of a particularly fine texture and made from the wool of the mountain goat. In their hands they carried small hoops, to which were attached a number of birds' beaks, and with these they produced a noise resembling the sound of castanets. While this diabolic concert is going on the dancers scatter the soft down of birds, until the air is filled with them, and it may be easily understood that to the stranger, who for the first time witnesses this scene, the effect is perfectly bewildering.

Most characteristic of all is the so-called death-dance, performed by one single individual, who runs through the village like a madman, wearing nothing but a loin-cloth. As he rushes past the houses, he imitates the hideous shriek of some wild beast, and, seizing any animal, which may happen in his way, he tears it to pieces and devours a portion of the raw flesh.

They do not appear to have any religious ideas, outside that of the great spirit, whose aid they implore, when embarking in any undertaking, and his opposite, which would correspond with the devil of other beliefs. They do not, however, have any graven images of either of these powers, and I imagine their ideas of them are somewhat vague.

They have at the same time, certain traditions or legends, which are handed down to them as myths from a remote antiquity. Thus they account for the creation of men by relating, that when the whole earth was covered with water, a raven, the only living creature left, heard cries issuing from a shell lying on a protruding rock, and upon examining it, discovered within a woman and a child, whom he brought forth. He married the woman, and thus became the father of the whole Indian race.

Another singular myth, explains the origin of the heavenly bodies. They say the raven also discovered that a powerful chief owned the moon, which he had hidden in some obscure place, that no one might find it. The same chief had a daughter, who was the mother of a young baby, and one day the raven did away with the infant, and assuming its appearance, took its place. He was petted and cared for, and when he discovered where the moon was kept, he begged so hard to be let in to see it, that the chief ultimately took him into the chamber. But no sooner was the supposed grandchild there, than he again transformed himself to a raven, and seizing the moon in his beak, flew away with it to Naas country. Here the Indians begged of him to let them see it, to which he ultimately consented, and, in the exhuberance of their joy, they threw it so high into the heavens that it broke into many pieces, forming the moon, the sun and all the stars. Both these legends are very striking, I think, and, may be, some student of mythology and revealed religions may see in them interesting corroborations of ideas, expressed in other religious systems.

The population of these islands was not very large and was steadily decreasing. I think it was estimated at about a thousand in the year 1883, but when I first visted them there were certainly a good many more. Still, the fact that they were decreasing was made quite manifest by the presence of a good many deserted villages in the different parts of the group, and there were large burial places with indications of funerals enough to show that the race had been far more numerous than when I knew it first.

I have dwelt upon these people at some length, because they greatly attracted me, and, however imperfect my account, it may still have some interest to my readers.

CHAPTER III.

Fort Simpson—On the River Skeena—"Pioneer H. B. C."—A Tempting Offer—Locating a Pass—What a Gold Band Did—Red Paint—*Bon Jour*—Frank's Curly Hair—Chief Saltow-tow—White Men in the Wilderness—Days of Privation A Poor Craft—Head Factor, Peter Ogden—A California Monte Bank in Victoria.

In the early part of September 1859 I was at Fort Simpson, ready to explore the river Skeena and penetrate as far as Fort Fraser, at the same time making a survey of the country with a view to finding a pass, as mentioned, for the Great Canadian and Pacific Railroad Route. My company consisted of two white men, William Manning, an Englishman, and Frank Choteau, a French Canadian, besides two Indians.

Fort Simpson was at that time a post of some importance. It is situated on Chatham Sound in the extreme northwest corner of British Columbia, adjacent to what were then Russian Possessions. Owing to its natural location and surroundings, it enjoyed a large and lucrative trade. It possessed an excellent harbor, the neighboring waters abounded in fish and the land in wild animals, thus making it the hunting ground of a number of large and thrifty tribes. It was the mart for all the various northern Indians and was frequented, not only by those of the mainland, but by a number coming across from Queen Charlotte Islands, and Alaska. The Fort was named after Sir George Simpson, a former Governor of the Company; and an extensive trade had been established between it and Victoria, steamers coming up from the latter place loaded with articles adapted for the Indian trade, and returning with such goods as had been obtained in exchange.

On the 5th of September I set out on my expedition with my little party. At our first camp we made the acquaintance of the Indians of these parts, who made haste to tell us, that they were very honest people, and demonstrated this by getting away with my coat, while I was asleep. We made a trip up a small stream, called by the natives Scenatoys, and here the Indians showed us some crystalized quartz, in one piece of which I detected gold. This was the first of its kind, I had seen in this locality, but, although I was shown a granite slide, from where the piece was alleged to have come, I could not find anything like a payable vein. We afterwards explored a small river, called the Foes, and then took to the Skeena again, making our way up the river, where the current was gradually getting stronger and stronger, and it took us all our time and strength to pull the canoe against it. The country looked auriferous, but, when we tried prospecting, we could only raise a few specks to the pan. We passed the village called Kitchumsala, and I went ahead of the party in a small canoe, only accompanied by an Indian. We came past the junction of the river Chimkootch, on the southwest side of which we found lead at the Plumbago mountain, and here my companion pointed out to me a tree, on which had been carved many years ago the legend: "Pioneer H. B. C." I was informed that this had been done by Mr. John Work, one of the company's officers, and the manner in which the letters bulged from the bark, testified, that many years had elapsed since this daring pioneer had visited the locality.

We were now approaching the village of Kittcoonra. The land became more level, and the mountains receded from the river bank, while fertile flats extended for four or five miles on each side of the river. This is decidedly fine farming land, and the Indians here pick berries and dry them for winter supply. We were taking a rest on the river bank, when my Indian companions suddenly gave a cry of alarm, and looking up I perceived, that a whole band of natives, inhabitants of the village, were running down towards us, evidently with no friendly intent; for they were all armed and shouting furiously, and behind them came the women and children, ready to carry away the plunder after the fray. In a case of that kind the exhibition of utter indifference is the only safeguard, as the least sign of fear would mean death by the Indians' bullets. So I motioned my men to lie down on the ground and remain quiet, while I filled my pipe and assumed an appearance of supreme ease. My tactics were rewarded with the desired result. The Indians, seeing no reason for hostility, quieted down, and some of the women came up close to me with the native inquisitiveness of their sex. To one of them I gave a needle, but this article, small as it was, seemed to please them all so much, that everybody came up for one, the men laying down their weapons to get a needle. But I was pleasantly surprised to learn these people's ideas of reciprocity. for they at once dispatched some of the young men to their village for venison, beaver and bear meat, all cooked and ready for eating, and we were all invited to sit down with them and feast. More than this, when we showed signs of departing they insisted upon us staying with them. They told me they would build us a house, be friends with us, give us all the land we wanted, and help us cultivate potatoes; but we had to refuse their profuse hospitality and push on up the river.

Arrived at the forks of the Skeena (called by the Indians Kittamaks, afterwards changed to Hazeton) we left the river and, walking overland, made for the Indian village of Agullgath. The country we traveled through was particularly pleasing, being especially well adapted for agricultural purposes. We dined at the village, having secured some fish from the natives in trade for tobacco and then crossed the river on an Indian suspension bridge, continuing our journey along a well-beaten trail. The timber consisted principally of small hardwood and some soft wood trees, far easier to clear than the tall pines. The land was rolling and well watered by little streams that flowed from the distant hills, and there were many indications of coal. Far away to the south we saw the snow and glaciers on towering mountains, which are white-capped all the year round, and down by the river bank the growth of cottonwood and birch pleasantly varied the scenery, which was indeed, exceedingly inviting. In this locality, finding the surroundings advantageous I put up the following:

"NOTICE—September 22, 1859.—I have this day located and claimed this pass, as the route of the Great Canadian and Pacific Railroad.   William Downie."

We were now making for Naas Glee and began to recognize, that we were on the down grade. In fact, we had really succeeded in coming through the only pass from Agullgath, which is suitable for a road. As we were traveling along here, we saw a wild goat, and one of my Indians made chase up the mountain for it, but, meeting with a company of three bears, he suddenly remembered that discretion is the better part of valor and returned express speed. As we neared the village of Naas Glee, we fired our pistols in the air. The effect might be likened to what might be produced by poking with a stick in an ant hill. In a moment we were surrounded by all the braves in the settlement. They came rushing towards us armed with guns and long bowie knives, but seeing that we manifested no fear they quieted down. I do not wish my readers to understand, that I consider myself a more courageous man than many others, although at the same time I have had plenty of opportunity of proving that I possess more personal courage than a good many. I am not prepared to say, that this is always an advantage, for while at times it helps to carry a man through great perils and hardships; the same man would probably have had a more comfortable life, minus this courage, which often leads him into most trying circumstances. In dealing with the Indians, I had soon perceived that the only way of getting along with them, was to show the utmost composure at the first meeting, and, while I adopted this as a rule and always succeeded in appearing calm, I am not prepared to say, that I always felt correspondingly at ease. Yet, I must admit, that as I now look back upon my many meetings with the redskins, and consider how many of my friends have fared among them I feel thankful that my scalp is still intact.

On this expedition I wore round my hat a gold band, and I had frequently reason to congratulate myself upon this fact, for it seemed to inspire the Indians with a good deal of respect, evidently impressing them with the idea that I was a great chief. On the present occasion they soon became very friendly, and their Tyhee, or chief, asked me to his house His name was Tal-tow-tow or Norra, they called him by both names, and I gave him what small articles I could spare. But my greatest stroke in the direction of making myself popular in this colony was made, when I devided three yeast cans, filled with red paint, among the women and children. Never was female vanity more satisfied, than when our new lady friends embellished their features with large streaks of red paint, and I doubt whether any belle of fashionable society could think herself more attractive, after using her cosmetics, than did these savages, after daubing themselves with the paint.

We discovered that this village was situated on the Skeena, and thus, having left this river five days ago, we had now struck it again higher up. We also here observed traces of French influence for the first time, for the Indians hailed us with the words *bon jour*; but later on we discovered that all through these regions many French words were used by the Indians as a result of their intercourse with French traders.

We were well entertained by the natives who feasted us in one of their houses, and I was given the seat of honor with my white companions next to me. The women seemed much amused at Frank's hair, which was very curly—a fact that evidently puzzled them a good deal, as the Indians' hair is always straight. They would steal up from behind and pull the hairs out of his head. Then they would hold it out straight between both hands and, letting go at one end, appeared much surprised when the hair curled up again. By and by Frank's head began to get sore, and he objected to the sport. "Never mind, Frank," I said, trying to soothe his ruffled temper, "It is only female curiosity."

"Female curiosity or not," grumbled Frank, "I don't want them to pluck all the hairs out of my head, as if I was some bird being prepared for cooking—oh! There, let go, you ——!"

And Frank brushed off a woman's hand, which was trying to rob him of another lock.

Naas Glee is a center, where all the upcountry Indians meet at certain seasons. The head factor of Fort St. James sends a boat down here at certain times, and a large trade in dried fish and other articles is carried on. I began to fear, that I should not be able to reach the Fraser, as I was told that it was about ten days' journey away from where we were, and the Indians were gradually robbing me of all I had to depend upon for further trade with the natives. I realized that I had to get out as soon as possible, and, after some persuasions, I succeeded in getting Tal-tow-tow to go with me. He provided a canoe and some dried fish, and we started up the river, exceedingly glad to leave our hosts, whose hospitality had been well counterbalanced by the persistency with which they had wrung from us a great many things, both necessaries and trading articles. About ten miles up the river we passed the village Whatatt, and above this we came to Babine Lake, traveling now through exceptionally fine country.

It was just about daylight the next morning, and I had crawled out of my blanket, when to my surprise I saw a boat approaching, filled with Europeans. The man at the helm turned out to be a Mr. Gavin Hamilton, and his crew were Canadians. He came from Fort St. James and was on his way to Naas Glee for dried fish, furs, etc. He was very much surprised to see us and told me that he had never heard of any other white man succeeding in traveling over the route we had come by. He insisted upon taking my Indian chief back with him, as he said he could do nothing at Naas Glee without him and would most likely be robbed of all he had in place of making trade, and when I remonstrated with him and told him, that I could not go on without a guide not knowing the way, he smiled and said, that a

MASSET, Q. C. ISLAND.

man, who had been able to visit Naas Glee as a stranger and come out as well as I had done, might go anywhere. He had no rations to spare us but finally arranged that we should take Tal-tow-tow's canoe, and that the chief should return with him, and he gave us a letter for Mr. Peter Ogden, in charge of Fort St. James, who was the same gentleman after whom the city of Ogden in Utah has been named.

I had sent both my Indians with Mr. Hamilton, and it proved a fortunate thing for us. We were supposed to be only five days' journey from Fort St. James, and on our first day's sail we made Fort Killman, which at that period was unoccupied. It reared its lofty palisaing in the silent wilderness with not a sound issuing from behind the closed doors. There was something uncanny about the lonely little fort, and we left it behind without regret. According to Mr. Hamilton we had now another four days' journey before us, but we soon realized, that we could not cover the distance in that time. Babine Lake is about one hundred miles long, and, whenever we could do so, we used our blankets as sails. The scenery along the shore was very pleasing, and, under more favorable circumstances, we could have enjoyed the trip very much, but rations were getting low and we had been out five days, when we reached the head of the lake and we took the trail for the next watershed, Lake Stewart. So we abandoned our canoes and made our way through the forest. Here, for the first time on our journey, did we see the track of a wagon, but, strange to say, it was over ten years since the ruts were furrowed in the soil. Previous to that time the Company had a wagon road to Lake Babine, but it was then abandoned. We packed our traps along the trail and came upon a camp at a small lake, where an Indian family was camping and hunting. They seemed much surprised at our appearace, and in exchange for some tobacco and paint, gave us a few dried fish, and helped us carry our pack to Stewart Lake, which was not far distant. Nevertheless the assistance was very welcome, for we had had so little to eat for a day or two, that the effect of privation began to tell upon us.

Arrived at Stewart Lake we looked in vain for a canoe, which we expected to find there. Things were beginning to look ugly. Fort St. James was away at the other end of the lake, but we could not possibly walk that distance in our reduced condition, and we sat down very much after the fashion of McCawber, "waiting for something to turn up." Driven by hunger and despondency, for I did not expect to get any more provisions till we reached Fort St. James, I attempted to eat grass in order to save our own scanty supply, but it would not go down, and the experiment demonstrated to me, that Nebuchadnezzar must have had pretty hard times of it, when he took to bovine fare.

At last we found a very old canoe. It was split from stem to stern and apparently of no use at all, but necessity is the mother of invention, and we lashed a drift log to each side of it, hoping by this contrivance and incessant baling to be able to travel down the lake. After experiencing considerable difficulty in making our frail craft answer its purpose, we succeeded in getting down about five miles, when we suddenly shipped a sea, that nearly swamped us, but just in the nick of time we perceived an Indian fishing close under the shore. We hailed him, and he at once came to our rescue and brought us safe to his camp, where we were fed on fresh trout and a meal, the enjoyment of which is yet fresh in my memory.

Once more we succeeded in making friends of our Indian hosts. They did not understand much English but could speak a little French, and Frank, who was a Canadian and could converse in that language, piloted us through this difficulty and arranged with the Indian that he should take us to Fort St. James, receiving as remuneration one blanket. It is strange, how soon a man forgets his troubles. We had now plenty to eat and a chance soon to get to Fort St. James, and all our troubles seemed to be at an end. We ran down the coast before a fair wind, going ashore when it became too rough. The scenery gradually changed, and towards the lower end of the lake the country became more rocky and barren looking, while the air became colder, and we experienced a slight fall of snow.

On the 9th of October we arrived at Fort St. James, just eleven days after parting with Mr. Hamilton. For four consecutive days we had had nothing to eat, and it had several times during the whole trip appeared to me as if our chances of reaching our destination were very slim. But now we were in clover. Mr. Ogden received us very kindly, and we soon recovered from our hardships.

After a two days' sojourn we left in company with Mr. Ogden. He was going to Fort Fraser, but we had determined to go to Fort George and from there to Fort Alexandria, and at the former place we parted company with the genial head factor, who had treated us so kindly. Fort Alexandria, or as it is generally called, Alexander, is an interesting place. It is called after the famous explorer and traveler, Sir Alexander McKenzie, and I believe it is the oldest fort of all, being founded in 1793. It was, when I visited it, a fort of much importance. The surrounding country was open and picturesque and afforded splendid hunting ground. Hence the Indians congregated here, and the Company did a large amount of trading in this neighborhood, while at the same time the post served as a depot for receiving produce, gathered in other distant districts.

We now made down the river and soon found ourselves in a mining region. At several places we passed mining camps, but I generally found the men as taciturn as they had appeared to me when I made my debut on the Californian gold fields. One of the few places, where we met with a welcome, was in a camp belonging to a Mr. Kirk and his partner Mr. Nichol. They were not working when we arrived there, because the ground was frozen; but they had been doing pretty well on their claim, averaging from three to four ounces a day. They were very pleased to see us, and shared with us what cheer they had, and in their agreeable company I dreamed myself back again to California in the early days and thought of many pleasant scenes under similar conditions.

There was now a good deal of ice on the river. It came drifting in floes and often menaced our safety, but we pushed on and soon reached the mouth of the Quesnelle river. There was quite an accumulation of men here. New diggings had been struck, and those on the ground had come to winter, so as to be ready at the first dawn of spring

We stayed here for several days to gather all possible information about the place and ascertained that some good gold had been already found here, while hopes were bright in anticipation of coming revelation, when spring should return. We also met several Californians here, who gave us a royal reception and spoke of old days. At Big Creek we abandoned our canoe and took the trail for Haskells. Here I met my old partner from California, Alexander McDonald, who was mining in this neighborhood, and I went to work with him for awhile, but the weather was getting very cold and the ground hard, and I concluded to make my way back to Victoria, where I arrived at the close of November.

I had been away for nearly three months and certainly seen a great deal of the country. His Excellency, Governor Douglas received my report very favorably and ordered my expenses paid, which was done accordingly.

CHAPTER IV.

Surveying the Inlets—Looking for a Wagon Road to the Fraser—Jarvis Inlet—An Awful Ravine—Desolation Sound—All by Myself—The Bears Came Rushing Down—The Kle-na-Klene River—Bella Coola—Dean Canal—A Land Boom—False Reports—Mr. Tovalloit Prevaricates—Spearing Salmon Indians from Fort Fraser—After Gold on the Nasse.

Having given an account of my trip in company with Mr. McKay, and my subsequent journey through the country to Fort James, I now come to my exploration of Jarvis Inlet, which is situated about thirty miles west of Howe Sound. It will be remembered that Governor Douglas, who by this time was known as Sir James Douglas, had an idea that it would be possible to find a shorter and easier ronte to the Upper Fraser than the one which we had pointed out to him, *via* Howe Sound and the Silooet Lake, and with a view to ascertaining whether such a possibility did exist, I traveled along the coast making a survey of the various inlets.

I found Jarvis Inlet piercing the coast line to a depth of about sixty miles, stretching inland in a northeasterly direction. There was every appearance of our finding a pass through the mountains here. At the entrance to the inlet we met several Bridge River Indians, and with them for our guides, penetrated to the head, and after two days' hard journeying we found ourselves in a canyon entirely closed in by steep mountains. Never in my life have I beheld such a scene as presented itself to our wondering gaze in this solitude. We were completely shut in by this wild nature. On either hand, lofty mountains reared their precipitous sides far above us pointing toward the leaden overcast sky, and looking like threatening giants guarding the entrance to some land of mystery. Not a vestige of vegetation; not a brush on the bare, solemn-looking rocks as they cast their gloomy shadow over the ravine below, making us feel like prisoners behind barred and bolted gates. Ahead of us lay a field of unsurmountable glaciers, forming a barrier to any further progress, and giving to the situation additional awe and grandeur. In the loneliness of nature, where the great architect has deprived her of the charms which in other places adorn her, I have always found something wonderfully impressive, far exceeding in force, the enthusiasm called forth by the smiling and pleasing scenery. It has always appeared to me in this solemn situation as if I stood face to face with the angry Jehovah, who stretched forth his hand to remind human beings of their utter insignificance.

Such was the impression I received in this instance, as I found myself absolutely enclosed in the ravine which had just one opening for ingress and egress alike. When I asked the Indians how they proposed for us to proceed any further, they said that we should have to ascend the glaciers in the best way we could, and pull one another up by ropes. "And the wagons—?" I asked. "Pull them up after you!" came the reply. It was very evident that this settled all prospects of making a wagon road by this route, when the only way was to climb glaciers and pull the vehicles up afterwards, and I therefore gave up all ideas of satisfying gubernatorial expectations on this point. We camped here for the night, and spent a wretched time waiting for dawn to break. The rain came down in torrents, falling over the steep sides of the mountains in cascades and filling the ravine, so to speak. Our traps—even our provisions—were carried away, and we had to stand up most of the night holding on to our blankets and utensils, for fear of seeing them carried away by the waters and the violent gusts of wind that came down upon us—the sweeping breath of angry elements.

In March, 1859, I made my first inspection of Desolation Sound, situated about sixty miles west of Jarvis' Inlet. This time I was the only white man in the company and was accompanied by a party of Indians. We went in a canoe up through the channel between the mainland and Redonda Island, and rounding Brettell Point and Snout Point, made our way into Toba Inlet. We penetrated to the head of this water, and then proceeded to ascend the river which has its mouth here. The land on either side of this stream we found to be low, sandy and overflowed, but some distance from the mouth the moutains began to rise to considerable altitudes. It was not possible to proceed in the canoe more than four or five miles from the Inlet, and we reconnoitered the land on foot. I found the mountains on the western shore to be higher than those opposite. On the eastern side there was an Indian trail crossing to Jarvis' Inlet, but the ridge on the western side could only be traversed by goats and bears, of which there seemed to be a great many. The bears came tearing down the mountainside, to welcome us, but we did not stop to shake hands, preferring to wave them our adieu from the canoe. I thought it possible to penetrate from here to Bridge River, but the Indians told me it would take at least a month to reach a group of small lakes where that stream takes its rise.

It was very evident to me that my purpose of making a wagon road by this route could not be accomplished, and I therefore prepared to return. I did a little prospecting first, and came upon slate, quartz and indications of copper, but nothing of any great significance, and as a memento of my visit, I carved my name upon a tree and departed from these quarters.

The next inlet upon this coast, is Bute Inlet. Of this place, and my experience of it, I will speak later, and meanwhile pass on to the next inlet, known as Loborough Inlet. It is situated about twenty miles west of Bute, and is surrounded by towering mountains, while glaciers abounded in these regions. During the summer months, the Indians from the surrounding tribes, come down here and fish, but none of them stay to winter in this locality. The place is wild and inaccessible, and when the winter gales sweep over it, and the snow lies on the mountains, it offers but a very uninviting abode for human beings. There are no settled tribes of Indians in this region, and when the summer season is at end, the whole country assumes an appearance of utter desolation and loneliness. I could not find any chances in this locality of building a wagon road, and once more turned my steps westward.

The reader who is unfamiliar with the map of British Columbia, by examining it for a moment, will easily follow my explorations of the various inlets, as they were undertaken, one after the other; and will also readily perceive the anxiety and vigor with which these explorations were being pushed, for the sole purpose of affording greater traveling facilities for the miners, who, coming from Victoria, made the upper Fraser their destination. At that time, when the country had been but little explored, and the exact course of the Fraser was but imperfectly known, it was naturally to be supposed that there would be some way of making a cross-country

A Group of Naas Indians.

road to the gold fields, by taking advantage of the rivers and lakes, which in so many places afforded excellent means of traveling. Moreover, the natives had shown the invaders how to utilize the sheets of water which intersected their home in so many places. The idea of portages originated with them, and the canoes were easily carried along the trail leading from one lake to the other.

I must admit that, in common with many others, I had long entertained the idea of such a traveling route. I had furthermore as an old miner taken much pleasure in looking for the possibility of finding one, and in order to realize this, had freely spent my money so far in vain endeavors to strike a trail that would answer the purpose. Having disposed of Laborough and found nothing there to work upon, I next turned my attention to Knight's Inlet.

This is one of the deepest and most formidable inlets on the coast. It runs east from Gilford Island for many miles and then turns north running in that direction, with a few curves, to its head, where the Kle-na-Klene River falls into it. At this point the land is open as far as the eye can reach, and we saw plenty of upland Indians, who came down here to trade for grease. I made two trips to the head of this inlet, but could not discover anything which would warrant a wagon road toward the Fraser. The natives, with whom I here came in contact, gave me some information about the interior. They said that it took one month and a half to travel to their country, which must therefore have been situated quite a distance away, but at the same time they had never heard of the Fraser river nor of the gold land. This made me think that these Indians lived considerably to the west of Fraser River, for my experience was that Indians living as far from the Fraser as Lillooet, knew all about the river, and the gold to be found there. More than this; an Indian on my trip through the Babine Lake district had told me how on the Fraser he had met the white men, and received a pair of pants in exchange for a salmon. The natives I met at Knight's Inlet gave me much information about the interior, and I had once more to abandon the idea of finding a starting point on the coast for the desired route.

My next expedition went to Bella Coola. This river, which rushes down from the Cascade Mountains, falls into the sea through Burke Channel, inside which the South Bentinck and North Bentinck Arm spread into the surrounding lowland. The North Arm may be called the mouth of the river, while the South Bentinck stops more abruptly. The entrance to the interior therefore goes through the North Bentinck, but it was soon found inpracticable to establish a wagon road by this route. The country further up the river becomes mountainous, and unfit for any such purpose as ours, and I had to give it up. But I was not the only one who had suffered defeat in this respect, as regards Bella Coola. Two gentlmen, Messrs. Harrison and Goolidge, spent several months in attempting to penetrate from the North Branch to the Fraser, but failed in their attempts, although they were particularly well equipped for the undertaking.

Separated from Burke Channel by a thin strip of land is Dean Canal, being the mouth of Dean, or Salmon River. My next expedition went up this inlet, and although I followed the river for quite a distance, I failed to find a suitable road. Toward the fall of every year the natives come down from New Caledonia to trade here and return again on snow-shoes, but just as surely as the flowers awake in the spring, these men come back with the returning season to trade. I had expected to see some of the Chilcotin Indians here, but was disappointed. At the time when I paid my visit to Dean Canal, there was quite an excitement in the real estate offices in Victoria, owing to the fact that a boom had been started in a quiet way in regard to the land on Dean Creek. It was predicted that land, bought in this district, would soon increase many fold in value, and that a better townsite could not be found. Consequently about one thousand acres were soon taken up by the knowing ones of Victoria, and expectations ran high.

I should have thought they might just as well have speculated in making a townsite on the sides of Mount Baker or Mount Hamilton, as at the head of any of the inlets that I frequented in my search for a wagon road, and I would not personally have given ten dollars for the whole area.

In connection with this I am put in mind of some of the tricks practiced for the purpose of inducing people to buy land in this locality. A Mr. Tovalloit, who was interested in the scheme, had the audacity to spread the report that he came on horseback from Fort Alexandria, on the Fraser River, to Dean Canal in seven days. I was told exactly where he claimed to have reached the water, and examined the place minutely, with the result that I doubted very much the truth of the story. Mr. Tovalloit also claimed to have come by Chilcotin Lake, but I learned afterwards from friends of mine who had been of the party, that this was not so. They left for Alexandria to go to the lake, but on the third day out they returned again, and up to that time Mr. Tovalloit had never seen it. This will show how easily people may be deceived in regard to location of country, the geography of which they know nothing about. Had it been possible to establish a seven-days communication between the coast and Fort Alexandria at this place, land would certainly have been of great value; but the possibility was entirely problematic. Mr. Tovalloit was a prevaricator of the truth, to use a polite term; and there was absolutely no reason to think that a wagon road would ever be built between the two points.

I next directed my attention towards Kitlobe River. In reference to this, too, gross misrepresentations had been published, and among other things it had been described as navigable. I soon discovered that it was not. The inlet stretches far inland, until the Kitlobe River falls into it, the latter springing somewhere in the southeastern corner of the Chilicotin plateau. But this river was far from being navigable as reported. On the contrary, I found it one of the most difficult rivers on the coast to ascend. The country was wild, in some places almost impassable, and while it was shown on the maps as nearly reaching to the Chilcotin, such was by no means the case. I had the satisfaction, through the press of Victoria, of drawing the attention of the public to these misstatements, and thus corrected a serious error in the minds of speculators in the Fraser river route, which I did not for one moment believe could be established here.

During the fishing season the Indians on the Kitlobe River sit perched upon the rocks and spear the fish. With marvelous aim they throw the weapon from considerable hights, and pierce the beautiful salmon far below. The Indians from New Caledonia cross this river in making their annual trips to Dean Canal

At the head of Kildalah Inlet is the river of the same

name. It rushes forth between steep mountain verges, and affords but a poor and dangerous navigation. I took much interest in conversing with the natives here. Some of them told me that they had come all the way from Fort Fraser, and described the country on the other side of the range, as level and easy to travel. The distance between this point and Fort Fraser is quite considerable, and they must have come by the way of the Fraser Lake, the French Lake, and across the Chilcotin plateau.

The Kitimax River comes from the north, running almost at a right angle to the Kildalah. It is a fine large river, which runs through an open valley that stretched its verdant pastures towards the Skeena, and as we traveled up the stream, we were much impressed by the surrounding country. The Indians here told us that it was only a matter of four days to reach the Skeena, and we made that river in the time stated.

Of my exploration on the Skeena I have already spoken. Myself and two companions were in reality the first white men who crossed from the coast to the Fraser River, but Mr. Alfred Waddington, who was jealous of my successful explorations of that part of British Columbia, took pains on several occasions to ignore the fact that I was the one who led the first expedition, and wrote about the route in such a manner as to make it appear as if indeed he was the first to penetrate the previously unknown country. However, I was quite willing that he should indulge in a little imagination on this point; I only wished that he should as well have some of the days of hunger and cold, with which we paid for the honor of being the pioneer explorers of this route.

I went up the river Nasse about one hundred miles. My expedition on this stream was undertaken principally for the purpose of prospecting, as I had been told that there was plenty of gold here. I spent quite a time on the river, making careful examinations of the various localities but not with any satisfactory results. There was undoubtedly traces of gold in many places, and in some the metal might be found in small quantities; but I could not find any place where it would pay over two dollars a day, and therefore it was not worth while working. From my experience, and examination of the Pacific Coast, I judge that from Washington Territory to Alaska, all along the coast of British Columbia, there are no placer diggings, which are worth working, whereas it appears to me that some of the baser metals may be worked to advantage.

From what has already been written it must be pretty evident that there was a strong desire to establish an outlet from the interior country, somewhere on the coast, and it will be also seen that I was not the only one who had attempted to locate such a station. Indeed, at the time I refer to, there were any amount of explorers in the field, but a good many of them did not amount to much. They would receive so much money for going out to look for a certain pass, and that would be the last heard of them.

I have hitherto spoken of such undertakings as aimed at locating a pass for a wagon road, but the idea had also become dominant that it would be possible to find, somewhere in the mountains, a pass that would allow of a railroad being brought down to the coast; and Bute Inlet was the favorite locality, where it was thought possible to realize this project. Bute Inlet goes far into the land, and at its extreme head the Homalko River falls into its waters, running almost due south, while the Southgate River joins the inlet on the eastern shore, a little further down. The mountains behind are wild and precipitous, the river is difficult to navigate, in some places rendering portage necessary, and at others being filled with drift wood, thus constantly menacing the frail crafts that come up here; the canoes of the natives being the only possible conveyance upon this swiftly rushing stream.

In order to ascertain whether a projected railroad might be brought to Bute Inlet, to be there connected with Vancouver Island, a meeting was held in the early part of '61 at the old government building in the city of Victoria, where now stands the postoffice. A number of prominent business men and professional men were present, and I also recollect seeing Lady Franklin there, the widow of the renowned Arctic explorer, Sir John Franklin, whose tragic fate had attracted so much attention some years before. Among others, who that night discussed the possibilities of Bute Inlet, were Dr. Helmcken, a Mr. Burnaby, and Mr. Alfred Waddington. I have already had occasion to mention the last named gentleman. He was much interested in the further development of the country, and to him the establishment of a railroad terminus at Bute Inlet was a matter of vast importance, wherefore, he also took a prominent part in the proceedings of the evening, during which it was proposed to send an exploring party to the head of the inlet, to report upon the conditions of the country.

In the general discussion that took place, I strenuously opposed the idea of paying anybody in advance. I suggested that parties willing to explore the country, might do so at their own cost, and if they returned with *bona fide* reports, they should be remunerated for their trouble, whether successful or not. I reasoned that paying in advance would give the men employed a chance to go half way only and come back without having attempted to find the pass; and, indeed, I knew a party just ready to start on some such proposition, waiting only to receive cheque in advance.

As soon as the meeting was over, I met my partners, and urged them to join me in exploring Bute Inlet. I was somewhat disgusted when they at once refused, saying that they had arranged to go higher up the coast, but after a little persuasion I made them agree to take me up there with them at all events, and we set out on the voyage,

I laid in a stock of supplies, enough to carry me through for several months, also brought with me an extra quantity of tobacco for the natives. Tobacco among the Indians, in many cases, acts as the golden key to the secret you wish to possess; and it is when this luxury gives out, that the explorer need have serious apprehensions as to the issue of his next negotiation with the red sons of the soil.

CHAPTER V.

My Partners—Visiting Friends—The Village of Tsawatti—Villainous Indians—Anxious Moments—Friends in Need—Bute Inlet—On the Homathco—Auxiliary Rivers—Wonderful Scenery—Glaciers Ahead—A Sick Indian—Great Hardships—The Tequahan and the Memria—Poor Luck—What a Newspaper Wrote.

I have spoken of my partners, and I may now introduce them to my readers. They were Aleck McDonald and Harry Harlan, both of them experienced miners and good fellows. I had mined with Aleck on the Yuba, years before; had camped with him on the Upper Fraser, when I succeeded in reaching those parts, and we had become fast friends, having shared the dangers and trials of a rough and adventurous life. Sometime prior to the meeting just referred to, the three of us had purchased a small schooner, and gone up the coast for the purpose of prospecting, and of this trip I will give a brief account.

Running along the west coast of Vancouver Island we called in at Nanaimo, where we spent a couple of days with old friends, among whom let me remember, Captain Stewart, Doctor Benson, Mr. Horne, Mr. Dunsmuir and others.

We next made a call at Fort Rupert, where Mr. Winter and Captain Mitchell received us with that lavish hospitality, for which the Hudson Bay Company officers had become famous among their friends, and, leaving them with some reluctance, we now cut across Queen Charlotte Sound and threading our way through the labyrinth of islands, with which this water is studded, we sailed through "One-Tree Passage," and steering for Knight Inlet, made our way toward the head of this water, where is situated the Indian village of Tsawatti. We had been up this way before, and it was now our intention to prospect the mountains behind the village, having previously found along the inlet, lead, copper and other minerals, one of which we took to be silver.

Our little vessel was richly laden with trade for the Indians, and we had blankets and tobacco in abundance. It was arranged that Aleck should go ashore at Tsawatti, taking with him a certain amount of trade and, while we made an examination of the coast-line, he should take the initiative in the hills.

We ran ashore as near the village as possible, and began discharging the goods that were to be left with Aleck, who proposed to take quarters in an Indian cabin a short distance up the hill, whither the boxes and parcels were carried. Meanwhile a number of strange Indians had put in their appearance. They filled the cabin which was to serve as a store-house and began to swarm around our vessel in canoes, looking anything but friendly.

If the reader has ever seen the heavy villain in a five-act drama of the blood-and-thunder school, overdoing, as he thought, the important role entrusted to his careful acting, he will have seen, as a rule, a fair representation of these Indians who were heavy villains without the least effort on their part. Their brows were knitted and their eyelids lowered, thus producing a hideous scowl.

The orthodox blanket was thrown over the left shoulder in the manner of a Spanish cape, and to the practiced observer the general posture of the body, as revealed by the folds of the blanket, demonstrated that their hands clutched some murderous weapon, whether a knife or a pistol, held ready to be used at a moment's notice.

I had been so busy arranging our cargo in the hold, that I had scarcely noticed the natives flocking around our vessel. Not so with Aleck. The space in the cabin had gradually become smaller and smaller, the air more stifling, the chattering of the natives grown louder, while the situation assumed a character, not at all pleasing to my companion, who left the boxes, which had been stowed away in the cabin, and came down to consult with me.

"I don't like the looks of these fellows, Major," he said, "those that belong here, I think are all right, but the strangers look ugly enough."

I made up my mind right then, that Aleck should not be left alone in this place. "Get the goods down again!" I said, "we will ship them and proceed."

My friend left me, but shortly after returned, stating that they would not permit him to take anything away.

I immediately went ashore; seizing the nearest fellow by the arm I pointed to a bale of blankets: "Put them on your shoulder and carry them down there!" I said, at the same time gesticulating to make my meaning clear.

I don't believe the man understood a word of English, but he obeyed me at once. There is a universal language, which everybody can understand, but only few can speak. It has no words of its own, but it depends upon accentuation more than anything else, as I learned in in the course of my life's schooling. It was but a matter of a few minutes when I had everybody carrying for me, and the goods were being returned wholesale, to the evident disgust of the wily Indians, who had hoped for plunder, while I now merely paid my carriers a few pieces of tobacco in return for their services.

But the trouble was not over yet. By this time the Indians were swarming upon the deck of our little vessel, and upon my return to it, they had blocked the gangway so that I could not get aboard for some time; when at last I reached the deck, I called my men below, and we at once made our arsenal ready for use. We had plenty of guns, pistols, balls and powder, and had just broken into a keg of the latter. I told the boys, and they agreed with me, that if we found we were getting the worst of it, I should throw a match into the powder-keg, thus showing our charitable disposition by taking our enemies aloft with us, rather than let them cut us to pieces.

Meanwhile the Redskins continued to hold possession of the deck. They were evidently in a quandary, not knowing how to begin the fray, for they had perceived that we had headed them off, and ever so much better armed than they were. Just as we thought that time was nearly up for the first round to begin, a large canoe shot across the waters toward our vessel, but to our surprise the warriors in the canoe came to render us assistance. They had heard of the plight we were in and now a few words from them quickly persuaded the enemy to abandon our vessel, but not till he had, with the polish of a thorough villain, assured us that everything was all right, that we were all friends and that we had quite misunderstood their move. I assured them in return that if that powder keg had been heard from there would have been no occasion for them to misunderstand our move in the matter, and from that day henceforth I never took a Knight Inlet Indian at his word.

On that same expedition we went up the Skeena and arrived near Fort Simpson just as the Indians were about to have a big fight. They recognized us, however, and kindly sent word to us, asking us to go below as they were going to shoot. Indian warfare differs somewhat from our mode of killing in battle. The Indians go on shooting till somebody is hurt, and then by a signal they stop to see what can be done further. After a little while the battle is taken up again. This somewhat retards bloodshed and limits casualties, unlike the more civilized mode of warfare, which takes particular pains to kill as many as possible. If the medicine man falls in battle, and he did not succeed in pulling his last patient through, his scalp is eagerly sought by the survivors. If the scalps of Medicos in more civilized communities were a little less safe than they are, probably there would be a good deal less quackery in that, otherwise most estimable, profession.

On this trip we made the discovery of what we took to be rich lead ore. We had a quantity shipped for London, and a man went to England to look after it, but neither man nor ore was ever heard of since and, while some charged fraud, I think it more likely that the ore was shoveled on board some other vessel as ballast.

I now proceed to speak of my expedition to Bute Inlet. It was one of the most important undertakings, with which I was connected in British Columbia, and, although I did not succeed at the time in crossing the range personally, our experiences there had much to do with the later success of Aleck McDonald, who was indeed the first white man to perform the feat of traversing the mountains at the head of Bute Inlet.

We arrived here on the third day of July 1861, having

traveled about 225 miles since leaving Victoria. On either side the shore rises boldly. The inlet is navigable for ships of any size, and there is particularly good anchorage at several places, where the fresh water streams join the inlet, which averages a width of one mile and a half and is clear of reefs and sunken rocks. At the head of the inlet on the west side, close to the shore, the bottom is sandy in twenty fathoms of water, and splendid shelter is afforded against the southwester blowing up the inlet. I have already mentioned the principal rivers, falling into the inlet, of which the Homathco is the most important. The back country Indians come down to the coast by this river for the purpose of obtaining salmon, and I determined to ascend it. We experienced considerable trouble in getting sufficient Indians to take us up the river. The natives here are not very easy to get along with, and I had to use all my tact and powers of persuasion in order to enlist eight men, who finally agreed to accompany McDonald and myself on our expedition.

On the 7th of July we started up the river. We had sufficient supplies with us to take us over the mountains, and we had three canoes, I heading the procession with two natives. The course of the river winds through sandy flats, thickly timbered. The timber however is very light, and the soil formed by the continual wash from the mountains. On the western shore we saw the snow mantling the distant hills and on the first day of our journey we passed two glaciers. We found that the tide came up as far as ten miles, thus rendering it possible for small steamers to go up that distance at high water. The formation of the rock varied somewhat, being principally granite on our western shore, while on the opposite bank we found slate, intermixed with straggling veins of quartz. At one place on this shore we observed a large mountain, the appearance of which indicated minerals, and I followed a reddish vein, thinking that it might contain something, but was disappointed.

On the second day the river current increased in velocity, and we foresaw that it would be a difficult task to ascend the stream. At one place my Indians failed to keep the head of the canoe to the current; she turned first broadside and then bottom up. In one moment we were all in the water. I saw what was coming, and warned my companions, but they did not heed in time. I caught my pistol belt and clambered on to a drift log which took me down the stream towards the other canoes, but for some time I looked in vain for the Indians. It did not take me long to meet McDonald and his crew, who picked me up, and by this time my late companions had reached the shore, where they stood shivering after their cold bath, while we went in pursuit of the escaping canoe, and soon overtook it. It had sustained considerable damage, while everything in it had, of course, dropped out, and it was quite a loss, under the circumstances.

The worst of it all was that the Indians had become so scared at the accident, that they positively refused to proceed further, and after much talking and arguing, we ultimately persuaded them to let us have a canoe in in exchange for blankets and shirts, as we were determined to push on towards the head of the river, Indians or no Indians. We now sent down to the vessel for more supplies in place of those we had lost, and, having received the goods, we made another start with only two Indians for my companions, one of whom was a chief.

Some way up the river we came to an auxiliary, join-

NANAIMO

ing the Homathco from the east. This stream was called by the Indians who live there, the Hickhanum, the name of their own tribe. It flowed swiftly, with stong current, but an Indian chief assured us that if we would only push up the stream, in the course of one day we should reach some very fine land, through a narrow pass further up. We took the man at his word, and set out to find the place.

The journey was a dangerous one, and we made slow progress through woodland, and flats covered with rocky bowlders, until we heard above us the deafning sound of rushing waters. Presently we came to a deep chasm. From between the narrow walls a muddy stream rushed forth, stirring the waters of the already turbulent stream, and filling the air with a thundering noise. I conjectured, at once, that the water came from a glacier, and we ascended the rocks forming the chasm, when, sure enough, we beheld the glacier lying between two mountains which rose abruptly on either side.

The glacier was distant about one mile, and we reached it by traversing a bowlder flat. This was the first glacier I had ever seen coming down to level ground. It was, apparently, over one mile wide, and extended back as far as the eye could reach, in an easterly direction.

I was much impressed with the surrounding nature of this locality. From behind, the woodlands wafted their fragrant breezes up the chasm, filling the air with an odor of life; and a number of small swallows playfully chased one another in the golden rays of a hot July sun. And there in front of us the grim picture of winter, as we descended the huge block of ice with all the varied hues of transparent blue, green and gold where the sunbeams were making inroads through the crevices, trying in vain to soften the ponderous mass. And these very crevices leading into caverns of eternal frost and darkness, traversed by ice-cold streams, but never lighted or warmed by the beneficent sun. As I stood there, looking backward and then again forward, it seemed to me as if I stood somewhere between life and death.

In this wilderness I naturally wanted to know what the trail was supposed to be, and my Indian guide looked somewhat blank, as he told me that the season was a bad one for traveling this way, and that the right time would be in the fall, when the crevices had frozen up again. I could have suggested that, myself, but having got so far, I thought we would try to skirt the glacier, along the mountain side, and thus find out where the gorge would lead us to. But the undertaking was a very risky one. We had to leap from bowlder to bowlder at the imminent risk of our lives, and when, after a while, we climbed the mountain, we could see nothing but snow-fields as far as the eye could reach, and the horizon itself seemed shut in by ice and snow. We concluded that we had gone as far as human beings could go in this direction, and, seeing no possibility of finding a pass here, suitable for our purposes, we retraced our steps, and having reached the canoe, returned to the mainland.

We had not proceeded very far, when we came upon another river, falling into the Homathco, and for the second time we left the latter, traveling up an auxiliary, coming from the east. We had hard work, journeying up this stream, which ran with great force. We had to make a portage at one place, while at others we were obliged to tow the canoe up the stream, making fast the line round a bush every now and again, while we cut our way along the bank. It was one of the most trying journeys I ever undertook, which is saying a good deal, and our Indian chief began to cry, said he was sick and wanted to go home. There are many who believe that the colored races surpass the Caucasians in endurance, but this is entirely a misaprehension. For endurance, tenacity, determination of purpose and moral courage the Caucasian cannot be equaled by any colored race I have ever met. On this occasion we suffered great hardships. We were most of the time in the cold water, warding off drift wood and pulling or pushing our canoes ahead, and we succeeded in retaining our Indian, without whom we could not have made sufficient progress, so we let him cry and complain but kept him at work. He was no doubt much relieved, when we discovered that we had been traveling up another outlet for a glacier and once more returned to the Homathco. However, before abandoning this route, McDonald and I followed the stream on foot for some distance and came to another small river joining it from the west. Here we learned that the Bella Coola Indians come down for salmon in the fall. They have a trail by which they come through this rocky pass at the head of the river, but our examination of this locality did not satisfy us that it could be used for anything but an Indian trail.

Having returned to the main river, we followed it further up, examining a few smaller streams that ran into it at different places. The country was very wild with deep canyons and steep mountains. Here and there large glaciers, and rushing rivulets with plenty of drift wood on the stream and large threatening bowlders on their banks. But in all this we could not find any place suitable for the desired pass, and after having spent sixteen days on the Homathco we returned to the schooner at the head of the Inlet. I was not at all satisfied with my expedition. I thought that under more favorable circumstances it might be possible to penetrate further up, and I felt that I should like to make another attempt.

We next ascended the river *Tequahan*, running into Bute Inlet from the north. Our experience here was very similar to that on the Homathco River, if possible a little worse, and we soon concluded that here, at all events, we should not find the pass, of which we were in search. At certain seasons of the year the Indians here cross the mountains, hunting the goat over the frozen snow, but this fact alone proved to us the absence of the desired conditions for our purpose, and we returned once more to the Inlet to try the third and last river, falling into it. This is known as the Memria or Southgate river.

We were destined to experience more hardships and additional failures on this expedition. The natives told us that the Lockwalla Indians came down here at times and that there was a trail across to Lillooet. We attempted to follow the latter but were forced to admit that it would not serve for a road of any kind, and having once more battled with the wilds of nature and suffered a good deal, owing to the roughness of the country, we again returned to the Inlet and set sail for civilized parts, having spent one month and a half in exploring the adjacent country.

As we had to bear the burden of expense, it came quite heavy upon us at the time, but we satisfied ourselves that we had, at all events, added to the general knowledge of the locality, and gathered information hitherto unknown. "The Daily Press" of Victoria, under date of 20th August, 1861, published the following editorial comments relative to our exploration.

"The problem which has caused so much agitation among imaginative speculators in Victoria, is at last solved, and the numerous gentlemen who have pre-empted land in the region of the inlet, (Bute) that they might cut it up into town lots and supply the overwhelming rush of business men and others that were naturally expected to beseige the place, have expended their eight-shilling fee for registration, to little purpose.

"The Bute Inlet route is a miserable failure. Major Downie has tested every conceivable opening to the interior, with a persistency that few but the Major would have exhibited, and has arrived at the conclusion that a road to the Fraser from Bute Inlet is, for any advantageous purpose, totally impracticable.

"We characterised sometime ago the glowing descriptions, which were circulated by interested or unthinking persons about the Bute Inlet route, as simply imaginative emanations, without any claims to substance or reality and the result has proved the correctness of our remarks.

We are glad the impracticability of the route has been demonstrated by a man whose knowledge of the practical science of exploration, few in the community will feel disposed to doubt.

"It will effectually set at rest this wavering, unsettled disposition about the route to the mines, a feeling that could only end in injury to those means of transit, at present under construction. We have no inclination whatever to discourage explorations of the coast for routes to the interior of British Columbia, but we have argued, that to attempt to draw the Governor's attention from the Lillooet road at the present time, when every farthing that can possibly be spared from the British Columbia Treasury should be devoted to that object, until we have one good, passable route to the interior, would be as injurious as it would be puerile. We are not exceedingly favorable to the British Columbia government; but we must admit that it has exerted the power placed in its hands so far as roads are concerned, in a manner that few can cavil at.

"We do not, therefore; wish to see the attention of the Governor drawn away to impracticable objects and deputations requesting the assistance of a gunboat, to humor the whims and 'castle-building' of a few erratic and fanciful speculators.

"We may be told that Bentinck Arm is still unexplored; that the rumors which were some time ago afloat with regard to its practicability as a coast route, are yet uncontradicted. But we think there has been sufficient evidence adduced to put a stop, for this year, at least, to any further attempt to show that the present route to the mines is a useless expenditure of money.

"If Major Downie's trip will have the effect, as it should have, of doubling the energy at present expended on the Fraser River route, it will be of infinite service to both colonies. At all events, the people of this and the neighboring colony, are under lasting obligations to Messrs. Downie and McDonald for the energy and disinterestedness which they have displayed in their explorations, and we hope that something more substantial than a public meeting will be awarded to the adventurous gentlemen.

"It is to be presumed, now that the spirit of exploring enterprise is in the ascendancy, that our colony will not be passed and neglected, as it has hitherto been.

"We have not the slightest doubt there are objects on this island awaiting the efforts of exploration, of infinitely greater importance to the colony, than any coast route to the interior of British Columbia. We hope, therefore, before any further voyage of discovery is made that Vancouver island, which can never exhibit the unsurmountable obstacles that Bute presented, will obtain some share of that attention which has recently been concentrated on the rugged mountains and impetuous rivers of the neighboring colony."

CHAPTER VI.

Unscrupulous Speculators—The Pre-emption Law—The People of Westminster—Two Explorers—False Reports—A Rowdy Audience—Cariboo Mining—Trying to Pump Gold—The Money Ran Out—Waddington's Enterprise—A Camp at Bute Inlet—Treacherous Indians—A Night of Horrors—The Avenger—The Killing of a Dear Friend.

The reader will propably excuse my indulging in a little self-praise, as it may appear, by publishing the above editorial; but I have not done it with an idea of personal agrandizement. I am rather actuated by a desire to demonstrate the sentiment prevailing at the time; or shall I say, one of the sentiments, for I shall presently show that opinions were somewhat divided.

The fight lay between the immigrants, who gradually became the *bona fide* settlers, and the speculators, who resorted to trickery and imperfect land laws, for the purpose of enriching themselves. The pre-emption law enabled men to take up land, purely as a matter of speculation; and many shady transactions in real estate were brought about by this fact. It was to some extent the motive power which resulted in a good deal of exploration up and down the coast, and in that respect it was commendable enough; but it also caused reports to be spread relative to these explorations, which were, in many cases, so far removed from the truth that no one would recognizedthe localities from some of the descriptions.

But of all places, none had attracted so much atten-

harbor facilities, the fine scenery, the location and the fact that three rivers ran into it,—all contributed towards a general desire to see it made a railroad terminus. The present railroad skirts along Kamploops Lake and follows the bend of the river Fraser below the junction of Bonaparte River, but had not the line been continued due west by Seton Lake, through the Lillooet district, it would have pierced the Cascade mountains near Bute Inlet, and come down to the waters of that splendid harbor. Then thousands of dollars would have been realized in that locality by a few speculators, who now either kept honest settlers out of the field, or sold them land under false pretenses, at unwarranted prices.

The one predominant idea was, as has been several times alluded to, to cut across the mountains from the river to the coast in place of following the windings of the Fraser. On the other hand, this river afforded a natural highway into the interior. It was a matter of course that the country around its outlet looked forward to the advantages which might accrue from such a fact, and hence a good deal of rivalry sprang up between the New Westminster people and the Bute Inlet speculators.

Every effort had been made to destroy the possibility of Westminster taking the lead. Even charts and maps had been published so absolutely wrong that one hesitates to speak of it for fear of being doubted; but nevertheless it is a fact that on such charts rivers were made to suit the convenience of the project; mountain ranges were placed where the alleged surveyor saw fit, and they were accompanied by reports, colored so as to throw the desired effect upon the scene, independently of the real truth.

Such, indeed, was the state of affairs, when the meeting was called which I mentioned in my previous chapter. Had I wished to get into the pay of the speculators, I could have made enough money on Bute Inlet to amply repay me for my outlay and hardships endured, but all I wished to do was to make a fair and unbiased report of what I saw and learned.

Not so with those whose only aim was to enrich themselves. McDonald and I risked our lives daily in the wilderness of the interior about the now famous inlet. A couple of men came up to make a survey of the coast, the same as we had done. They came in a small vessel, and when they learned that we had gone up one of the three rivers, they put their craft about and sailed for Victoria, where they at once reported the magnificent discovery of an easy pass at the head of the inlet, and a safe road across to Fort Alexandria. This garbled statement was clad in all the fanciful language of the novelist, and no efforts were spared to make the country appear advantageous, while the paper that published it, went into elaborate details regarding the projected railroad with its terminus at Bute Inlet and all the rest, giving land in the vicinity a wonderful rise in the market.

Of all this, however, I was not aware. I first learned of it when sometime after I arrived in Victoria and determined to make my experience known in proper style. So I hired a hall, calling a meeting and arranged my papers in such a manner as to give my audience an intelligent report of my explorations in the interest of the common weal. I had a fair-sized audience, and as I appeared upon the rostrum, flattered myself that I was going to make quite an impression, which indeed I did; but it was the wrong way. No sooner had my hearers understood from my remarks that I could not recommend Bute Inlet, when it seems that one and all took it for granted that I was in some kind of a collusion with the Westminster people to squash the big land schemes of Bute Inlet. Yells went up in different parts of the audience, such as "Put him out!" "What's he talking about?" "Bully for you!" And then various articles were thrown across the hall, breaking sundry lamps in their route towards myself, who had certainly become the central point of interest.

I was surprised beyond description. I could barely realize that in return for telling people a truth which had cost me many weary marches at the peril of my life to ascertain, I should be treated as a charlatan, while a couple of imposters walked off with the glory of having accomplished what they never attempted, probably well paid, while I got nothing. Strangely enough, to-day, after thirty years, there are still people who allow themselves to be gulled into speculating in Bute Inlet land, not content with the experience reaped by different parties during all these years, all pointing to the fact that nature will resist any engineering in those regions, excepting at a cost which would be considered absolutely unreasonable.

In the spring of 1862 I was mining at the mouth of Mink Gulch in Cariboo. It was evident that I had more luck, when looking for gold than when trying to find mountain passes, for I struck it rich in the gravel and took out lots of the precious metal. Indeed, during that period the miners in this locality did well and filled their sacks fast, and when I remember such places as Conklin Gulch and Williams Creek, I am thinking of some of the richest placers that ever were.

But here again the old demon whispered the words into the miner's ear, which sent so many to destruction into the miner's ear, which sent so many to destruction —the word Excelsior! The gold seekers did the same thing in British Columbia, as they had done in California ten years before, always eager for better chances they let go of a good claim to pursue a phantom—I with the rest as a matter of course. And thus I came to look for gold in the Cariboo Swamps, where rumor had it there was lots of the yellow stuff. But alas for gold hunting in swamps! We pumped mud day and night to find some kind of a trace, but it kept out of our way. Under the title of the Long Point Company we dug ditches and pumped enough brown mud out to fill an ocean. To make a long story short, we pumped there till my finances were pumped completely out, for I had to foot the bills. At last I gave up. I told the boys to help themselves to a sack of flour, or whatever they required, and to look for better chances somewhere else; and while the diggers down the creek said that we had struck it rich and were making "two fish to the pan," I made my way down the Fraser River on foot—a sadder but a wiser man.

I have mentioned Mr. Waddington's aspirations in the direction of exploring, and that he was vastly interested in Bute Inlet and the adjacent country. In course of time he planned a townsite there and began to make roads as best he could. It proved a dangerous work for the men; not only because of the wild nature in this vicinity, but also owing to the indisposition on the part of some of the Indians, who objected to any road being made through their country.

Such an objection was not altogether uncalled for. The Indians were not slow to perceive that at the same time as the approach of the white man brought them advantages, there were also other sides to the question, not the least of these being the diseases, spread among the native tribes by the invaders. Thus, in the year 1862, small-pox was carried by the whites to Bella Coola, whence it spread as far as Benshee and Chisicat lakes, and in an incredibly short time no less than five hundred Indians died at the last place. Again, the manner in which unscrupulous adventurers had repeatedly broken faith with the natives, had done much harm to the white man and reflected even upon those who came among them with honesty of purpose and good intent.

Among the chiefs who opposed the progress of Waddington's Party was one, Tellet by name. At the time I speak of the party consisted of seventeen men, in charge of Mr. Brewster, and a man named Jim Smith looked after the store and ferry. One day, during the month of April, 1864, Tellet arrived at the ferry with his sons-in-law, known as Jack and George, and also accompanied by Klattasine, a young Indian of nineteen years; Indian slave, Chraychunume, twenty years of age, and three more Indians. It was afternoon when they neared Smith's place and Klattasine was sent ahead, commissioned to ascertain the whereabouts of the white chief, as they called Waddington, and to murder Smith. The Indian demanded that Smith present him with some blankets, which the storekeeper refused to do, whereupon Klattasine suddenly fired at him, killing him instantaneously. Then he ransacked the house, and having returned to his companions, a plan was laid to surprise Brewster's camp at the Third Bluff during the night, and thither the Indians now proceeded.

Arrived there the scene that presented itself was the customary picture of a surveyor's camp after the days' work is over. The men had gathered round the camp-fire. and the smoke of their pipes curled aloft in the still

BARNARD GLACIERS ON THE SKEENA RIVER.

evening, while the smokers were chatting about current topics, entirely unconscious of the tragedy that had been enacted at the ferry, and the awful fate that awaited themselves. As the party had apparently always been on the friendliest of terms with the Indians, their arrival did not arouse the least suspicion. The Redskins joined in the general conversation, and time passed by agreeably enough, until the hour had come, when every white man went to his tent, rolled himself in his blanket, and slept the sleep of the weary.

But the Indians did not sleep. They lay watching for the moment to arrive when their fiendish mission could be fulfilled, and just before the sun rose to throw its glimmer upon the landscape, and call all creation to life once more, these demons rose to put the peacefully slumbering and unsuspecting men to death. The men were divided in the tents, sleeping two or three together, and the Indians rushed upon them, throwing down the tent poles and with knives and pistols began murdering the sleepers, who, taken entirely by surprise, were stabbed or shot at through the canvas. For a moment all was confusion. The whoops and yells of the Indians rang through the clear morning air and mingled with the groans and imprecations of the struggling surveyors, who tried in vain to escape their cruel enemy, and when the hideous work had been performed, only three men out of seventeen had escaped death, as if by a miracle. They were Peter Petersen, a Dane; Philip Buckley, an Irishman and an Englishman by the name of Moseley, the last one being the only one who escaped unscathed.

The terror of the situation may be imagined from Moseley's statement, who, in his own words, described the scene as he saw it: "I was in a tent with J. Campbell and J. Fielding, a Scotchman and an Englishman respectively, when just about day-break I was awakened by two Indians coming to the tent door. They did not enter, but merely raised the door, then, whooping aloud, they fired on either side of me. I was lying in the center of the tent, and as they let the ridge pole down it fell upon me, and the tent nearly smothered us. Presently I saw the canvas on either side of me being pierced with knives penetrating the bodies of my companions. I could see through the canvas, and observed the Indians going to another tent, when I jumped up and extricating myself plunged into the river, which was but a few steps from me. I swam about a hundred yards and then crawled ashore, when I noticed Indian men and women shouting and yelling, where the cook's provision tent was. I fled further down the river and then met Petersen, with whom I proceeded. We never had any difficulties with the Indians previous to this."

Both Buckley and Petersen had a most miraculous escape. The former received two knife wounds and was hit in the head with the butt-end of a musket. He fell to the ground like a log, and the Indians thought him dead; but he afterwards recovered his senses and made his escape. Petersen's wrist was crushed by a musket ball, and it is a wonder that they were not murdered with the rest.

After the Indians had assured themselves that their victims were all dead, they finished up their bloody work by horribly mutilating the bodies; tearing the tents into shreds and looting the camp, carrying away all the stores, including two hundred pounds of bacon. Brewster and two of his men were not in the camp at the time of the bloodshed. They had gone up the trail to examine it, and the Indians at once went in search of them, and all three were murdered like their companions.

The three men, who escaped, all made for the ferry, where they found the mutilated body of the storekeeper.

They had great difficulty in crossing the river, wounded as two of them were, and for fear of being overtaken by the Indians, baricaded themselves in a log house, where they remained for several days, until two packers came past, who took them away. They were then conveyed to Nanaimo, where they were cared for at the French Hospital, under the care of Dr. Pujol.

The news of this massacre created the greatest excitement, and no time was lost in dealing out severe retribution and checking these savages in their wanton course, but as they went on to the junction of Bute Inlet and Bentinck Arm, it was feared that Manning's party, and McDonald and his party, known to be, at the time, packing considerable freight into the Cariboo mines, would share the same fate as the Waddington party, and true enough, it was confirmed later by some of the scouts under McLean, of Bonaparte, that Mr. Manning and others were murdered at Benshee Lake.

The gunboat "Forward" was dispatched to Bute Inlet with twenty-one volunteers. The flagship "Sutlej" was dispatched to Bentinck Arm with a party of marines, taking with them two Clayhoose Indians who were acquainted with the murderers and witnessed the massacre. Commissioner Cox started from Cariboo for Soda Creek with forty hardy miners, well equipped and armed with good rifles and revolvers, where he expected to meet with Captain McLean, but this gentleman together with Aleck McDonald and others, had started out to reconnoitre, only to be trapped by the Indians.

Hiding in the thick undergrowth, Tellet and his

men fired at the party from ambush, and McLean fell dead to the ground. The fire was returned, but as the enemy could not be seen, no certain aim could be taken, and the white men were forced to retreat. The Indians now made their appearance to pursue the enemy when McDonald and a few more turned round, and, firing from behind a tree, sent several of the hostiles to the grass. At last McDonald was the only one left, attempting to cover the retreat and check the Indians. His friends shouted "come on," but he replied: "Just one shot more at that fellow, and I will come!" It was too late, however, and his horrified friends saw the musket falling from his hands, while he sank dead to the ground with a bullet through his head.

Thus died one of the bravest of men, one of the truest of friends, trying to cover his companions, fearless to the last; one of the many unknown heroes, whose lives were lost in the great wilds, in trying to build up a grand and beautiful country.

But retribution was near at hand, and the murderous Indians soon after met their fate. They were surrounded in the mountains, and cut off from escape; fear and hunger forced them to surrender into the hands of the law. They were all hanged in quick order, five of them being strung up on one beam, while Chief Tellet boasted to the last of the number of white men, whose blood he had shed.

Thus was enacted one of the greatest tragedies of the early days of British Columbia, and while the invader lay scalped and mutilated in the woods, the rightful lord of the soil hung dangling from a gallows tree. Strange, indeed, that it should be thus, that after all, the difference between the human being and the savage brute is so small; for it should at all times be borne in mind that, although Waddington's party had committed no attrocities on the Indians, yet the usurper of the country had in so many instances caused the Indians to suffer indignities, which even more civilized races would have considered that only blood could atone for.

CHAPTER VII.

The Gold Export Tax—Captain Evans and His Son—In the Editor's Room—The Russo-American Telegraph—Two Different Routes—How to Go to Work—Once More at Dean Canal—Some Beautiful Land—Predicting a Bright Future—Hon. John Robson—The Famous Granite Creek—Lumps of Gold—Advice to Disheartened Miners—Comparing Past and Present.

The idea of introducing a so-called gold export tax met with much favor among the miners of British Columbia, who in the early sixties clamored loudly for a measure, the object of which was to keep the gold within the country where it had been found, and I admit that I was, at the time, one of the supporters of the project. Having had an opportunity, in after years, to more thoroughly consider the matter and view it from other points than those which then presented themselves to me, I am inclined to think it was well for the country that the measure was never made law.

I remember a curious incident in connection with this, which caused some amusement among the initiated ones. During the year 1866 a meeting was held at the The Theater Royal, in Victoria, for the purpose of discussing the matter of the said tax. Captain John Evans was in the chair, and a great many people were present, most of them miners or men interested in mines, and, while a good many speeches were made, the general sentiment expressed, seemed to be in favor of the tax. Captain Evans was a Welchman, and one of the best known Cariboo miners. From Billy Barker's down to Cameron's, there were few who did not know him, and he was held in much esteem among the miners of that district. He was a fluent writer, and frequently contributed to the newspapers of the day, and was a personal friend of Alexander T. Bell, of the Victoria *Times*, to the columns of which paper he had contributed many valuable articles; and when the tax question arose, he was a fervent advocate of its introduction. The Captain had a son, Taliesen Evans, who is now well known in California, as a journalist and writer on various subjects, but at the time of which I speak, he was a coy youth who had not, as yet, made his debut before the public, in any manner.

Young Evans was at the meeting referred to. He listened to the speeches and could hardly refrain from making one himself, being checked only by his youthful modesty, but it appeared to him that the argument in favor of the tax was wrong, and he was anxious to say so. After his return home that evening he set to work and I am told, for the first time ventured upon an address through the public press. He wrote a letter, commenting upon the meeting and its object and urged that, as the miner was taxed for everything he ate and drank, for his clothes, his tools, his necessaries of life and his luxuries alike, it would be unjust and out of reason to place a tax upon the product of his labors, gained amidst hardships and perils, moreover as there was virtually but little use for the gold within the country itself.

With this message to the interested public young Evans approached the Editorial Sanctum. He had attached a fictitious name to the letter and, taking advantage of the absence of Mr. Bell, placed the communication upon his table and hurried away, presently the

Editor entered, picked up the Manuscript, read it and was just digesting its contents, when Captain Evans made his appearance.

"Look here Captain," said Mr. Bell with a smile, "Here is an anonymous writer sitting down upon you folks pretty well, and he is right too, I tell you. I am going to publish what he says at any rate. Just look at that."

With these words he handed the Captain the newly received communication, but his friend had hardly glanced at it, when he exclaimed in utter amazement: "Why, that is my son's handwriting."

But the letter was published just the same, and young Evans had written his first newspaper article to the satisfaction of the Editor, if of no one else.

In the year 1865 the Russo-American Telegraph Company began to cast about for the most advantageous route, by which to lay their lines across British Columbia from the Fraser River to the coast. The chief Superintendent of the company was Colonel E. Bulkley, and I was advised by Mr. Allan Francis, the United States Consul, to report upon the country, situated between these longitudes and bordering on the Russian possessions, so as to assist the Colonel in his choice of a route. Having traveled over the whole of that vast territory more than once, I could easily comply with the suggestion, and I reproduce here the greater part of my report, as it will serve to show the reader the intimate knowledge, I had acquired of a country by perilous wanderings and hazardous explorations.

After a few preliminary remarks I go on to say: "Starting from Fort Alexander on the Fraser River the distance to Fort George is about 150 miles; from Fort George to Fort St. James on Stuart Lake, following the course of the river, the distance is about 120 miles, thence following along the bank of Stuart Lake to the Portage about fifty miles, the portage is ten miles, from here to Naas Glee at the lower end of Babine lake 100 miles, and from this point to Port Essington is a distance of about 250 miles, making a total of about 700 miles.

This was the route which naturally suggested itself, but I knew of another more practicable, and suggested the following: "Starting at the junction of the Quesnelle and Fraser Rivers, keep along the east bank of the Fraser for about fifteen miles till a small canyon is reached, and there cross the river, the width from cliff to cliff being only two hundred yards at this point. Follow up the west bank of the river about thirty miles further, then strike across in a northwesterly direction towards the Stuart River; follow this river for about sixty miles to Fort St. James, on Stuart Lake; thence keep along the south side of Stuart Lake to the ten-mile portage between this water-shed and Babine Lake. Continue along the south side of Babine Lake to the Naas Glee; follow down the river from this point, until a canyon is reached, distant from Naas Glee about one hundred miles, and as far from the coast.

"This course appears to be more favorable for running the line. It is tolerably level, and is but lightly timbered, and the river, from this canyon to the sea, is navigable for batteaux, thus facilitating the transport of wire, tools, etc. From this point, take a northwesterly course till the river Stikine is reached, a distance of about one hundred and fifty miles, and thus avoid the Peak and Babine mountains. This will strike a point on the last named river, which may be reached from the coast by boats or canoes, and thus further facilitate transport, while this course carries the line nearly two hundred miles further north, through a good country, easy to travel and work upon, and accessible by several water-ways."

I further recommended that the Skeena River be avoided, as it is very mountainous and difficult to travel. I also advised as to the best method of traveling, by making all possible use of the water-ways as the easiest means of transporting material and supplies.

My report went on to say: "Boats adapted to the Fraser River navigation, and capable of carrying five tons dead weight, can be built at Fort Alexander, or at the mouth of the Quesnelle, where suitable timber may be found in abundance. The size required would cost about five hundred dollars, and none larger could be used to any advantage. These boats would be required between the Quesnelle and Fort Alexander, and the head of Stuart Lake, as well as on Babine Lake, while a good wagon road can be made along the portage between the two lakes.

Boats of the size mentioned, will require a crew of eight men. Four of them may be Indians who will be found to work well, and the balance may be made up of half-breeds or old servants of the Hudson Bay Company, who can be hired in this locality for very moderate prices. They are most excellent boatmen, good pilots and capable of rendering much information and assistance.

As soon as the boats are ready, I would send a party to the Junction of the Fraser and Stuart rivers to commence operations from this point, keeping the boats engaged in carrying up supplies in the meantime. Too much attention cannot be paid to the management of the boats for the distribution of material and supplies at the proper time and places which will facilitate operations more than anything else, and I would therefore recommend to have a well qualified man as superintendent of the boats and to keep the same crews in the boats all the time, provided they do their duty, as by so doing much confusion and discontent will be avoided. Leaving the junction of the two rivers, I would go to Stuart Lake and commence operations, choosing the south side as the one best adapted to the purpose.

"Having commenced on Stuart lake I would take a party to the portage and start the making of the road there. This should be easily made, as the distance is only ten miles, and the country presents a fine stretch of rolling land; the pasture is good here, wild hay growing in abundance, which may be cut and stored in sufficient quantity for any number of cattle and horses it may be found desirable to keep through the winter. At the same time men should start in, whip-sawing and building canoes at the head of Babine lake, as the canoes obtained here are made of cottonwood, and not well adapted to carrying freight.

"In carrying cargoes across the lakes it may be found necessary to do the principal work at night, when all is calm, as in these high latitudes the wind often rises during the day to a perfect gale, at times making the sea so turbulent as to surprise any fresh water sailor.

"In running the line along Babine Lake, the south side will be found the one to be preferred, although the hills are rugged, but at the same time not very high. On the north side there are many large bays, while in other places the land is rolling and clear for considerable distances. The country is open to the northwest from Naas Glee, where lie the Indian villages of Kiss-pi-yaks and Kith-a-rath.

"In regard to the necessary operations to be undertak-

KOSKEEMO INDIAN CHIEFS.

en on the seaboard, I would recommend that an expedition, supplied with all necessary materials, be dispatched to Stikine River, as this will be a central point upon the coast, on account of the river being navigable, as far as is necessary, to a point through the coast range, from whence a line may be run northwest to Sitka, and another southeast to connect with Naas Glee."

The reader knows what it meant to be able to write so exhaustive a report of a vast, and mostly unknown territory. My experience had cost tremendous efforts and great suffering. I had gone hungry and weary for many days, in danger of my life among savage Indians, never knowing when they might turn upon me, and it may, therefore, appear excusable that I felt hurt and indignant at the fact that no proper acknowledgment was ever accorded me in regard to a report which contained much valuable information, and some practical advice.

Let me not pass over this period of my stay in British Columbia, without reverting once more to Dean Canal. It will be remembered that my first visit to this inlet was not fraught with any result as regards penetrating the mountains, and finding a route into the interior, but later on, I succeeded in this respect. I found that having overcome the difficulties which first presented themselves to me, my efforts were richly rewarded. I came upon a magnificent country of rich, rolling forest land, splendid pastures, and altogether, a country presenting the possibilities of thousands of homes being built in this region. Rivers and lakes, forests and meadows, varied in pleasing order, and here, indeed, is the shortest route from the coast to Fort Fraser, and further on to Fort James or Fort George. The river Nechaco runs southwest from Fraser Lake, and dividing itself, runs through a number of other lakes, until it is finally lost in the Tazella Lakes. I understand that lately a move has been made to settle this land, upon the advantages of which I reported to the government years ago, and I verily believe that this will become one of the most prominent portions of British Columbia. Through this country will, no doubt, run the projected railroad from Fort George to the coast, and I predict a splendid future for the settlers on Dean Canal and Salmon River.

In 1886, when the Hon. John Robson was Minister of Mines, I was again in British Columbia. At that time the Granite Creek District had attracted much attention, and I was bent upon making a close examination of the various localities in this district. I subsequently made an official report to Mr. Robson, and as it may serve to illustrate the condition of that region at the time of my visit, I here append the principal points of its contents, which may not be without some interest.

I begin where I pass the so-called Summit House, and soon found the geological formation to be real granite, below which the slate formation commences and continues all the way down. Following the trail down Whipsaw Gulch, I struck the gravel benches and rolling ridges, covering a large extent of country and clearly showing the great wash of an earlier period of the earth's history, when, I take it, large bodies of water, receding from the lakes, caused the formation of gravel ridges, gulches, creeks and ravines, where, indeed, one would expect to find gold. The wash is very extensive, and some of the creeks and gulches had been prospected and a small quantity of gold found, but not enough to pay for working.

Nine-Mile Creek and Whipsaw Gulch had been prospected chiefly by Chinamen, and the Mongolian had stuck to it with all the tenacity, characterizing his race, but had been forced to give up and abandon the diggings. The south fork of the Similkameen had also been prospected for a stretch of fifteen or twenty miles, but nothing of consequence had been found. Here is situated Allison's copper mine, and I saw some very fine specimens of peacock ore from this section.

All the way down the ridges gravel occurs, and, as I neared the river, some of the low benches looked very favorable. I found several Chinamen at work and further up the stream a company of white men were preparing to go prospecting. The gravel was heavy and did not wash off readily, and the gold, being fine, no doubt got away through any sluices with fall enough to carry off gravel. I took it for granted that these extensive gravel benches will never be washed off and that working on bars and bends will be the extent of work done on the Similkameen for many years to come.

Leaving Allison's I took the trail for Granite. It led up steep grades at the back of Tulameen, and on this road I met numerous prospectors returning disgusted, in fact, I had not seen so many sad miners in a heap since the days of '49 in California, and I could not refrain from telling some of them that their poor experience should serve them as a warning not to leave house and home again to tempt fickle fortune.

Arrived at the flat opposite Granite city, I camped and made a thorough examination of the far-famed Granite Creek. The distance from the river to the forks of the creek is four or five miles, and the hills, bordering it, rise very abruptly forming, so to speak, a natural ground-sluice so that any gold on the hillsides must find its way into the creek; but nothing like bench or hill-diggings had as yet been worked with success with the exception of the larger flats at the mouth of

Granite Creek. Opposite the town a quartz ledge had just been located and work started, and a number of claims on the Tulameen below the mouth of the Granite were also being worked.

Leaving Granite I took the trail for Otter Flat, situated about seven miles distant. On the large Flats above Granite Creek I noticed several Chinamen, who divided their attention between mining on the river and raising potatoes and other vegetables in large quantities higher up. The upper part of the trail led through a most beautiful country of the finest pasture land and to all appearance affording a better location for the herd than for the miner. The town of Otter is situated on a large fine flat at the junction of the river and creek, being originally a Hudson Bay Company's Camp, and the old Brigade trail from Hope comes down the ridge on the opposite side of the river, but it had ceased to be used and was blocked with fallen timber. The town, when I visited it, consisted of two stores, two saloons, a bakery, conducted by a chinaman, a branch postoffice and a news depot, but its few residents looked forward to, what they considered, a promising future.

I then took the Nicola Valley trail and went to Bowlder Creek, where I found several companies holding on to their locations with great determination, although they were scarcely making wages. One shaft, sunk forty feet, proved a failure, while others, sunk in shallow ground, paid well, and Collins' Gulch on the other side of the river paid wages but was about worked out. Here I was shown a piece of gold, weighing one ounce and three-quarters, but it was regarded as something phenomenal in these parts. On Cedar Creek, two miles above Otter Flat, several companies were at work, some of them making small wages and others nothing at all;

there was but little excitement, and everybody felt like giving it up.

On the Tulameen, above Otter Flat, a San Francisco company had located, but they were not ready to test their claim, as they required special machinery to work their diggings, which were very deep.

The Golden Crown Company was getting ready to commence operations, and the Beaver Company had a ditch out of Slate Creek and a powerful overshot wheel working an eight inch pump. Upon striking the granite sand, which seems to prevail generally on the Flats of the Tulameen, the water came in too strong for the pump and stayed any further progress for the time being. This company owned thirty-five claims and had a frontage of 2,000 feet on the river. It was undoubtedly the finest mining property on the Tulameen; and the facilities for working could not be surpassed, as there was a fall of twenty-five feet in the entire length of the claim. When I was there the company was about to sink another shaft in a more favorable place.

At California Company's claim expectations ran high, two dams had been put in, and good results were anticipated. It was located in a canyon and there were several other companies in the vicinity, some of them worked by Chinese. The Colorado Company had just taken out a lump, weighing nearly six ounces, but that sort of nuggets were not so common here as they were in certain places on the Yuba gold-fields in the early days. But such revelations of gold may never be seen again in this era of geological events. Slate Creek was considered the best location among the many Tulameen claims, and yet it yielded barely five dollars a day. This creek runs through the center of the Beaver Company's property.

A well-defined quartz ledge could be located near Eagle Creek, on the Tulameen, but nothing had been done, as yet, to test it. After all, I came to the conclusion that there was considerable gold to be taken out of the Tulameen River when the requisite appliances should be put upon the ground.

As I glance over the early pages of this book, I review, at the same time, the early history of modern gold-finding. It has never been surpassed; it will never be equaled, I believe. The gold which the forty-niner beheld in the dawn of California's most remarkable epoch, was like the dawn of day, when the sun throws its roseate hues over all the heavens. As the day wears on, the golden sunbeams still shine down upon us, but from a much smaller compass. So, to-day, the gold-hunter has a much smaller field in which to operate. And as the sun at meridian, appears to be much further removed from us than when it rises, so, to-day, the gold appears to be much further removed from the miner than it was of yore. Will the day end with another glorious burst of gold, or will the sun be veiled with heavy clouds as it sets upon the present era? Who can tell.

CHAPTER VIII.

Indians—The Value of Natives—Medicine Men and Superstition—An Incident at Yuclatan Villege—Heart Disease and no Bullet—Memoir From the Naas River—Singular Customs—The Price of Flour—The White Man and the Red Man—How They Died—Scarlet Fever—Indian Mechanics—A Promising Country.

I cannot here refrain from once more reverting to the Indians of British Columbia, who indeed played a prominent part in the early history of caucasion invasion of their country. In many instances they contested most bitterly, the forward march of the white man, while in others they became his faithful friends. Perhaps it would have been impossible to penetrate to the fastnesses of some of these regions but for the guidance of a native, who directed the steps of the adventurer, showed him the trails and conducted him, on foot or in his canoe, into the interior of the country.

The relation which we assumed toward some of the Indians was that of guardians who became responsible for their welfare, and must render account to their friends and relatives in case of anything happening to them whilst traveling in our company. They were valued as so much cattle by their own people, and in case of an accident, restitution could always be made by presenting their friends with blankets or other goods, much after the manner in which modern grief is assuaged by demanding hard cash from a railroad company to make up for the untimely death of a relative who has lost his life through their neglect, or whilst traveling in their care. I still have a lively recollection of nearly losing two Indians, who would have cost me something like sixty blankets, had they perished in the river where we capsized, and I admit that, as I saw them carried down the stream, I was more concerned about the heavy damages, than I was about the lives of the two natives whose struggles finally brought them safely ashore, much to my relief. In fact, in all such cases the first thought that seemed naturally to occur to one, was a quick calculation of how many blankets one would have to pay for so much native flesh and blood.

Superstition reigned supreme among the Indians, and it was considerably increased by the weird and singular action on the part of the medicine man who held sway over the natives by mystifying them with his phantastic actions. The medicine man played altogether a curious part in the Indian community, and was in many cases both revered and abhorred at the same time. He was looked up to because of the superior knowledge which he was believed to possess, and feared because of the evil power he was often supposed to exercise, and I am here reminded of an incident which goes to prove the superstition of the Indians in regard to the possibilities of the medicine man.

According to the usual custom amongst the Indians, of leaving their villages in a body, every man woman and child in the Yuclatan village was about to take to their canoes, carrying with them all their belongings; but, just as they were pushing off from the shore, it was discovered that the medicine man was not in his accustomed place in his canoe. His reputation was bad in the village, and he was feared as well as hated, and had it not been considered an omen of bad luck to depart without him, they would gladly have left him behind. Wondering what could have become of him, the young bucks called him loudly by name, but receiving no response, fear began to take possession of the departing Indians, when suddenly an old squaw cried out in a suppressed tone: "See him on the top of the house!"

Everybody looked in the direction, and, sure enough, beheld the hideous form of the Medicine man on the ridge of a roof, crouching in a half-sitting posture, pointing at them with one long lean finger and assuming an air of mystery which was well calculated to puzzle the Indians. Suddenly the attention of everybody was drawn from the old man perched on the roof to a young buck who had been standing in the shallow water alongside of his canoe, and with the others viewing the singular scene. With a loud piercing cry he fell forward without warning; there was a splash in the water, and his astonished and horrified comrade drew his lifeless body into their canoe.

Although not a sound but the voices of the Indians had been heard, still the general impression was that the medicine man had killed the youth by silently sending a bullet into his heart. The women set up a wail, and the bucks stood about in a sullen and defiant manner, waiting only for one word of encouragement to avenge the cruel death of one of their number.

Suddenly a brave in red paint stepped to the front. "Let us kill the murderer!" he cried; and with a yell and a whoop they made a mad rush for the hut, upon the roof of which the old man had perched himself. They were bent upon murder, and the medicine man perceived it; so he let go of the ridge and allowed himself to drop down behind the hut, but in so doing he rolled over and inflicted a hideous wound in the head.

FORT SIMPSON.

The Indians found him behind the hut, lying on the ground and bleeding profusely from a gaping wound. They dragged him out and would certainly have murdered him, had not a white man who happened to be present, dissuaded them by arguing to them that the medicine man, not having a gun, could not have fired a shot at anybody.

For awhile the natives seemed pacified, and the white man, being something of a surgeon and desirous of discovering the cause of death, undertook a post-mortem examination. He took out the heart of the dead man and found in it a clot of blood which had undoubtedly stopped the circulation and caused the sudden colapse; but the natives, seeing it, immediately took it to be the substance that had been fired at the dead buck by the wicked medicine man and once more prepared to kill the alleged slayer of their friend. Again the white man interfered and saved the object of their hatred, but the incident will show the mysterious powers attributed to the medicine man and the manner in which he was regarded by the natives

The Indians on the Naas River were very numerous in the early days. They were generally clad in fur coats and dirty blankets and did not present a very inviting appearance. But they were a careless, indifferent lot; they spent the greater part of the time in dancing, feasting and smoking and were so much given to the indulgence in pleasure that they entirely forgot to put something by for a rainy day, and, when winter came, they generally had to go starving for months, notwithstanding that the river abounded in salmon, and they might have secured enough food to carry them over the winter, had they not been so given to amusements.

The medicine man exercised the greatest power also

in these quarters and often held the people in abject subjection. I have seen many singular proofs of the manner in which one man's mind may direct that of another until it becomes perfect master of the weaker one to such a degree that the latter may be made to imagine almost anything. These "doctors" professed to be able to "ill-wish" anybody or to throw any particular spell over their subjects who not only believed in the possibility of such a thing but went so far as to suffer both physical and mental pain in the firm conviction that it had been forced upon them by the invocation of the medicine man, who could command the evil spirits. Thus it has often happened that a young buck would look ill and suffering and when asked what was the matter, would explain that he was sick, the doctor had cast his spell over him, and he was dying. And, indeed, it was not by any means a rare occurence, that young men in this plight would positively refuse to take either food or medicine and would gradually become weaker and weaker through sheer exhaustion and fear. These illustrations would tend to show that if the Indians do not know what we call mind-cure they certainly understand its opposite-mind-killing, and the success with which they practice it may demonstrate the correctness of a theory entertained by some white people in our days.

But it must not be supposed that these doctors practiced their noble profession for nothing. On the contrary their greed often knew no bounds, and this was one of the reasons, why they were so much detested. They carried with them a small box corresponding with the orthodox satchel of their medical confreres of more civilized communities; but, in place of costly instruments and an assortment of pills, the box contains bones and beads, feathers, stones and all sorts of trinkets. Naturally the owner surrounded his casket with a great deal of mystery and it did at times contain some curious objects, such as fingers and other parts of the human anatomy in a ghastly display. And, when the learned doctor has exercised his influence over any particular individual, or number of individuals he put in his charge with the same discretion as does the physician of a civilized community who never forgets to distinguish between the millionaire and the pauper, and the wealth of the medicine man was measured by the quantity of furs and blankets he had exacted from his unfortunate victims.

The Indians practiced polygamy in proportion to their wealth. Ordinarily speaking an Indian would have but one squaw, but, if he were rich and a chief of importance, it was a common thing to increase his household by adding one or more wives to the original one. When a girl was of marriageable age her lower lip was pierced and a pin inserted. This pin had a flat end, which remained in the mouth, while the rest protruded through the lip and over the chin an inch or more. As a matter of course it gave the girl a very hideous appearance in the judgment of a caucasian connoisseur of female beauty; but according to the ideas of savagedom, Venus herself is defective, in as much as her lip was never pierced. The marriage ceremony was the simplest one imaginable, being entirely void of any rite or other imposing formality. A great feast was arranged and at it the names of the bride and groom were called out, this constituting the tying of the nuptial knot, while the bride's brothers, uncles, and other relatives received handsome presents, consisting of blankets and furs often in large quantities. The wedding feast generally concluded with dancing and singing, which was kept up for many hours. They had a perfect system of dividing their community into groups. This I have found to be the case among the Indians all over North America, and the object seems to be to prevent too close intermarriage. The groups or "crests" are usually called after some animal, such as the wolf, the bear, the eagle and so on; and members of the same crest do not marry.

In no civilized community does a more complete code of etiquette exist than I found among the Naas River Indians. Every chief was accorded the privileges of his particular rank, and any attempts to assume a higher rank than the one to which he was entitled, was at once resented The chiefs on the Naas used the totem poles as indications of their social standing, the same as I afterwards found to be the case in Alaska; the hight of the pole denoting the rank of its owner, and it was not uncommon for two chiefs to disagree upon this matter. I remember one such case, where a chief put up a pole, much taller than he was entitled to, the result being a fight with another chief whose rank he had encrouched upon. The offender was wounded in the arm at the beginning of the fight, whereupon he immediately submitted and cut his pole down to the regulation hight.

Their principal food consisted of dried salmon. During the summer months the fish was caught in the rivers, sun-dried and put away for winter use. The natives also gathered different kinds of berries, which they preserved in grease; but one of their most important articles of food was a loaf, made from seaweed. The seaweed when gathered, was properly prepared and pressed into cakes or loaves, which were much relished by the natives.

Now-a-days, as a matter of course, the Indians eat many kinds of food, which have been introduced by the white men, but even as late as 1877 this was not the case. At that time flour cost ten cents per pound, and the Indians could not afford to buy it. The Hudson Bay Company was the first to give the native an idea of trading, and the latter soon learned that he had to pay for trade. In the spring and fall he would come to the trading posts with his season's catch of furs or fish and, if he wished to buy a Flint-lock musket, the bargain would be made by placing the musket, end up in the ground, after which the Indian was told to put his furs down, one upon the other, until the level of the other end of the gun was reached. Then the trader took the pile of skins, and the Indian took the musket.

Among the many curious traditions existing among the Naas river Indians, none perhaps is more characteristic than the narrative of how the red and the white man met for the first time. The story in substance is as follows: A number of Indians were fishing in a large canoe at the mouth of the Naas River, when suddenly a thick mist surrounded them. After awhile they heard a strange noise, not far distant, and they at once thought that some evil spirit of the great ocean had risen from the deep to swallow them, wherefore they hauled in their cedar lines and seizing their paddles, pulled for the shore as fast as they could. But the dread noise did not subside, on the contrary it seemed to follow close upon them, and in fear and trembling they expected every moment to encounter some fearful monster. At last they reached land and jumped ashore, and there they stood looking into the dense fog, anxiously watching the sound, which grew louder and louder, as it evidently approached the terror-stricken Indians. But what can describe their amazement and consternation, when they suddenly saw a large boat of a strange and unknown build gliding out of the mist towards the very place where they stood, the boat being filled with white men?

The strange appearance of the pale-faces created the greatest surprise among the Indians, who now witnessed the white men landing and preparing to camp; but they were soon to behold even greater wonders. The strangers beckoned the Indians toward them and signed to them to bring some fish. One of them carried something resembling a stick, which he pointed at a bird flying overhead. Then they saw fire and smoke issuing from the stick, while a thundering sound called all the echoes of the mountains to answer its sharp, sudden crack, and the bird fell lifeless to the ground with blood upon its feathers. Then died all the Indians, by which expression is meant in the language of the Naas River people, that they were fairly taken back with surprise. When they had again recovered themselves, they questioned one another as to how they felt, and whether they were all alive, and then, in response to a sign by the white men, they prepared to make a fire in their usual way by rubbing two pieces of wood together.

But the pale-faces laughed, and one of them, seizing a handful of dry grass, applied a flint and steel to it and all of a sudden there was a blaze. Then the Indians died again.

The white man now gave them to understand by signs that they desired some fish, boiled, and the Indians prepared to heat stones in the fire, according to their way of boiling by putting hot stones into cedar vessels, filled with water. But the white men smiled at them, and placing an iron pot over the fire, began cooking in their fashion. The Indians had never seen anything like this, and they could not understand why the bottom did not burn out of the vessel, and, indeed, so great was their surprise that they again "died," as is explained above.

But, after the fish were eaten, the white men put in some rice to cook. By and by it began to swell, and the astonished Indians saw it rising and moving about in the bubbling water, and, thinking it was something alive, they cried in disgust; "Maggots, Maggots!" But when the rice had been properly cooked, the white men prepared to eat it by pouring molasses over it, and the natives at once surmised that this was the grease of dead people and refused to taste it when it was handed to them. But, when they saw the white men eating the boiled rice and apparently relishing it, they died again.

Other similar things occured, which in the consideration of the Indians appeared like miracles, and whenever another wonder was worked they died. Then came the time for the white men to die. The Indians went away a little distance and when hidden from sight, they put on their paint and head-dress and besought the great *Nok-Nok* to assist them. Returning to the camp, they walked slowly and majestically, with firm and steady, step and head bowed, into the presence of the strangers, but when they raised their heads and the white men looked into their wonderful faces, they were surprised beyond measure, and they also died.

As traders, the Indians have always impressed me as being very keen, although as a matter of course, they never received the real value for their goods. But as they could not possibly ascertain how much their furs were worth in the market of the white man, the question became entirely relative, and so far as their knowledge of the transaction went, they were often particularly sharp. One incident occurs to me just now, which will show their manner of calculating. The Hudson Bay

Company had hired a number of Indians for the purpose of taking freight up the river Skeena in their canoes. The party was in charge of a white man, and the Indians were paid so much per day, everyone who owned a canoe receiving double; in other words, a canoe and a man counted the same. The company supplied part of their provisions, but on this trip they nearly ran out of stores; for, having covered only one-half of the distance to be traveled, the freshet in the river so increased the current that no headway could be made, and the whole party was obliged to go ashore and camp for ten days. Gradually as provisions became scarcer, rations were reduced, and at last orders were given that only one spoonful of sugar would be allowed each man per meal. The Indians are very fond of sugar, and in this party was an old man, who had a particularly sweet tooth. He was the owner of a canoe, and he made use of this circumstance to help himself to an extra supply. When the sugar tin was passed round, he helped himself to one spoonful, "This is for me," he said. Then taking another spoonful he remarked dryly "And here is for the canoe."

Their idea of justice is often very striking. At one time some young Indian girls in a mission school on the river Naas brought the charge against a young man that during prayers he had looked at them through his fingers and made grimaces. The Indians summoned the accused before their council; and severely reprimanded him, reminding him of the reverence which was due to the occasion, and which he had so sadly forgotten. The youth admitted the offense, and after a scorching lecture was fined in a small amount. The council then called the young girls in and admonished them, saying that if they had kept their eyes closed and attended to their prayers, they would not have noticed the indecorous action of the young man; and they in turn were fined for their alleged impropriety.

The Indians have a great dread of diseases. Rev. E. A. Green informs me that when scarlet fever broke out on the Naas, in '87, for the first time, the Indians held a council to discus the matter. It was reported among them that the fever had been sent up the river in a box, and was being served out among them as a punishment because some of them had not joined the mission, and it was decided to murder Mr. Green and his family. ' Just then, however, the fever broke out in the Missionary's own home, and they at once saw their mistake, and were profuse in offering their sympathies to the family. Mr. Green has lived among the Naas River Indians for many years, and done much good work among them. The Reverend gentleman holds a high opinion of the natives, characterizing them as a manly people.

But, as the Indian of British Columbia has advanced in the course of years, so has that splendid country increased in importance as the explorers laid open to the world at large the rich fields it contains, where prosperity may be reaped. Foremost among these explorers stand the pioneers of the Hudson Bay Company, but they left much undone, which was not accomplished until the Fraser River Gold-diggings were discovered. Then came the miner, and with his natural lust for adventure, he repeated what he had done in California years ago, and forced open highways and by-ways that had never been thought of before, thus taking the first active step in the general and final development of a magnificent country. Let all who took a hand in the work rejoice! Their trials were great, their labors hard to perform, but the result will prove a great and glorious one.

ADVENTURES

IN

PANAMA.

CHAPTER I.

Taking a Rest—A New Friend—Queer Conversation—How Vansickles Dug Gold—My Greatest Chance—Panama the Place—Departure—A Curious Old City—Difficult Mountain Trails—Down With Fever—An Indian Graveyard—Digging For Gold—Pottery Galore—A Curious Whistle—My Collection Spoiled—Moving to Other Parts.

In the fall of the year 1874 I was staying in San Francisco, taking a rest. During this period I paid frequent visits to my brothers-in-law, Artemis and Douglas Davison, who, like myself, were old California miners, and always on the lookout for any new enterprise in the way of gold-hunting. We were often talking over former days and wondering to ourselves when and where the next excitement would break out, for, although we all realized that we were not "so young as we used to be," we were all in good health and full of vigor eager to plunge into some fresh undertaking for the sake of shining gold.

There is an old adage which says: "Once bitten, twice shy." It may be true in certain respects, I have no doubt, but in regard to the pioneer miners of California, I never found that it held good, on the contrary, defeat seemed to urge them on to new ventures. And so it happened that the three of us had not yet given up our worship of the golden calf, principally because it had always got away from us, after we had caught it, and was yet roaming at large in some, to us, unknown place. If the opportunity, however, should present itself to run it down in whatever clime, we were prepared to chase the symbolical bovine until we had penned him, and like a spider watching for a fly to get into his web, we were laying wait, anxious for our chance. It was introduced to us by a young gentleman by the name of A. T. Vansickles in such a manner that it fairly took us old miners aback and made us think that we had the softest "snap" on hand, ever presented to anyone, hunting for the precious metal.

One day we were talking to our new friend, Vansickles, when he told us something about Panama, whence he had just arrived. "Gold," he said in answer to an inquiry. "You bet there is gold; why, the country is full of it. Hard to get at, you say? Not a bit of it. I found lots of it and can get as much more as I care for."

We pricked up our ears, as a matter of course, and began to talk mining to him right away. But he did not know a rocker from a pan, nor a sluice box from a diamond drill, and we commenced to think he had merely been having a joke at our expense.

"But how in the world did you get the gold?" I asked.

"Dug it out of the graves!" he said, perfectly unconcerned, speaking as if it was an every day occurence in that country to dig gold out of graves.

I must confess I did not at once relish the idea to turn suddenly from the honest occupation of a gold digger, to something bordering on the nefarious trade of body snatching, and I asked him to explain a little further, what he really meant.

"Well," he said, "I learned that the old Indians in their days used to bury their dead—that is the wealthy ones—with large portions of the treasure they possessed. I was told furthermore that old Spanish adventurers had opened the graves of Inca chiefs and had taken as much as 200 pounds of gold from a single grave, and so I made up my mind that I could play the same game. Consequently I made friends with an Indian, who pointed out to me one of the old Inca cemeteries in the Interior, and showed me where I might dig with some success. My guide was so scared of the possible advent of the spirit of the deceased chief, that he quickly made off, but, as I had no fears on that score, I set to work with a spade I had bought, and very soon found that I had struck something. I was fairly dazzled, when I came upon gold and silver bracelets of heavy patterns, and other ornaments, mingled with all kinds of useful and decorative articles, many of them exceedingly costly. I felt as if I had suddenly entered a fairyland of wealth, and hiding as much of the precious find as I cared to carry away, I made off for the time being, and upon arriving at the nearest town, soon realized quite a handsome sum, on what I had brought with me. Since then I have done a good deal of grave digging, and with pronounced success, and on the last grave I emptied, I realized about a thousand dollars for a couple of hours work."

As Mr. Vansickles finished his story, he jingled a couple of twenties in his pocket, and the words he had spoken, together with this sound, produced an effect upon us, as though we had been listening to some charming song, accompanied by sweet music. Here was a proposition. To exchange the hard rock in the dark tunnels for the easy work of uncovering dead Indians, and in a few hours enrich ourselves with treasures they certainly had no more use for. Artemis was no less struck with the idea than I was, and it did not take us long to make up our minds, that, after all, Panama was the place where we were destined to make our fortune, and as Mr. Vansickles offered to go down with us, we made the necessary preparations to proceed to the Isthmus and make the big haul of our life.

It was but the matter of a few days to get all in readiness, and the next steamer for Panama carried all three of us southward. I do not think that I have ever felt so elated in all my life, as I felt when we steamed over the waters of the blue Pacific. The waves, as they danced about the bow of the steamer and glimmered in the light of the sun, looked like so much golden spray. The sky, as it reflected the setting sun in the far horizon, appeared like one mass of golden banks. Hope itself glittered like gold in my thoughts and dreams alike, and I felt more certain than ever that at last the hour had come, when I should attain that reward which every gold hunter has a right to look for. We had money enough with us to suffice for four or five months; we had a splendid outfit, conprising everything we could possibly have need for, and accompanied by a man who had dug the gold in these parts before, failure seemed impossible. We did not think for a moment that the steamer, which carried us, went quickly enough. The days passed slowly, and the nights were sleepless; for the anticipation of our coming fortune rendered us nervous and restless, and when we came to the end of our voyage and stepped ashore in Panama, we were greatly pleased.

I cannot pass over my entrance in Panama without briefly mentioning the impression I received of this ancient town, which has since become so famous, while its name has cost men millions of dollars, for the sake of enriching a few unscrupulous speculators, who have now received the just punishment for their unsatiable greed. The city, which has, or had then, about 15,000 inhabitants, is of very old Spanish origin. It is built upon almost level ground, and the site of it is located on a narrow peninsula, extending into the bay of Panama, and on the extreme eastern point of this peninsula stood the walls of the old citadel, built of brick and faced with cut stone. These walls were used as a promenado, being twenty-five feet wide on the top. They were from thirty to forty feet high and were provided with seats, and notwithstanding their age, they were in good condition. The view from here was very pleasing, and embraced not only the vast blue expanse of the Pacific with the islands in the foregound, but also the hills and forests of the country.

The streets were narrow, winding and badly paved, and the city altogether appeared dirty and full of disagreeable odors. The houses had never more than three stories and were provided with balconies, projecting, until they almost touched one another. The atmosphere was damp, hot and generally disagreeable, and, apart from the historical interest, I could find nothing attractive about the little city. The old fort and the Cathedral are the only buildings of any interest, and as an architectural curiosity, it may be mentioned that the cupolas of the two towers of the Cathedral have an edging of oyster shells by way of ornament. French and English were spoken in most places, and the restaurants were frequently conducted by either Americans or Frenchmen. From Panama we went to Chittrae, and here we rested, while a man was sent ahead to La Mesa for horses, to take us up into the mountains for a distance of about 120 miles, and as soon as the animals arrived, we started out.

The horses were small, although sturdy, but the road was like the rocky road to Dublin—hard to travel. The nature in these regions is certainly unique, and it impressed us, as strangers, with its wonderful variety of scenery, fauna and flora. I believe the vegetation embodies everything, from tropical to Alpine, as the altitude rises from the level of the Pacific and the Atlantic to the summits of the Cordilleras, which rear, so to speak, from a plateau formed by other mountains, palms grow here in great varieties. From some of them, so-called palm wine is extracted, while on others cocoanut grows, but many of them are very beautiful trees. While the soil is said to hide, in addition to gold and silver, also platinum, amathysts, emerald, copper, lead and other valuable products, the forests supply cinchona and log wood, while such plants as Aloe and Sarsaparilla are found.

Among the animals, inhabitanting this nature's drugstore, if I may use the expression, the monkeys are most numerous. They are as a rule very small, but there is said to be about twenty varieties of them, and they would sit on the branches of the trees, and throw twigs or fruit at us as we passed by. There are various kinds of animals, belonging to the feline race, also deer and bears, while Alligators swarm in the rivers. In the upper regions of the forests parrots and peroquets vie with cockatoes in making the most noise, and over them again soar the condor; cranes wade through the swamps; the wild turkey hides in the undergrowth; and the beautiful pea birds display their rich plumes. There are plenty of snakes in the country, and the boa constrictor makes his home in certain places, while the Yaruma and Casabal are more frequent. In the valleys are excellent pastures, and nature in these regions is wonderfully grand, while rugged mountains of phantastic outline, and rushing streams, add to the effect, produced by the animal and vegetable life.

It was no easy task to travel through the forests of Panama. The trail was often dangerous or hard to find, and the mountain streams ran with a velocity, which rendered them difficult to ford. However, we pushed on until we arrived at the place belonging to a Don Juan Barrio. It did not take us long to discover that the noble Don was a near relative of our guide, in fact the home of the latter seemed to be in the bosom of Barrio's family, and it was evident that he was determined to stay here for a few days before proceeding any further. It would not have been of much avail had we opposed his desire in this direction, for we had not been long in this place, ere both Mr. Davison and myself were down with fever. For several days we were *hors de combat*, and I felt so bad that for awhile I thought the only grave digging I should have the privilege of being concerned in, might be the one preceeding my own funeral, and I was not at all cheered at the prospect. The complaint was evidently a malarial one, and no doubt had its cause in the wretched drinking water we were treated to in this locality. Meanwhile our host was very kind to us, and in a little while we found ourselves recovering, and as soon as we were able, we set out again on our weird mission. It was more struggling with the wilds of nature, more pelting by the impudent monkeys, and a continuous anxiety for fear our small horses would not be able to carry us and the pack through, but I must give them credit for their wonderful powers of endurance, which I learned in time to appreciate.

One animal, which we here encountered in large numbers, I nearly forgot to mention, although indeed it played quite a part in our adventures—it was the wild hog, the peccarico, as the natives call it. It is only a small animal, but very ferocious, and especially, when it appears in hordes, quite unpleasant to meet. It will attack a man with its sharp teeth, and should one chance to be unarmed, Mr. Hog can make things quite lively for a time. In such cases the general thing is to climb a tree and allow the enemy to get tired of waiting for one's descension. I sat in a tree the greater part of one day, looking down upon my pursuer, who evidently had more patience than I. He stayed below, resting on his haunches with his head turned skyward, one eye apparently asleep and the other every now and again blinking up at me, to see how I was getting on. At last a native came to my relief and speared the peccarico, which settled the contest in favor of me. I was beginning to get pretty tired of being a tree dweller, and made haste to get down. The natives are very skillful at spearing these animals, but I never could understand why they disrobe themselves of their nether garment when they go in pursuit of them, except it be that they would rather keep their trowsers than their legs intact. As to myself, I felt as if I would prefer wearing six pairs of pants, rather than none, when waging war upon the wild hog of Panama.

At last we arrived at a place where our guide introduced us to an Indian graveyard. We were told that a few months previous somebody had dug out forty-seven pounds of gold in this neighborhood, and sold it in Panama for fourteen dollars a pound, and we felt sure that there must be many graves left from which other treasures might be unearthed. I admit that it was with a singular sense of anticipation that I invaded this ghastly gold field. I recalled to my mind a dozen different instances, from former years, when I had approached a place where gold was supposed to be. We had judged then by the surrounding nature; the geological condition had in most cases given us some kind of assurance; but here was absolutely nothing to go by, save a little mound, and in some cases not even that, but rather a slight hollow in the ground. Nevertheless it was not material where we dug. In the graves of the rich we might expect to find what we were looking for, in those of the poor we had no chance. But there was nothing to indicate the one from the other, for these dusky heathens, in going to their forefathers, had not provided for forty thousand dollars' worth of carved stone piles, so as to denote their rank and keep their bodies safe below the soil at the same time.

Consequently we had to "go it blind," and we set to work. We soon came to the conclusion, that our departed friend had taken some of his household articles with him, for we dug up a quantity of curious looking pottery. I had not gone to Panama for the purpose of collecting old crockery, or set up a curiosity shop on my return home, and I was therefore not wholly satisfied with my find. At the same time it interested me to some extent, and I went on digging, but to my disgust our success was limited to the unearthing of pottery, until it appeared to me that all the old earthenware vessels of ancient Panama must have been dumped in this cemetery. We heaped the articles up at one place, and gradually we had accumulated enough to start an ordinary museum. Grave after grave was broken into, and amidst bones and skulls, that seemed to grin at us from their eyeless sockets, we drew vessel after vessel, swelling our supply of ancient ware.

Suddenly we came to a grave in which the pottery

RELIC FROM AN INCA GRAVE.

seemed to be of more delicate texture, and we concluded that some chief had found his last resting place among these pieces, and so dug on with renewed hope, expecting certainly to strike some of his silver or gold plate. But no! It was crockery, and remained crockery. But among it we found one curiosity, the like of which I had never seen, neither before nor after. It was a whistle, made to represent a puma, or leopard. The tail was cut off stumpy, and arranged for the mouth-piece, and on each side were three holes. The instrument was a very curious contrivance, and so ingeniously arranged as to render it possible to play sundry different tunes upon it.

After several days, spent in digging up pottery and finding nothing else, we determined to try other regions. Meanwhile, I had collected the best samples of what we had found, and packed them in a basket, intending to bring it back to California with me. But my intentions were thwarted in a singular manner. In a moment of misplaced generosity I had given the native, who found the curious whistle, a dime, and as soon as he had an opportunity, he spent the money on grog. Whether he added to his purchase of the fiery fluid by expending his own money, or whether he could really get drunk for such a small amount (he afterwards insisted that he did) I cannot tell, but he came back to camp in a state of intoxication, which prevented him from distinguishing the objects around him, and he laid down to sleep on the basket, containing my precious pottery. The result was fatal to the curios. The native came out intact, but not one piece of the disinterred property of deceased Indians was saved from a devastation, which rendered them entirely unfit even for a dime museum, and I left these parts heartily sick of my first experience in digging for gold in the graves of the Incas.

CHAPTER II.

The Chirique—Another Graveyard—More Pottery—David City—The Shuber Brothers—A Native Hog—Singular Tombs—Above the Clouds—Abandoning Grave Digging—Looking for Copper—A Perfect Hoodoo—Farewell Panama—Bric-a-brac.

Although it is true that we felt greatly disappointed at the poor results so far attained, we did not lose courage, and with the tenacity and perseverence, which I think is characteristic of the pioneer miners of California, we determined to give other localities a trial before giving up the venture, and so pushed eastward, towards Costa Rica, in hopes of meeting with better success. On the 5th of April 1875 we arrived at the Chirique and prepared to cross it. The waters came down with much force, for we were experiencing a rainy season, and had endured a good deal of hardship on our journey, in this way; moreover, the river was very deep in some places, and when we attempted to cross it, reached to our shoulders. We all linked hands, and in this manner, succeeded in crossing without any accident. It is strange that directly on the opposite side of this river, the territory is called Costa Rica, although the boundary of the State of Panama does not occur till further east

Our journey, so far, had been impeded by numerous difficulties, more especially afforded by the thick underbrush, through which we had often been compelled to cut our way; but we now expected to get along much more easily. We soon came upon a camp which had been built by cattle men. It was of singular construction and covered with palm leaves, serving well enough as a shelter against the sun, but forming a poor protection in the rainy weather. As there was a plantation patch near by, we concluded to camp here and rest, and we made a good fire and placed one of the natives on guard to keep the peccaricos away. These little animals were very daring here, and hung round the camp like a pack of wolves. Our friends, the monkeys, were also very numerous in this locality, and every now and again one of us would be hit by something, thrown at us by these mischievous brutes, whom Darwin flattered by calling them the progenitors of the human race. I have seen the human race in many varieties, and all through my stay in Panama I lived in daily exchange of missiles with monkeys, and I consider it a consolation that in Mr. Darwin's theory there is a missing link, which cannot be found.

The trees around our camp were covered with moss to a remarkable degree. It enveloped them like a thick mantle, from the top down to the very roots, and the effect was exceedingly striking. Here, also, we saw a great many wild turkeys, the so-called "Royal Turkey." It is a very pretty bird, and affords an excellent meal, but the natives will not kill it on account of some superstition.

I tried to prospect several creeks in this neighborhood, but with no success. The appearance indicated gold, but my experience would not bear it out, and I began to wonder whether all the mineral wealth attributed to this country, is confined to the graves, in which so far, I had not found it. Shortly after leaving this camp we came upon large droves of cattle, which were being driven towards the coast to be sold in the market. The drovers, or cow-boys, looked very picturesque, wearing large sombreros and mounted, Spanish fashion, with all the display characteristic of their race.

At last we came upon another graveyard, and with renewed hopes we entered upon an examination of the burial place. Again pottery and nothing but pottery. It seemed to me as if all the pots, vases, vessels and everything else, made out of clay, had been heaped together here, and as if the deceased chiefs had measured their wealth by the earthenware in their possession. There was, however, one curious feature about these graves, which rendered them more interesting than any we had hitherto seen. They had been constructed on the principle of tombs, and were enclosed with thin slabs of whitish spar, from two and one-half to three inches thick. I examined this material, and came to the conclusion that it would do first rate for building purposes. I found it very remarkable that in all this neighborhood there was not a quarry to be seen, and it made me think that the stone, used in these tombs, had been brought from a considerable distance; but these graves contained neither silver nor gold, and it began to dawn upon me that our trip to Panama was as much of a wild-goose chase, as, in days gone by, the search for the Gold Lake had been.

We traveled by way of David City and here rested for a few days, putting up at the house of Mr. and Mrs. Agnew. Mr. John Shuber, a prominent Panama cattle dealer, was staying here, and he and his brother Henry, owning certain claims on the Atlantic Slope, where there was supposed to be copper, I entered into an arrangement with them to prospect the locality, and of this undertaking I will speak later on. We enjoyed the utmost hospitality during our stay here. The city of David is located on a plain about thirty-five miles west of the volcano, known as Mt. Chirique, and its inhabitants are mostly engaged in stock-raising and coffee culture.

Not far from this city we visited one of the greatest natural wonders I have ever seen. It was a huge cave situated in a limestone formation. We entered it with blazing torches to light our way, and the effect was truly magic. The stalactites and stalagmites pointed their long thin fingers at one another from above and below; the walls glistened with spar, and the bats flew like phantom birds into the farthest darkness, as the glare from the torches partly lighted up the uncanny scene, leaving dense gloom like a circle beyond the periphery of their reach. The cave was probably sixty feet high at its lowest point, increasing toward the back. The air within was oppressive, and the whole situation affected our senses in a disagreeable manner, although it roused our wonder, and I felt relieved upon once more breathing the fresh air and having the sunlight fall upon me again. One thing, less pleasant to contemplate when we issued from the wonderful cave, was the appearance of fresh tiger-tracks, but we never saw the animal, which had left, and continued our way without any further adventure.

Again we camped on the banks of the Chirique. While here I saw a native woman carrying a wild hog on her back. She had evidently speared the animal, for she held the weapon in her hand. The flesh of this animal is very savory, not unlike our tame pig but has an additional flavor, which is particularly pleasant. I was amazed to see this woman thus burdened, for although the peccary is not so large as the one that goes in as pig at one end of Armour's establishment, and comes out as pork at the other end, still it is a heavy weight to carry. I engaged in conversation with this woman. She told me, among other things, that she had been engaged in digging gold out of Indian graves, and exhibited a small piece which I bought of her for six soft dollars, meaning dollars worth eighty cents apiece. All along here the natives told the most harrowing tales of Spanish cruelty, as practiced in the early days upon the aborigines. I listened to accounts of whole families who chose self-destruction rather than falling into the hands of the invaders, and if the tales related to me were only half true, the revolting treatment to which the early settlers subjected the native sons of the soil, is almost unparalleled in the history of the world, and on a par with any torture practiced upon early Christian martyrs.

Once more we tried gold-hunting in graveyards, but with the same result as previously. Pottery, again; pottery forever; nothing but pottery, until we became so disgusted that I believe if a stranger had come up and said "Indian graves" to us, we would have laid him alongside some of the ancient pottery, considering ourselves justified in so doing, on the ground of gross provocation.

Before disposing of the subject of Indian graves, however, let me say that in many parts of South America, very valuable ornaments have been found in Inca graveyards. Probably one of the most interesting of these finds is at present in the possession of a Mr. Thorndike, of Lima, and consists of a pure, solid silver bust of a male being, eight inches in hight, and weighing about eleven pounds. Mr. Frank Vincent, the well-known traveler, says of this wonderful relic: "The head is decidedly Homeric in aspect, but wears a sort of Persian cap, surrounded by a large, radiating sun. The moulding and carving of the sun in such a position, would appear to indicate a Persian origin, and thus, again support the theory of trans-Pacific migration." I think these remarks are very suggestive and full of interest. There can be no doubt that many valuable antiquities, outside of pottery, have been buried in these tombs, and may, in due course of time, in the hands of ingenious interpreters, serve as an explanation of some of the mysteries that at present meet our retrospective glance, as we try to penetrate the past. I am informed that at Molendo, a limited liability company has of late years been organized, with a capital of $50,000. It bears the singular name of the "Anonymous Company for Exploration of the Inca Sepulchres," and has for its object the search for antiquities and valuables, in the old burial grounds in the district of Cuzco, the government having granted a concession to the company for this purpose. To all those who may have any intention of taking stock in this somewhat remarkable company, I give here my own personal experience in digging for gold in Indian graves, that they may consider well, ere they embark in an undertaking which has, on the other hand, been crowned with such success as that attained by Mr. Thorndike.

I was now thoroughly disgusted with my efforts to find gold in Panama, and determined to give it up, and at once attended to Mr. Shubert's business. The mines he wanted me to prospect, were situated on the other side of the range, and we therefore made for the summit, so as to reach the Atlantic slope. Our journey was a very difficult one. The rain was coming down in torrents, and not till we arrived above the cloud-belt did we experience any sunny weather. There, on the tops of the Cordilleras, pretending to put one leg on the Atlantic, and the other on the Pacific side of the mountain ridge, I made a speech to my companions for the purpose of enlivening the somewhat dreary situation. I reminded my audience of the Spanish heroes, whose perseverence in days of old, had first guided them to these mountain tops, and then pointed out how Anglo-Saxon energy was in no way behind that of the Spaniards, and how, through Americans, it had led us on to unqualified success throughout the known world, excepting, of course, when it came to extracting gold from Indian graves. Then I gave three cheers for California, after all, the only genuine El Dorado, and we started away from the cheering surroundings of sun-lit mountain scenes into the clammy region of mist and rain, towards the borders of the Atlantic.

The trail was bad and dangerous, and we suffered considerably on our journey, but we pushed on with unabated vigor, hoping that we might achieve in copper, the success we had failed to find in gold. All along I examined carefully the formation over which we were traveling, for I had been told that we might find traces of lead and copper throughout the whole distance, from the Atlantic to the Pacific, but I failed entirely to benefit by the tips given me in this direction, and could find no indication of the metal I was in search of.

At Horcansists I was joined by Mr. Santiago Hovenue, whom I found a most pleasant companion. He was an exceedingly gentlemanly man, and gifted with rare conversational powers and general knowledge, which rendered him very interesting, and his presence did much towards alleviating the hardships of the trip. The location which we had to examine, is situated about sixty miles from Horcansists. We camped in the can-

DANCING THE FANDANGO.

yon known as Aliares Reo, and paid a visit to Mr. Rills' trading station, some fifteen miles further on.

Arrived at our destination, we found that a tunnel had been started into the hill about fifty feet above the creek that runs through these parts. This tunnel was cut into the rock about twenty-five feet, and ran in upon a reddish brown slate lying horizontally. Along the face of the hill outside of the tunnel a slate formation appeared, running at right angles with the tunnel, and in this formation I found small seams of crystalized quartz. It was here that the virgin copper was found, and I was told that when first discovered, the metal lay in large lumps just above where the mouth of the tunnel was situated.

But that was the last seen of the copper in any appreciable quantity. I worked into the seams, but could not find much of anything. They became narrower, until they ran out altogether. The hill had the appearance of a drive, as the rock did not lie in a regular position, such as is generally the case when true leads of mineral are found. I made a careful examination of the seams, but could find only faint traces of the mineral, and not even a good specimen, where the copper was first discovered. I must say, that the more I saw of this place, the more I was at a loss to understand what the people, who drove the tunnel, were thinking of when they did all this work; for there was nothing whatever, that I could find, to warrant the expenditure of any such engineering.

I followed the ledge up the canyon, and found slight traces of copper in various places, but nothing like a lode. There was no appearance of carbonate of copper, but here and there were stains along the ledge, just enough to indicate that we were in a copper country, but not by any means enough to justify any outlay of money for the purpose of speculation, and I can safely say that I did not see, during my journeying up and down on the Atlantic slope, one bucket-ful of copper. In this same section of the country I made an examination of a ledge of cinnabar, which had been described to me as exceedingly rich, but again I failed to find anything worth working. The soil here consisted of brownish clay with red patches, but if there really was cinnabar to be found, it was in such small quantities, that it would not pay to work it.

Altogether, it would have cost considerable money to undertake any mining in these parts. The places I was directed to examine were only accessible over almost impassable trails, and the dense undergrowth on the hillsides rendered even the task of prospecting particularly difficult. Closa Canyon was the name of the place where the Shuber brothers more, especially expected to find successful mining, but I failed to meet with anything which would give the least encouragement, or warrant my writing a report advising operations for the purpose of opening mines in this section.

Strange to say, while I was in these parts, a native chief, by the name of Ruez, came to me and told me that he would show us a place where we could take out plenty of gold. By this time my reader knows me well enough to know also that such a thing merely had to be whispered in my ear to cause me to start in search of the promised fortune. I persuaded Mr. Hovenne to come with me, and accompanied by two natives, we set out on a new venture. But Luck and I, did not go to Panama together, and after having traveled in the rain, and slept on the damp ground for several nights in wretched camps, we arrived at the place pointed out to us, only to find that once more we had been on a fool's errand.

I now prepared a report for the benefit of Messrs. John and Henry Shuber. I much regretted that I could not write an encouraging report, but conscience prompted me to advise them to abandon all idea of working these supposed mines. It appeared to me that there had been a hoodoo over my whole expedition to Panama, and no previous experience had so disgusted me as my visit to this, the most famous of Columbia's United States. It must not be inferred from this that the metals I went in search of, do not exist on the Isthmus. Undoubtedly they do, but somehow I did not happen to come their way. Columbia, and for that matter the greater part of South America, is one of the favored quarters of the globe, and I have already mentioned the many products, minerals and precious stones which may be found there. But even up to the present day the country has been, comparatively, but little worked. The Spaniards are not the ones to develop its natural wealth, and the North Americans, or I would rather say the Anglo-Saxons, are so far scarce there. Moreover the climate is not congenial to the latter; malarial complaints often break out, and now and again the yellow Jack is experienced with a death rate as high as 150 in 1,000. Had the Canal been realized, no doubt this country would have benefited by it, or rather others would have had an opportunity to take advantage of its resources, but since the great disaster which overtook that undertaking, I should say that many years will elapse ere Panama will afford any other interest to the rest of the world, than the line of rail possesses, which carries the traveler from Aspinwall to Panama.

I was favorably impressed with the Spanish element

of the population in this country. They were exceedingly courteous, and would go to much trouble to accommodate a stranger. But they were great gamblers, and the gambling houses in the city of Panama were numerous. The favorite games were roulette, and that other game of hazard, which a few years ago set the tongues of the gossip "a-wagging" in aristocratic England. When I first saw baecarat played, there was no historical interest attached to the game—it was as ordinary as draw-poker, or seven-up, is today, and I do not believe any heavy sums were staked upon it. The dancing of the Spanish Fandango afforded me much amusement, as a spectator in the dance houses. The attitudes assumed by the dancers, and the contortions gone through by them, were very ridiculous to behold.

I was now glad to turn my back upon Panama, which to me had been a land of continued disappointments. I had wasted six months of time and spent at least six hundred dollars, in a vain endeavor to find something worth my time and trouble, and all I had to show for it was a few pieces of pottery, which now help to make up the bric-a-brac on the What-not of a friend, being the only trophies, brought home by a Forty-niner, who went abroad to worship at the shrine of Dame fortune.

A TRIP

TO

ALASKA.

AMONGST THE ICEBERGS IN GLACIER BAY.

CHAPTER I.

Off for Alaska—Review of the History of the Country—Russian, American and English Influences—The Tolstois and the Astors—A Wonderful Region—First Impression of Scenery—Quoting Kate Field—Mountains and Glaciers—Lieutenant Schwatska's Surveys—A Phantom City.

I went to Alaska solely for the purpose of taking a cursory glance of this wonderful country. I had no idea of staying there for any length of time, merely desiring to visit some of the localities, where gold was said to exist in sufficient quantity to induce men to go in search of it. But, brief as my visit was to that northern province, I am anxious to add a few remarks to the many, which have already been published in regard to one of the most interesting quarters of the globe.

It will be remembered that in May, 1867, the United States paid Russia the sum of $7,200,000 for the territory of Alaska, which in area is about one-sixth of the size of the States, and probably money was never better expended than on this occasion, when we secured a province, abounding in natural resources to an extraordinary degree. The Russians were the first to recognize the worth of Alaska. As early as 1646 they had pushed their explorations eastward in Siberia as far as the Koly'ma River, and, eager for trade rather than for discovery, they attempted the first voyage east of the Koly'ma, thus finding a narrow channel between the grounded ice and the shore. They landed in a small bay, where they met with a number of Chirkchees, from whom they obtained a quantity of walrus ivory, thus establishing the first trade with the natives. From that day to the present the development of Alaska has continued incessantly. Discoveries of great resources followed one upon the other. The merchant found an inexhaustable field for operations in various markets. When in 1741 Bering made his discoveries in the northern waters, an additional impetus was given to trade in those regions, and the daring navigator little foresaw the seemingly endless troubles, which his undertaking should bring about, and which are today so prominently before the world. It was more particularly the furs and skins that then attracted the trader, but afterwards the fisheries became of world-wide importance; then the presence of costly metals was discovered. In addition to all this, the Alaska of today is a place, where the tourist and the scientist, alike, may go into ecstacies over wonderful scenery or the discovery of natural phenomena, which seem to connect the remote antiquity with the present day and explain some of the mysteries that meet us in the consideration of our own immediate surroundings. As yet Alaska is but little explored. The coast is the only part that is well known with the exception of some few inland places, more especially on the rivers. But there are vast territories in the interior, where probably no human foot has ever trod, and in that mysterious wilderness we may still expect to meet with wonders, which shall puzzle our imagination and surprise our senses. It has been asserted that there the giant mastodon still roams, and who knows what their wondrous animals, which we have believed to be extinct, may still be found, when this *terra incognits* shall be properly traversed.

These nations used their best energies to develop Alaska, although up till '67 Russia was the only one that did so as a national enterprise, the others being in the field as private speculators. It is interesting to notice, that while today Count Leo Tolstoi exercises a remarkable influence in the matter of social problems, one of his ancestors, Andrean Tolstoi, in 1760, fitted out a vessel, called the "Andrean and Nathalen," which in command of Maxim Lazeroff sailed from Kamschatka and wintered on Bering Island. Lazeroff explored the islands, which have since been called the Andreanoffsky Group, but it is to be regretted that the cruel treatment, to which his men subjected the natives, had much to do with the revolting attrocities practiced afterwards by the aborigines in retaliation of the conduct of the Europeans. Twenty years before this the first student of science visited these regions. It was the naturalist Louis de la Croyere, who went with Chirikoff in the St. Paul at the same time as Bering and Steller in the St. Peter sailed from Avatcha in search of the American coast, and the man of science paid for his venture with his own life.

But Tolstoi is by no means the only literary man of the present day descending from one who helped to develop Alaska. America threw her enterprise into the matter, and the grandfather of the brilliant editor of the Pall Mall Magazine, Mr. William Waldorf Astor, was the man who first brought about a business relation between this country and Alaska. In 1810, the late John Jacob Astor formed an association in New York under the name of the Pacific Fur Company, but already the previous year, he had fitted out and dispatched the ship, Enterprise, which, in command of Captain Ebbets, arrived in Sitka in July 1810. The following year Mr. Astor dispatched the second detachment of traders under William P. Hunt, and the trading station of Astoria was established. The so-called Russian-American Company was then pushing trade in Alaska to the best of their ability, but the arrival of Mr. Astor's force gave a new impetus to business. In October, 1811, he made an agreement with the Company, according to which he pledged himself to furnish provisions at fixed prices and to take pay in furs from the company. They were to mutually protect each other against smugglers and respect each other's hunting ground. Astor was to take the Company's furs to Canton and sell them on commission, and both agreed not to sell any liquors to the natives; but this arrangement was broken up by the subsequent war between England and the United States. It is of interest to notice that the agreement was ratified and approved by the Emperor of Russia, Alexander the first.

During that period also, in 1812, the first Russian settlement in California was established. The idea was to furnish Alaska with certain products, which could not be produced there, but were easily carried along the coast, and the settlement was established with the concurrence of the Spanish Government, though against the wishes of the Roman Catholic missionaries. On the 30th of August Kriskoff removed this colony to a hill, near what the Russians called the Slaveanka River, now known as the Russian River, and the inhabitants were principally devoted to agriculture and the drying of meat. Wheat was also raised in large quantities and sent to Sitka, but the Spaniard regarded the Russians with anything but friendly feelings and did all in their power to impede their operations. This will show how one nation, which had a splendid chance of benefiting by the opportunities afforded in Alaska, refused to do so principally on the ground of religious differences, owing to the rivalry existing between the Greek and the Roman Church.

In 1824 the convention between the United States and Russia was signed at St. Petersburgh. It provided that the North Pacific should be open to citizens of both nations for fishing, trading and navigation, except that the trading posts of either of the contracting parties should not be visited by subjects of the other party without the consent of the officer in command. The Russians were not to make any settlements south of latitude fifty-six degrees forty minutes, nor could the Americans form any north of that parallel, and it was also provided that arms and ammunition should not be sold to the natives. One clause in the convention was to the effect that the liberty to navigate the Russian waters, might be abrogated after ten years, and the privilege was withdrawn in 1834 on the ground that unscrupulous traders had carried on the sale of fire-arms and spirits to the natives.

England was the third nation to contribute, to some extent, towards the further development of Alaska. The Hudson Bay Company, ever on the alert to extend trade, conceived the idea of establishing a fort on the Russian territory, before the termination of the agreement between Great Britain and Russia, which had been made on the same basis as the one previously referred to. So they fitted out a vessel and dispatched the same to the mouth of the Stikine River, but Baron Wrangel, who was chief director of the colonies, learned of the project, and the English were not allowed to land. Subsequently, however, the dispute was settled, and the Hudson Bay Company received a ten-years lease of a strip of land, agreeing to pay an annual rental of furs, and to furnish a certain amount of provisions annually, at fixed rates, consisting of 560,000 pounds of wheat, 19,920 pounds of flour, 16.160 pounds of peas, 16,160 pounds of barley, 36,880 pounds of bacon, 19,920 pounds of beef, and 3,680 pounds of ham.

During the year 1848, the Russian mining engineer, Doroshin, was sent by the government to examine into the mineral wealth of portions of Alaska, and his report shows that already in the same year when gold was discovered in California, it had become evident to the Russians that their province on the Pacific Coast was gold-bearing. In the same year, the American ship Superior, under Captain Roys, passed through Bering Straits, being the first whaler that undertook this enterprise, thus inaugurating a series of unforeseen difficulties.

There was, probably, no circumstance which more contributed towards bringing Alaska to the front, than the disappearance of the unfortunate Franklin in the Arctic regions, whither he had gone in the year 1845, in search of the northwest passage. The subsequent expeditions, sent out to find some trace of the Franklin party, although unsuccessful in this respect, did much towards adding to our general knowledge of the northern country, and Alaska received her share of mention. Yet it was not until the country became a territory of the United States, that the greatest attention was attracted to Alaska. American enterprise, in every conceivable branch, has placed its stamp upon the newly-acquired land. The wonderful canneries have been established with American money. Gold, silver and cinnabar mines have been opened by American labor, and worked by our ingenuity. Our whalers yearly place upon the world's market thousands of gallons of oil, and thousands of pounds of whalebone, while American skill and business capacity has made it worth the tourist's while to visit these distant parts, and view the wonderful scenes presented there. For, to the man of liesure, or the studednt of nature, Alaska possesses a charm which is, probably, not excelled by any other country. Its wild forests, towering mountains, wonderful glaciers; its rugged coast, vast expanse of a sea nearly always calm as its name—all these are features in the great panorama which unfolds itself to the visitor.

A pretty picture of Alaskan scenery is presented in the following lines by Kate Field:

"The sea is glassy, and a procession of small bergs, broken away from the glacier, float silently towards the South. It is nature's dead march to the sun, to melt in its burning kisses, and to be transplanted into happy tears. Wild ducks fly past, and from his eyrie, a bald-headed eagle surveys the scene, deeply, darkly, beautifully blue, apparently conscious that he is the symbol of the Republic. There are glaciers and glaciers. In Switzerland a glacier is a vast bed of dirty, air-holed ice that has fastened itself, like a cold porous plaster, to the side of an Alp. Distance alone lends enchantment to the view. In Alaska, a glacier is a wonderful torrent that seems to have been suddenly frozen when about to plunge into the sea. Down and about mountains wind these snow-clad serpents, extending miles inland with as many arms, sometimes, as an octopus. Wonderfully picturesque is the Davidson glacier, but more extended is the Muir glacier, which marks the extreme northerly points of pleasure travel. Imagine a glacier three miles wide and three hundred feet high at its mouth. Think of Niagara Falls frozen stiff; add thirty-six feet to its hight, and you have a slight idea of the terminus of Muir glacier, in front of which your steamer anchors; picture a background of mountains fifteen thousand feet high, all snow-clad, and then imagine a gorgeous sun lighting up the ice crystals with rainbow colorings. The face of the glacier takes on the hue of aqua marine, the hue of every bit of floating ice, big and little, that surround the steamer and make navigation serious. These dazzling serpents move at the rate of sixty-four feet a day, tumbling headlong into the sea, and as it falls, the ear is startled by submarine thunder, the echoes of which resound far and near. Down, down, down goes the berg, and woe to the boat in its way when it again rises to the surface."

Such, indeed, was the impression I received on visiting Alaska. But no less wonderful is the sail along the coast as one passes through a perfect labyrinth of islands. One's admiration is constantly challenged as scene after scene unfolds itself with unexpected grandeur, and the traveler fails to find words with which to express his wonder, as he beholds the glaciers and the mountains of perpetual snow.

Among the travelers of the present day, who have added to our store of knowledge regarding this wonderful region, Lieutenant Frederick Schwatka is one of the foremost. According to him the territory is larger than all that part of the United States lying east of the Mississippi river; its coast has the deepest soundings in the world; its mountain peaks are the highest in the whole of the American continent; its coast line is more extended than that of the United States; its farthermost western point is a greater distance west of San Francisco than the State of Maine is east of the same city, and its great river, the Yukon, 16,000 miles long, has a mouth wider than the distance from Keokuk to Davenport. It is more in particular in his survey of this river that Lieutenant Schwatka has become famous. Up to the year 1886 it was but imperfectly mapped out, but he penetrated to its head waters, which he found were made up of about one hundred lakes. On this journey the party passed the ruins of the old trading station of Selkirk, which was established in '53 but afterward abandoned. A short distance above this point the river passes through the mountains into the great plains, where it spreads to a width of twenty-five miles. In the middle of the plains it turns directly west at a right angle and cuts through the mountain range at a point, where is now established the last of the trading posts.

But Lieutenant Schwatka's most interesting journey was probably his second expedition, during which he accomplished the ascension of Mt. St. Elias, which rises to an altitude of 18,000 feet above the sea. On this occasion the party encountered the greatest difficulties throughout, and the landing, which took place in Icy Bay, proved a most dangerous task. Three glaciers lie between the bay and the mountain, of which the first covers an area of 1,000 square miles. It is 2,650 feet deep and has a frontage to the sea of fifty-three miles.

The scenery here is grand beyond description and the avalanches, the chasms, the ice mountains, the floating bergs—all combine to produce a scene, which is most wonderful in its effect. It fairly dazzles the onlooker, and as one views the surrounding nature, he realizes that in no language known to human tongue can words be found, which will adequately express the sensation, experienced in this majestic nature.

If Mount St. Elias be imposing to behold, with its surrounding scenery, the Muir glacier, in Glacier Bay, is not less so. So many descriptions of these wonderful ice-fields have already been written, that I do not feel called upon to compete with the practiced writers whose fluent descriptions of nature so ably depict the grandeur and beauty as it appears. But I cannot close this chapter without remarking upon one of the most wonderful phenomena, which yearly occurs in Glacier Bay during the longest days of the month of June. As the midsummer (and one may almost say the midnight) sun is setting behind Mount Fairweather, there appears upon the bosom of Pacific glacier, a singular sight. It is a phantom city; the mirage of an ancient, and to all appearances, oriental town. Directly in front, apparently surrounding the city, is a high stone wall, behind which are seen immense buildings looming toward the sky. The architecture is quaint and seemingly eastern. The building material appears to be mostly stone, the roofs are flat, and smoke may be seen issuing from the chimneys. The streets appear to be narrow and the buildings, some of which are evidently in course of erection, are closely packed and do not look as if they were placed in proper blocks or arranged according to our ideas of a city plan. It is apparently a very large city, extending back as far as the eye can reach, and tall spires and cupolas intersperse the contour of the picture, which is so distinct, that it has been possible to take well defined photographs of it. It is a fact, that, since 1880, every returning year at the same period and hour this remarkable phenomenon repeats itself. But where the real city is situated, which is here so strangely reflected, no one can tell, nor have I ever heard any scientific proposition trying to solve the problem of locating the actual city. There, in the waning light it may be seen in the far northern land, where the ice king reigns all the year. There it seems to float before the vision of the puzzled spectator, whose mind involuntarily grapples with the wonder and tries to locate its reality. But who dwells there, no one knows. What hopes, what fears, what longings are fostered there remains a mystery. On the barren icefield of the glacier it rises nightly for a few fleeting moments like a phantom, called into existence by the magic wand of a fairy—a most wonderful optical deception, a freak of nature, a *fata morgana.*

CHAPTER II.

Mining Matters—On the Stikine River—San Francisco Speculators in the Field—Large Mining Machinery—Fish Oil and Gold Dust—The Yukon Diggings—Comparison Between Past and Present—Interesting Indians—Artistic Carvings—Innocentius Veniaminoff—The End.

As a matter of course I paid particular attention to the mining districts of Alaska, during my brief sojourn there, and did not forget to visit the Stikine River where the first mining camp of any account, was located in 1876. At the mouth of the Stikine is Fort Wrangle, called after one of the Russian Governors who, during his term of office, did much for the benefit of the territoy. That Alaska is a rich gold-bearing country, there can be no doubt, and at the time of writing this, reports are frequently heard as to new mines opened up there; but I do not think it will ever compare with the first find on the California gold-fields, nor, indeed, with the present supply, reserved for the capitalist to reveal by means of modern machinery. The coast of Alaska, like the coast of British Columbia, indicates immense geological revolutions, and in my opinion, it is during such a period that the gold, which would otherwise have been easily accessible, has been forced downward to a lower stratum, whence only large capital can bring it to light, if accessible at all.

Comparatively speaking, our knowledge of the geological conditions of Alaska, is somewhat limited, for obvi-

WRANGEL ISLAND, ALASKA.

ous reasons. On the Stikine River, the gold deposits, which are now nearly exhausted, were only worked on the placers; but there are, no doubt, quartz veins in the neighborhood, and the miners who had the courage to penetrate to the headwaters of the Tahco River, were rewarded by finding coarse gold. Gold has also been found in the sands of the Yukon, near Fort Yukon; it exists on the Kaknu River and around the Taku villages. Of late, however, a number of enterprises have been started in Alaska, on a large scale, for the purpose of extracting whatever wealth the soil may hold in gold or other precious metals. On Douglas Island the largest quartz mill in the world has been lately put up. Two hundred and forty stamps are in operation, and the machinery is conceded to be not only the largest, but the most complete of its kind in existence, its monthly output of gold bullion being roughly estimated at about $150,000.

Douglas Island, I should say, is at present that part of Alaska, where the richest deposits of Gold are to be found. Here is located the celebrated Paris Mine and Eastern and European speculators have lately bought claims in this locality, sinking as much as $1,500,00 in mines which will now be worked by improved machinery. It is supposed that the country holds several gold-bearing ledges of great size and value, and tunnels are being driven into the mountain sides with a view to opening them. On the mainland, also, rich lodes are claimed to exist in the so-called Silver Bow Basin, near Juneau, and this locality is regarded with a good deal of anticipation. It is expected that some rich revelations will take place here in a near future, and the sanguine ones contend that one of the most prolific gold-fields in the world will be found in this locality. An extension of the Silver Bow Basin is supposed to crop up at one of the forks of Sheep Creek. Here, at all events, recent discoveries have revealed ore that carries galena, zinc blende, and copper pyrites, while the assays show plenty of gold and a small percentage of silver. As a matter of course this ore has to be treated in a smelting furnace, but I understand that there are other lodes in the same belt, which bear rich ore as a free milling quartz, wherein the gold can be readily detected with the naked eye.

A Wisconsin company has lately put a small mill into operation in the Sitka district. It is asserted that this locality is rich in different lodes, and that gold is found in payable quantities; but I am not aware that the Wisconsin people have so far done any great strokes in their venture.

On Unga Island several San Francisco companies have engaged in developing a dozen or more claims, and I believe that with comparatively little outlay some good results may be expected by the way of rich returns. The ore carries about equal parts of gold and silver and from thirty to seventy per cent. of lead, and it is taken to San Francisco to go through the smelting furnace there.

On Onolaska Island gold and silver ledges have been disclosed, and it is expected that they can be worked to advantage. Some years ago prospectors thought that they had found gold in paying quantities in the so-called black sands of the shores of Yakutat Bay and of the ocean in that vicinity, and large quantities of the sand were assayed in Sitka, showing forty dollars to the ton. There was a rush at once, but most of the miners soon returned disappointed. A few, who remained and had brought with them proper appliances for the extraction of the precious metal, were more fortunate and succeeded in making fairly good wages, when all of a sudden they discovered that the gold had totally disappeared. A singular explanation was given of this fact, which I repeat here for the benefit of miners placed under similar circumstances. A large quantity of dog-fish had been left to die upon the shore by the receding tide, and the oil from these fish was drawn out by the heat of the sun's rays. The oil permeated the sand and operated in such a manner as to prevent the quicksilver on the plates from picking up the gold, which was therefore carried away in the tailings and lost.

The miners having discovered the reason for their loss, selected sand which had not been permeated with fish oil, and were once more making their labor pay, when a tidal wave swept into the bay and washed away all the sand within reach containing gold. But the incident would tend to prove that it is possible to extract gold from the sand all along the coast of these parts, with proper appliances and care.

In Golovin Bay a San Francisco company has opened a silver mine, with good results. It is located in the mountains running through the peninsula between Bering Sea and the Arctic Ocean, in latitude 65 degrees. The ore here is rich, carrying all the way from seventy to eighty-five per cent of pure lead, and from one hundred to two hundred and fifty dollars of silver to the ton

During my stay in Alaska, I was unable to learn much of the diggings on the Yukon and its tributaries. In conversation with men who had been there, or who knew about the locality, I ascertained, however, that no great operations had been carried on, although a good many daring prospectors had ventured far into the interior, fighting the natives and the elements with equal valor and tenacity. Here, to my mind, was carried on the kind of mining mostly resembling what I had known in the early days of California's gold history. Men would go up there in parties and work the placers, the same as we had done. Some of them pentrated as far as the Shetando, and the pan or the rocker was their main-stay as they drew from the gravel the golden specks. I learned many things about these diggings that interested me and recalled to my mind incidents of my own life on the Yuba. The fortune-seekers on the mining fields of to-day, seem to have much in common with their predecessors of the long ago. They are just as restless and just as credulous. I listened with a smile on my lips, when they told me the wonderful stories that would come into camp, of rich discoveries of untold wealth. The wild-goose chase for Gold Lake or Lone Tree, returned to my memory on such occasions. Then again they would describe to me how they might have become rich had they not left good-paying claims to go in search of others which were either phantoms, or did not pan out. Alas! How often had I done the same. And how many are there among the early pioneers who might now have spent the evening of their life in comfort and ease, had they been content with the claims that afforded them a rich yield, instead of leaving them to go in search of still more magnificent fortunes which did not materialize. In other respects I recognized features similar to those predominant on the Yuba. It appears that the route into the upper Yukon country was through the Dyah Pass. But this trail is difficult and dangerous to travel, and the miner is not in a position to take with him any great amount of supplies, and therefore, when he gets to the diggings, is entirely at the mercy of the traders, who take the same advantage of him, that they did of us in the early days. When I visited Alaska, I was given to understand that on this gold-field flour was sold at thirty-five dollars a barrel; bacon forty cents per pound; sugar thirty cents, beans twenty cents, rice twenty-five cents, lard thirty-five cents, and everything else in proportion.

I was, naturally, more interested in the gold mining of Alaska than in anything else appertaining to the products of the country; but I must admit that I was somewhat impressed by the grand possibilities of this territory, in other directions. I have already mentioned the silver mines, but in addition to these are, as a matter of course, large deposits of lead; and copper, iron and quicksilver are also found. The fisheries and canneries cannot but attract the attention of the observing traveler, and the wonderful variety of furs is not less interesting.

I would not close my brief outline of this wonderful country without mentioning the natives, who dwell therein. The aborigines are divided into a number of tribes but Mr. William H. Dall contends that they consist of two principal races, of which he calls one the Indians and the other the Orarians, the latter name being derived from the Latin, meaning: appertaining to the coast. He claims, and it would seem with much justification, that the inland natives and those who inhabit the coast, are two entirely different races, and probably no Caucasian has ever more dilligently examined into the affairs of the native Alaskans, than has Mr. Dall, who, as director of the scientific corps of the Western Union Telegraph expedition, traveled over these northern regions and made scientific researches of all the conditions of the natives. To the Orarian group is counted the inhabitants of the northern and western shores of America, the islands of the vicinity and that part of eastern Siberia, which is known as the Chukchee peninsula, and Mr. Dall divides them into three branches—the

Innuit, the Aleutians and the Tuski. The Indian group Mr. Dall divides into two branches, calling them the Thlinkets and the Tinnels, but each of these again is divided into a number of other branches or tribes.

All these different divisions of mankind vary in language, in custom, in appearance from the Eskimo to the Kygani, in whom I soon recognized my Indian friend from the Queen Charlotte Archipelago. In fact the Kygani and the Hydah Indians both belong to the Thlinket group. They were the ones with whom I came mostly in contact, and whom I therefore had the greatest opportunity of observing, and I was much impressed with all that I learned concerning their habits, customs, beliefs and traditions. Singularly enough, although these people live so close to the Queen Charlotte Indians and are, as already stated, somewhat related to them, they have traditions, in which notwithstanding the subject matter is common, the expression is entirely different. One of these relates to the origin of the heavenly bodies, and I refer my reader to the myth, as told in the chapter of the Hydah Indians, while I here produce the version, given by the Thlinkets.

Yehl or Yahl is described as the maker of woods and waters. As he grew up he had many adventures, but the most interesting one was experienced, when he put the sun and moon and stars in their places, and this is the way in which it was done. There was a rich chief in those days, who kept the sun and moon and stars in different boxes, which no one was allowed to touch Yehl knew that only a grandchild of the old chief would be permitted to handle the brilliant lights, and he determined to take upon himself this part. To this end he transformed himself into a blade of grass and was swallowed by the chief's beautiful daughter, who in due time gave birth to a child, in whom Yehl was embodied. The grandfather soon took such a liking to the young child, that he could not refuse him anything. One day he asked to be allowed to play with the box, containing the stars, and, having obtained permission, he removed the lid, when, behold, the heavens suddenly became starlit. He received a severe scolding, but still his grandfather could not refuse him, when he asked permission to play with the other box, containing the moon. Again the same thing happened and the old chief swore that he would never consent to let him have the third box, containing the sun. But Yehl kept fasting, until he made himself sick, and then the grandfather gave in, Yehl having solemnly promised not to open the box. No sooner had the mischievous grandchild obtained the box, than he transformed himself into a raven and flew away. He then removed the lid from the box, and the sun shone over the earth, but the dwellers thereon, dazzled with the unusual light, ran into the woods and mountains, some of them diving even into the waters, and many of them were transformed into animals and fish.

These Indians do not seem to have any definite idea of a Supreme being, and with them Yehl seems to be the only recognized deity, if deity he can be called. He arranges everything for the comfort of the Thlinkets, and then retires to his abode, where neither men nor spirits can penetrate. Among their traditions there is one which bears upon the theory of a general deluge, thus accounting for the difference of languages. A few human beings were saved on a raft, but this broke in twain. On one part of it were the ancestors of the Thlinkets, and on the other the rest of the nations of the world; and hence, to this day, the Thlinkets do

GLACIER BAY, SHOWING SECTION OF MUIR GLACIER.

not speak the same language as do the rest of men.

Baron Wrangel, of whom mention has been made several times, has collected many of the legends of these people, as has also Mr. Dall. But in the opinion of the latter, the Baron's accounts have been considerably mixed with the superstitions of the Greco-Russian Church, and is not to be relied upon in every respect.

The most remarkable feature about the Alaska native, is his wonderful idea of carving. In this regard his skill is absolutely singular, and his imitative powers often very remarkable. Among these people we find the totem-pole artistically decorated, the same as I have described in speaking of the Hydah Indians, the grotesque masks and the curious carvings on all the implements and domestic utensils. But it appears to me that in Alaska the art is carried to a still higher degree, and the many visiting tourists which now-a-days travel over the territory, have no doubt done much to develop the practice by ordering things carved which were never thought of before, such as paper-knives, salad-forks, salt-spoons, etc. They also understand the art of carving one thing within another, such as several balls within balls, and so on, and I have seen a watch-chain with proper links, most skilfully carved from one piece of a a walrus tusk. Neither do these people confine themselves to any particular material, but will apply walrus tusk, wood, silver, gold or anything that their primitive tools can form into articles for use, ornament or curiosity.

This talent they seem to have in common with the Chinese, and, indeed, the native people of that northern province, strange as it may appear, belong more to the Mongolian type than to any other I can think of, and is certainly not at all like the North American Indian in appearance or habits.

It is roughly estimated that there still remains about 35,000 natives who are entirely outside the boundaries of civilization. There are about 3500 partly civilized natives, while the Aleuts number 3,000. These latter people are highly interesting and inhabit the Aleutian archipelago. They nearly all speak Russian and profess the Greco-Russian faith. They owe their present degree of civilization almost entirely to the undying efforts in the cause of humanity of the late Rev. Innocentius Veniaminoff of the Irkutsk Seminary, who labored among them with a devotion and self-sacrifice, that have born everlasting fruit. It is said of these people that they are most excellent chess players. They are very singular in their habits and ideas, and they certainly afford interesting subjects for the student of mankind in its various manifestations.

I have submitted these few remarks about Alaska in hopes that they may be of some interest to the reader. I paid but a brief visit to that wonderful land with no other intent than to see it and ascertain a few facts about its mining prospects, some of which I have related above. But my journey thither comprised part of the experiences of my life, which by this time has been a long and varied one, and for that reason I have presented in these chapters, what I thought would be a fitting termination to an account of a gold hunters travels on the Pacific coast.

THE

NATIVE SONS.

W R Hearst

CHIPS OF THE OLD BLOCK.

A CHAPTER DEDICATED TO THE NATIVE SONS.

The Author's Address—Pioneers and Native Sons—Two National Days—An Organization Established—A Moth-eaten Bear—General Winn's Efforts—A Young President—Telling Speeches—A Birthday Party—Grand Secretary and Free-Mason—A Relic Saved—Men of Action.

I am approaching the close of this volume and have soon to fall back upon the kind indulgence of my readers, who shall decide whether it has imparted to them any additional knowledge or afforded amusement. I have devoted a few of the closing pages to the memory of some of my pioneer friends, whom I have known in California and British Columbia. Some of them still walk in the path of life, enjoying the pleasing results of successful labors, whilst others have crossed the bourne, from which there is no return.

It is safe to say that these men have been among the builders of the respective countries which they represent. My readers will have seen what tremendous progress has been made on the Pacific Slope within the past forty-five years, Alaska has been made accessible and promises to become one of the world's most interesting parts. British Columbia is daily being opened up more and more and develops immense resources in its interior as well as along the coast. California, the country where the "citrus blossom" and the midwinter roses scent the air; the country that became the second Colchis, has so developed since '49 that it is on a level with many parts of the old world and ahead of others; and Panama has been the scene of the most gigantic engineering projects of the present age, which, although they have so far failed, will eventually be written upon the pages of the world's history as one of its wonders.

In paying a small tribute to a few of the pioneers who in one way or another had something to do with the success and development of the various countries, it has not escaped my observation that there are many whose names ought to have been particularly noticed in these pages, while want of space has not permitted me to follow my own desire on this point. Yet, as I reflect upon my first entrance in California and review the changes that have passed over that country since those days, I cannot help remembering such names as Fremont, Sutter, Marshall, Winn and others, while it appears to me that even the name of Mariano Vallejo demands consideration.

But, in remembering these men, one is apt to carry his reflections into the generation that followed them. The pioneers were sturdy, but their children were no less so; that which the former founded and commenced to build the latter covered with a roof and cared for, and when to-day one visits the far west and sees the progress and the continued development, which is taking place there, it should be borne in mind that in no parts of this great continent is the advancement of the country due so much to the Native Son of the soil as here on the Pacific Slope, where distance and the expense of traveling have kept immigration within limits more so than in any other parts.

It was a happy thought, which first brought about the idea of establishing the order of Native Sons of the

HON. STEPHEN M. WHITE   HON. GEORGE C. PARDEE   HON. LEVI R. ELLERT   HON. THOMAS FLINT, JR.
ROBERT WIELAND   HON. R. F. DEL VALLE   FREDERICK C. CLIFT

Golden West, and it was conceived by a pioneer. To General A. M. Winn is due the credit of having originated the desire to form such a society. It is somewhat amusing that, when the thought first occurred to the enthusiastic pioneer, he could not find a Native Son old enough to become a duly responsible member. It was in 1869 that the General, having been made Grand Marshal for the Fourth of July celebration, issued a call to young native Californians, urging them to meet him for the purpose of forming a company in the parade.

His idea was that having created a patriotic enthusiasm amongst them, he could easily persuade them afterwards to organize an association, and he evidently foresaw that such a society would not only become an ornament to the state, but also act as one of the driving wheels in the machinery which should bring this young but ambitious state to the front. For, although, in its ultimate organization, politics were not among the topics which might be discussed by the order, the sense of patriotism is yet the mainspring of its existence, and nothing will more thoroughly permeate the principles of men, guiding and directing them into one groove.

But on that June day 1869, when a number of young Californians met in response to his summons, the General was doomed to disappointment. It is a fact that they attended in large numbers; that they exhibited much enthusiasm and formed a pleasing feature of the parade; but they were too young for organization, and disbanded when the festivities were over.

But their only short-coming was one which in time mended itself. The idea of a Native Californian Society had been conceived, the enthusiasm created, and like an avalanche, it increased until the time arrived when everything was ready for formation.

During the preparations, incidental to the celebration of the Fourth of July, 1875, General John McComb Grand Marshal of the parade of that year, inserted in the advertising colunms of the daily press, on the morning of June 24th, an invitation to the Native Sons of San Francisco, over fourteen years of age to meet in the Police Court room, Tuesday night, June 29th and organize for the purpose of taking part in the celebration of the national day. This public notice was the means of bringing together the young men, who finally carried into execution the formation of the order of *Native Sons of the Golden West*. In accordance with the call, a small but enthusiastic body met and organized for the purpose of taking part in the parade, and further determined to perpetuate the organizatiou under the name of the *Native Sons of the Golden State*, while a number of those present, who were under sixteen years, were debarred by vote from participating. Among those who met on that occasion were many, who have since become well known, and the followimg names are recorded: Myles F. O'Donnell, Louis Patrick, James McDermott, Abraham Meyer, John Wilson, Walter Loveland, Charles D. Olds, F. C. W. Fenn, Louis Harris, Raphael Prager, Robert Aitken, James Bayliss, E. F. McKenna, E. Block, Broderick Temple, George Winslow, and John A. Steinback.

General Winn, who had not forgotten his plan of six years before was present. He now saw a chance of having his pet idea realized, and in calling the meeting to order, he briefly stated that its purpose was to form a society of Native Californians.

After resolving to parade on the Fourth of July, the society adjourned to meet again on the First of July, when General Winn in a spirited address to the young men, used the following expressions: "This organization of young men under the name of the *Native Sons of the Golden State* is to become the future pioneers of California. Such men as James Lick and others are fast passing away; and the rising generation will surely fill their places, and the course adopted by you is one that I have long looked for among young Californians. As to the future of our State, never was there such an outlook known in the annals of history."

That year, '75, the national day was celebrated on Monday, the Fourth falling on Sunday. The Native Sons made their debut in a new role; they carried a handsome silk American flag, lent them by a patriotic citizen, and as an emblem they exhibited a stuffed bear, which had been found in a deserted room in Anthony's Hall. The bear was rather the worse for moths; it was a cub about three feet long and had been used as one of the insignia of a disbanded club, but it answered the purpose, and few, who to-day see the bear emblem upon the breast of a Native Son, would think that it originated with a musty, old straw-stuffed cub that had been discarded by its rightful owners.

The band of young natives made a splendid appearance in the parade and it was noticeable that there was hardly a difference of ten years between the youngest and the oldest of them. After the parade the boys marched to Anthony's Hall, where they held impromptu literary exercises, and one of their number, F. G. W. Fenn, read a poem, which he had composed for the occasion.

The next meeting was held on Sunday, July 11th, 1875, and from this dates the beginning of the Order, which here finally took the name of "Native Sons of the Golden West," and John A. Steinbach was chosen the first President, although at the time he was scarcely twenty-one years of age. A few months after, on October 21st, a party was given at Sanders' Hall in honor of the young President, who on that day became of age. On that occasion President Steinbach made a speech which, for force and eloquence, was singular as coming from a man so young. In it he said: "Our society is the beginning of an Order that, will proudly wave its banners over more than half the territory of the United States, while its power and influence may control the destinies of the Golden West. We were born in a country of gold and silver, at a time when the world was looking for some great change, and when we presented it with more metals than the nations of the earth had ever seen before; with agricultural products in such quantity and quality as to astonish mankind, it is not to be wondered at that we are proud of the land of our birth; and when we consider that none but self-reliant, energetic families could get here at that early day, we are equally proud of our parentage."

In these last words, indeed, is the key-note to the success of the Order, which was organized for the mutual benefit, mental improvement and social intercourse of its members; to perpetuate in the minds of all native Californians the memories of the days of '49, to unite them in one harmonious body; tied together by the bonds of friendship, irrespective of individual opinion on religious and political matters, the discussion of which is not allowed at the meetings of the Order.

Thus was established an organization which was destined to exercise a decisive influence upon the state that gave it birth, and to-day it is regarded as one of the mainstays of California. Its members include professional men of all branches; lawyers, physicians, writers, artists and others; men engaged in mercantile pursuits, politicians, bankers, men of science and in short nearly every branch of intelligent occupation is represented among the members of the Native Sons of the Golden West. And among them are so many bright men whose names shine in larger or smaller communities, as their chances have allowed them, that it would be impossible here to enumerate them, and in mentioning a few it must be understood that they are gathered at random, like the flowers plucked from a bed upon all of which the sun throws its lustrous light.

One of the brightest men of the order is undoubtedly Henry Lunstedt, the present Grand Secretary, who is a native of Tuolumne County, but was educated in San Francisco. Mr. Lunstedt was not satisfied with the knowledge he gathered at school, and applied his leisure hours to diligent study, making himself aquainted with the literature of various periods and countries and subsequently becoming a writer himself, contributing to the columns of local papers and giving interesting accounts of the proceedings of the organization. He was one of the founders of the order, and has for twelve years held the exalted office he now occupies.

This fact will show how much Mr. Lunstedt's services are appreciated. He is considered not only a man of culture and learning, but also of action and excellent judgment. He exhibited from boyhood up a predeliction for public life and has for years served with competency and credit in various important and responsible capacities under the Municipal Government of San Francisco.

He is essentially a man of the world, and in the undertakings on which his energies have been focussed, he has shown phenomenal strength of purpose and sound judgment.

HENRY LUNSTEDT   J. A. STEINBACH   HON. C. H. GAROUTTE   HON. R. M. FITZGERALD
DR. C. W. DECKER   COL. C. F. CROCKER   J. T. GREANEY.

Mr Lunstedt is a Mason of the Scottish order, and was the first Native Son to receive the thirty-second degree of this famous rite.

In Col. Charles F. Crocker, the Golden West has a fitting representative of the remarkable energies exhibited in the State of California at the period when his father and a few others built the first American Railroad which made transcontinental traveling possible. Col. Crocker was born in Sacramento in 1854, and was therefore only a boy when the great engineering work was carried out, but he inherited his father's practical judgment, and with the advantages of surroundings excellently fitted himself for the high position he now holds as First Vice-President of the Southern Pacific Railroad Company.

Colonel Crocker received a liberal education both at the State University of California and in Germany, where he studied for several years, and also attended the Polytechnic Institute in Brooklyn, New York.

Few men with Colonel Crocker's advantages, and enjoying his great wealth, are as retired and modest as he. But he has won a name as an excellent manager with great executive ability, and one of the trustees of the Leland Stanford Junior University, the order rejoiced that one of their members, so representative, had been honored with the call.

As a Native Son, Colonel Crocker performed most graceful acts, when by his liberality he recently saved the Sutter Fort property from destruction, and thus perserved one of the most important historical monuments of the Golden State.

Among the politicians who have done credit to themselves and the far west, is Anthony Caminetti, who now represents the Second Congressional District of Cali-

fornia, having been re-elected at the last general election-
He, too, has worked earnestly in the interest of California history, and to his untiring efforts is due the erection of the John Marshall Monument. During '83 and '84 as an Assemblyman and in '86 as a State Senator he persistently urged the matter until he finally obtained a favorable appropriation for the desired statue. He was appointed President of the Marshall Commission, and as President of the Day, delivered an eloquent address at the unveiling of the statue, which took place in May '90.

Mr. Caminetti is a lawyer by profession, and studied for some years under the direction of the late United States Senator, James T. Farley. He has established a reputation as a fluent speaker and sound logician, and possess extraordinary endurance and power of work.

It appears that law has had a particular attraction for the Native Sons of the Golden West, and many bright and prominent lawyers have stepped from the parlor of the order into the bright daylight of public renown. They have indeed done credit to themselves and the bar and have occupied, or do at present occupy, many prominent positions from the Judge's seat to the lawyer, who eloquently pleads the case of his client.

Among those who have especially distinguished themselves should be mentioned, Frank L. Combs, who is a native of Napa, and who, having received his education at the public schools, finally graduated at the Columbia Law College, Washington, D. C. Mr. Combs early distinguished himself as an orator and his fine natural talents soon brought him to the front. In 1879 he was elected District Attorney of Napa County, succeeding himself at the next election, and in 1886 he was elected to the legislature and served two terms. He soon became a leader in politics, and during the Harrison administration he was sent to Japan as Minister plenipotentiary as a fitting recognition of talent well applied.

Jo Davies Sproul was born in Solano County, in '59. His father was a pioneer and prominent physician, who removed to Chico ten years after the birth of his son. Young Sproul received the appointment for West Point Military Academy; but after two years' sojourn there he gave up the idea of wielding the sword and returned to take up the study of law, which he successfully completed under the guidance of F. C. Lusk, the leading lawyer of Northern California. The change suited the former aspirant to military honors, and he soon gained a lucrative practice and hosts of friends.

One of the most remarkable members of the Order of Native Sons is Frank D. Ryan. Scarcely thirty-four years of age; he has already been sent to legislature from Sacramento, has officiated as chief clerk of the assembly during two sessions thereof and is the present District Attorney of Sacramento County. Mr. Ryan is also a member of the Sutter Fort Commission and will undoubtedly prove one of the most efficient workers in that important body.

When Hasting's Law College sent out John T. Greany a young man went into practice, who is likely to reach the top of the ladder. Mr Greany, who was born in '60 had previously studied at St. Mary's College and taken the degree of M. A. Shortly after he was admitted to the bar he was intrusted with the management of the famous Blythe estate, which was then in the hands of Philip A. Roach, as administrator. While in this important position, managing an estate worth several million dollars, he displayed phenomenal ability as an accurate and careful steward, and when, in the course of time, he gave up his stewardship; he was highly commended for the excellent manner, in which he had performed his work.

One of the most active of Native Sons is Robert M. Fitzgerald, who was born in San Francisco in '58. Shortly after, his parents removed to Sonoma County, and later on to Contra Costa County. Mr. Fitzgerald attended the Oakland High School, and during this early period of his life he was called upon to assist his widowed mother and before graduating spent one year on her farm, managing it for her. He then returned to school and, taking up his studies with a will, was admitted to the State University, with the class of '83.

Mr. Fitzgerald soon gained a lucrative practice as a lawyer as well as the confidence and love of the community in which he lived. Although he never made himself conspicuous as a politician, he has been repeatedly called upon to run for prominent offices and was on the first board of Commissioners of Public Works in the city of Oakland, California.

Another legal light, which was kindled at Hastings', College, may be found in Marcellus A. Dorn. He is both physically and intellectually a typical representative of the sturdy Pioneer, being a man of high mental attainments and commanding presence. He is a native of Los Angeles and graduated from the State University, and he has always been noted for his fine address and more than ordinary power of oratory.

Among the Native Sons, who went abroad for their education and returned home, bent upon showing their splendid achievements, should be mentioned Albert F. Jones, who was born in Colusa County in '58 and finished his studies at Yale University in 1879. That same year he was admitted to practice in the Supreme Courts of

Connecticut and California and in '82 he was elected District Attorney of Butte County, where he has resided since 1880. He was afterwards sent to the State Senate and became Chairman of the Judiciary Committee, being the youngest man who ever filled that important position in the California legislature. Governor Bartlett appointed him Aid-de-Camp with the rank of Lieutenant Colonel, and he held the same office with Governor Waterman.

In Yolo County there was, some years ago, a young plow boy, known as Charles H. Garoutte. When his day's work was over he would take to his books, and, when opportunity afforded itself, he frequented the state school, studying with a wonderful zeal and finally obtaining a collegiate education at Hesperian College, Woodland. He taught afterwards in the public schools, devoting his leisure hours to the study of law, and in 1876 he was admitted to practice by the Supreme Court of the State. The following year he was elected District Attorney for Yolo County and was re-elected upon the expiration of the term. He finally went into active practice and succeeded in gaining the good will and respect of the community to such a degree that a few years after he was elected Judge of the Superior Court of Yolo County, being the youngest Judge on the entire bench of the State. In this office also, he gained the confidence of the people and filled it with credit to himself and to the satisfaction of his constituents, resulting in his final elevation to the Supreme Court bench.

During his official term as Judge he has heard some of the most important cases ever tried in the State, and as a member of the order of Native Sons, he enjoys the grand distinction of having broken the greatest electoral deadlock, known in the annals of the order. In 1886,

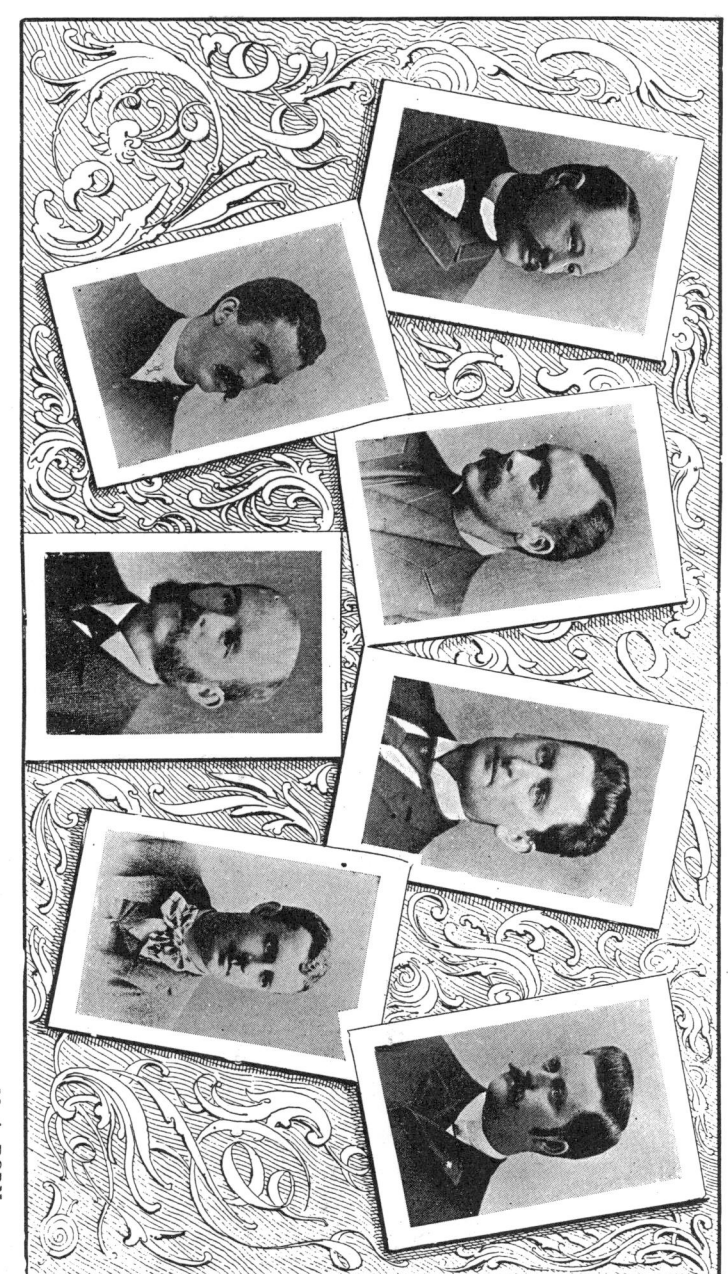

HON. FRANK L. COOMBS H. CLAY CHIPMAN FRANK D. RYAN M. A. DORN
FRANK J. HIGGINS JOHN H. GRADY JO D. SPROUL

when the Grand Parlor met in Woodland, he was a grand trustee and displayed marked parliamentary ability, by reason of which he was with one accord selected to dissolve the triangular contest for the grand vice-presidency. His choice for the place was made by an unanimous vote, and in the following year he became Grand President.

As has been already shown the legal fraternity is liberally represented in the order of Native Sons, but no member of it reflects more honor upon his chosen profession or possesses more friends and admirers than does Frederick C. Clift, who was born in Grass Valley in 1867. Justice Clift is an Oakland lawyer and Magistrate, who pursued his studies under the guidance of Nathaniel Bennett, one of the Judges of the first Supreme Court of California, and P. D. Wigginton, an ex-member of Congress. In 1890 he was admitted to the bar by the Supreme Court, then in session in Sacramento, and two years after he was elected Justice of the Peace for Oakland Township with an overwhelming majority.

Although the discussion of politics is not permitted in the parlors of the Order of Native Sons, it will be observed, nevertheless, that the members take a lively interest in political affairs.

But, it should be observed, that the Native Sons have at all times endeavored as far as possible to purify their government. In a young country as a matter of course, certain elements often appear in the persons of adventurers and other undesirable intruders, who wish to take advantage of the crude circumstances existing, and raise themselves to positions for which they were never qualified. When the pioneers first came to California, law and order were at a premium; but, as the Native Sons grew up, the country, step by step, assumed the shape of a well organized State, and in their hands, more than in any others has been left a precious trust, of which they are indeed taking good care.

It is interesting to notice the vigorous, and it should be said successful, attempts made by the native element to introduce means for the furtherance of pure politics. California was one of the first states to adopt the Australian ballot system, and everything is being done in the State for the purpose of putting down corrupt practices in legislature.

In this respect William R. Hearst comes prominently to the front as the founder and proprietor of a newspaper, which from first to last has fought for pure principles. His father, the late United States Senator Hearst, was one of the lucky pioneers, whose wealth enabled him to satisfy the cravings of his ambitious son. Young Hearst wanted a newspaper and he finally established the San Francisco Daily *Examiner*, which as a newspaper enterprise, ranks as one of the first in the States, at all events relatively speaking. Through its columns Mr. Hearst has fought for everything that is right and just. The scheming politician, the unscrupulous manipulator of municipal affairs, the man in power, who abuses the trust reposed in him—all, in fact, who evade the law of morals and conscience, have in Mr. Hearst their arch foe. Armed with a most popular and widely circulated paper, assisted by an army of talented men, he pursues the offender to the bitter end, and in legislature, in the courts of justice, in the various public departments has the Native Son, through William R. Hearst sent a warning call to all evil doers who attempt to cast a blemish upon the fair name of California.

At the time of writing this two other names naturally suggest themselves to my mind as being those of politicians of the clear-cut school. They are Dr. George C. Pardee of Oakland and Levi R. Ellert of San Francisco, each in his place enjoying the honor of being Mayor of the community he represents, and both elected on the so-called citizens' or non-partisan ticket.

This ticket is the outcome of vigorous attempts to resist dastardly onslaught on pure political principles, brought about by a foreign element, which took advantage of national political enthusiasm to work some hidden schemes in local affairs.

But these two Native Sons took up the battle for the just cause, and were victorious. The reason is obvious; they had the sympathy of the native element, which recognized the fact that their affairs must be given into the hands of right thinking men. Mr. Ellert has extensive business interests in San Francisco and has held important offices in the Order, and Dr. Pardee resides in Oakland, where his father has lived for many years. He is held in marked esteem for his personal qualities, his professional attainments and his integrity and honesty of purpose in all that he undertakes. He is a graduate from the State University and afterwards studied in Germany, where he made ophthalmology his specialty.

Stephen M. White, another Native Son, has come prominently to the front as a true patriot. On the 18th of January, '93, he was elected United States Senator, even his political opponents voting for him. His own character is well depicted in the closing words of his address, when he said: "For those, who opposed me from duty, I have nothing but the kindliest feeling, and for those who opposed me from other motives, this hour is my triumph." The Oakland *Enquirer,* a paper opposed to White in politics, but an advocate of pure politics, wrote about his election: "It is a great deal better to send to the Senate a man like White with brains in his head, than to elect an old money-bags, whose qualification consists merely in giving $50,000 to a campaign fund."

Mr. White's career, throughout, has been one incessant triumph. He was born in San Francisco but early removed to Los Angeles. He inherited Democratic sentiments from his father, who was a lawyer, a writer and a politician, and in '79 was nominated for Governor by the working men. Young White studied law and early gained a reputation as a speaker and a logician, and when he engaged in politics rapidly rose to distinction. At the time of Governor Bartlett's death White was President of the Senate, and when Waterman became Governor, he took the office of Lieutenant Governor. At the Democratic National Convention in St Louis, in '88, Stephen M. White was made Chairman of the Convention, proving that the appreciation of his rare abilities are by no means local but have secured for him a high national reputation.

A very popular man among his many aquaintances is Dr. Charles W. Decker, who has met with much success in his practice as a dentist. Dr. Decker is a member, it is said, of more orders than any other Native Son, and has made himself best known as the author of the ritual and secret work under which the order has now been governed for several years.

H. C. Chipman, one of Sacramento's prominent men, was born in that city in '53. He has followed the trade of a Sign painter all his life, but his rare intelligence has secured for him public honors, of which he may well be proud. For three successive terms Mr. Chipman held a seat on the Board of education, where he did some excellent work, and in the fall '92 he was elected to the assembly to represent the twenty-first district

In the order of Native Sons, Mr. Chipman has always been particularly active. He is a charter member of Sacramento Parlor, No. 3, and attended the first Grand Parlor in '82, when he was elected Grand President, thus being the first upon whom that exalted office was bestowed. He is also at present the Senior Past Grand President, and expresses his appreciation of the Society by saying: "I have never thought enough of any others to join them; the Native Sons are all I care for."

If there be a class of men upon whom the welfare of California more particularly depends, it is the agricultural, and among the farmers the order of Native Sons is most worthily represented. One of their brightest members, Thomas Flint, jr., whose sterling qualities and peculiar fitness for his chosen vocation has made him one of California's most extensive and wealthy farmers.

Mr. Flint was born in San Benito County, and has lived there most of his life. He received a liberal education at Dartmouth College, New Hampshire, but laid aside his books, after graduating, in order to follow the pleasant life of a rural occupation. His clear judgment and sound sense soon attracted the attention of all who came in contact with him. He was one of the most active members of the County Board of Trade, and also has a seat in the State Board of Trade. His sterling qualities secured for him a seat in the Legislature, where he has done good work, and he is spoken of by all who know him, as a man generous to a fault, and ever ready to give his fellow-man the benefit of his own experience. In the order of Native Sons, Mr. Flint stands high, and no one is more devoted to its cause than he, notwithstanding that he is a prominent member of other important orders

The year I left California for British Columbia there was born in Yuba County a boy whose future career testifies to the sterling qualities with which he had been endowed at his birth. His name is Fred H. Greely, he is a native of Galena Hill, and no one more truly depicts the full vigor of the youth of the California soil. After graduating at the Marysville High, School he went east and finished his studies at the Maine Wesleyan Seminary, at Keats Hill, Me., where he graduated in 1880.

But Mr. Greely's mind was bent upon mercantile pursuits, and upon his return to the Yuba he took up his residence in Marysville, where he obtained an engagement as Secretary to the Buckeye Flour Mills with which he has been identified ever since. It was not long ere his fellow citizens fully recognized his superior qualifications for the prominent offices in their community, and in 1886 he was elected Mayor of Marysville and filled this position with credit to himself and satisfaction to his townsmen.

Two years after he contested with Congressman Berry for the Senatorship of the twelfth District, which had become vacant by the death of A. L. Chandler.

Once more his many friends rallied to his support, and he was sent to the post of honor with a handsome majority. Mr. Greely comes of the real old pioneer stock, the early settlers in the wilderness of California, whose energies, perseverance and undaunted courage made it possible for others to follow in their foot-prints, and build the cities where stood before the canvas tents.

Another Native Son, who has engaged in mercantile pursuits is Robert P. Wieland. He inherited from his father a large fortune, but also a temperament which did not allow him to take any undue advantage of the favors thrust upon him by the fickle Dame. He is modest, unpretentious and generous, and is noted for his splendid business talents and sound common sense.

After leaving school he attended Heald's Business College, and subsequently graduated from a business college in Louisville, Kentucky. Upon his return home he at once entered upon active duty in the Philadelphia Brewery, as shipping clerk, and is now the senior member of that extensive establishment.

Few men possess greater business abilities and activity than M. Wieland. Besides the important position he holds in his own firm, he is President of the California Bottling Company, President of the A. Folsom and Company, a big carriage-building concern, and Vice-president of the Clinton Consolidated Mining Company, of which his brother Charles is President. But in addition to all this, he is widely identified with fraternal organizations and other institutions. He is a member of every German fraternal order is San Francisco, of several Masonic Fraternities, and is a life member of the Olympic Club. He is also Lieutenant in the Light Battery A, N. G., and holds a commission as Second Lieutenant in the California Drill Corps.

As a member of the order of Native Sons, Mr. Wieland has enjoyed many distinctions, the foremost of all, perhaps, being the great popularity he has achieved among his associates.

Among those of the Native Sons who have distinguished themselves whilst holding public office, should be mentioned John. A. Grady He was born in San Francisco in '52 and is among the patriarchs of the Order, and no one has worked more zealously for its advancement than he. He assisted in organizing the first Grand Parlor and was afterwards elected the first Grand President. In the public departments Mr. Grady has served terms as Tax-collector of San Francisco, and also as Deputy State Treasurer, and in both offices he has proved himself a man of integrity and sound business management, reflecting great credit upon his administration of public affairs.

I cannot here pass by the memory of one who was dear to all who knew him—the late Frank J. Higgins, who died in San Francisco on the 3d of January, 1889, after a most active life, in which he used his best efforts and energies in the public service and for the benefit of the order of Native Sons.

Mr. Higgins was for many years a special revenue officer, stationed in San Diego, where his native affability secured him many friends. He lived there during the good days of Southern California, and accumulated quite a fortune through careful management and judicious investment, and his early death was a grief, not only to his fellow-members of the Order, but to all who had enjoyed business or friendly relations with him during his very active life.

Mr. Higgins was born in Tuolumne County and was educated in San Francisco. He was a life-long friend of Grand Secretary Lunstedt, a charter member of the Order, and one of its early Presidents. At his funeral was expressed, in many fitting ways, the great esteem in which he was held, and the sorrow that his death brought to the hearts of all who knew him. But his memory is garlanded with the flowers that never fade— the immortelles of love, and friendship, and respect.

I have now, to the best of my ability, brought out the native element of the Golden West, in its brightest colors. I would not presume to say that outside the Order to which I refer, this element does not distinctly exist, nor do I even know, for certain, that everybody I have mentioned here, belongs to the brotherhood. But it must be conceded that this fraternity of Native Sons is productive of much good, and if, as an old pioneer, my opinion is worthy of notice, I would urge upon all the desirability of joining an organization which holds together so many excellent forces, and is established with such a noble aim.

I have shown, too, the presence within its limits, of representatives from nearly all walks of life. The farmer, the merchant, the physician, the lawyer, the editor, the artisan, the politician, and I presume it would be possible to follow this up until all and everybody has been included in the ranks of the Order. When I reflect upon the establishment of this society, and review the part that the native element has taken in moulding the State into its present shape, I am bound to admit that the foresight of General Winn was keen, and the realization of his pet dream was a most fortunate event in the history of this State. I began my book by describing the early days of California, and it is but fitting that in closing it, I should pay a tribute to those whose patriotic enthusiasm has helped so much towards establishing and organizing the Golden State. "In union there is strength," is an old but true saying, and it is by remembering this, that the Native Sons of California will ultimately succeed in raising this to one of the foremost States, pursuing their onward march, but revering as they advance, the milestones left behind them, not forgetting the very first one raised by the early pioneers.

SOME OF

MY

EARLY FRIENDS.

DAN T. COLE.

There is probably no man identified with the early days of pioneer settlers on the river Yuba, who has come more prominently to the front, than Dan T. Cole, at present a member of the board of Harbor Commissioners. But notwithstanding this, there is no man occupying a high office or holding a responsible position, more modest than Mr. Cole. He is a thorough American and to-day more proud, by far, of the hours he has spent in hard work and honest sweat, than he is of the greatest distinction thrust upon him by an appreciative Executive who recognized his worth and ability.

Mr. Cole is a native of the state of Vermont and came to Sacramento in the year '52. After a sojourn of three years in that city, he spent one year in Alvarado, and then removed to Sierra County, where he has resided most of the time since, his home, "Mountain House," being well known to a large circle of friends.

Mr. Cole is an ardent Republican. For thirty years he has been a delegate to the State Convention, and last year he was sent as a representative to the National Republican Convention, held at Minneapolis.

Mr. Cole owns large property interests in Yuba County, and is one of the directors of the Northern California Bank of Savings in Marysville. He is also largely interested in hotel and mill property in Yuba County, and about four years ago he invested largely in

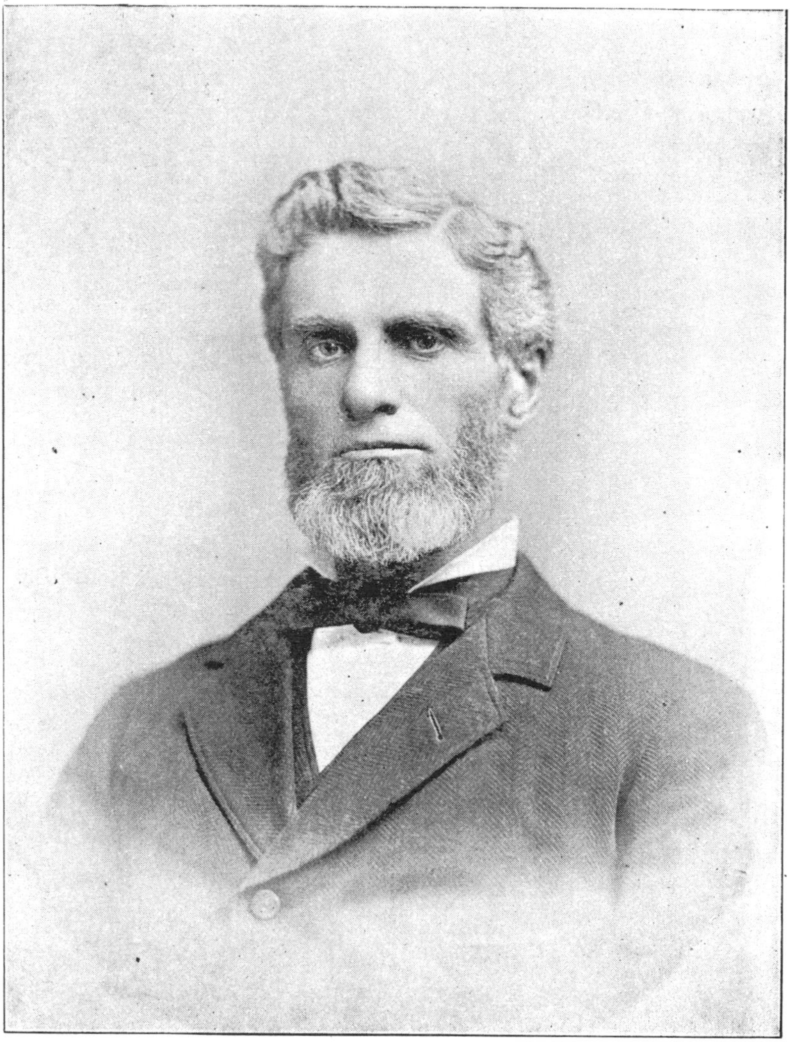

W. T. Cole

real estate in San Francisco, expending about $60,000 on buildings in that city, where he now resides.

During many years of incessant activity Mr. Cole has been engaged in staging, saw-milling, mining and teaming, and for ten years he was a member of the board of Supervisors of Sierra County. At the time when his appointment as Harbor commissioner was rumored, his enemies foolishly tried to besmirch his character by publishing that he had been a stage-driver. As a matter of fact Mr. Cole never drove a stage himself, but he is the last man to blush at the idea of having handled the reins in the pursuit of an honest living, and the accusation, false as it was, ratherer flattered than annoyed him.

Referring to Mr. Cole's appointment to the Board of Harbor Commissioners the *Marysville Democrat* remarks under date of January, 16, '93: "His appointment will be received with general satisfaction, and he will be found an efficient and honest official, who will at all times stay with the people and oppose boodle measures, whether in the office he fills, or in the attempt to force an unfit man on to the people of California in the office of United States Senator."

This comes from a paper opposed in politics to Mr. Cole, but having known him personally for many years, and the high opinion expressed for the Commissioner in these lines, is well backed by all who know him and have had an opportunity to watch him in his private and public life. In both spheres Mr. Cole enjoys the highest regard and it would not be out of place here to mention that he is blessed with a home where a model wife, who has stood by him during his years of struggle, presides over a family circle in which he is considered the best of fathers and a most devoted husband.

GEORGE C. PERKINS.

No man is better known throughout the State of California than George C. Perkins, and it safe to say that none is more highly esteemed in the Golden State. In saying so, one may not fear being accused of empty flattery, but rather, perhaps, of having expressed too inadequately the great worth of a most excellent man.

Mr. Perkins arrived in California from his home in New England, in the fall of 1855. At that time he was a beardless youth, but had, nevertheless, seen much of the world as a sailor, having made his first voyage as a cabin-boy when only twelve years of age. A few days after his arrival here he went to Sacramento, by schooner, and saw for the first time the city in which he should afterwards play a part entrusted to only the highest officers of the State. From Sacramento he walked to Oroville, a distance of one hundred miles, and displayed that energy and persistency which gave the impetus to his splendid career.

At that time his resources were few, but his enterprise and ambition were great. He first followed mining, and afterwards teaming and lumbering, but not being satisfied with the small remuneration he received for his labors, he finally engaged in mercantile pursuits as a clerk in the store of Hedley & Knight. Here he laid the foundation to rapid advancement. He became instrumental in establishing the Bank of Butte County, built the Ophir Flour Mill, and also became interested

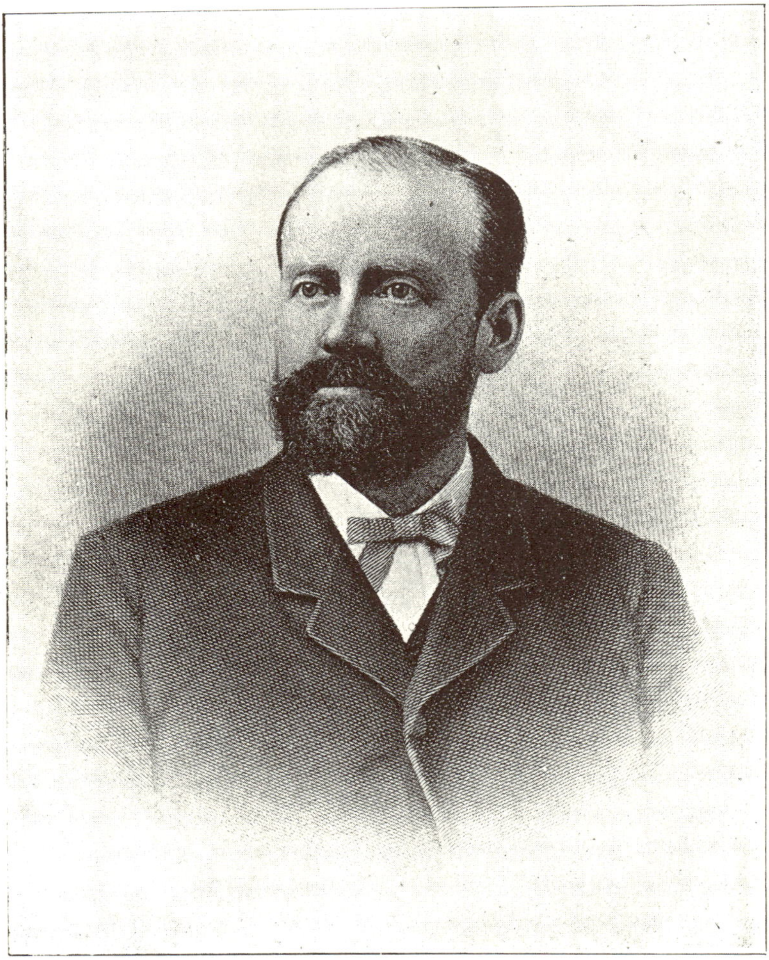

Geo. C. Jenkins

in mining, sawmills and sheep-farming. He throve wonderfully, and the success of his various enterprises not only redounded to his own advantage, but added to the wealth of the entire country.

No wonder, then, that Mr. Perkins soon became a very popular man. In addition to his rare abilities as a business man, he was possessed of many personal traits which endeared him to a large circle of friends, and at their earnest solicitation he entered the political arena on the Republican side, being also here destined to meet with unqualified success. He became a State Senator, and during his stay at the Capital, formed a friendship with Captain Goodall, of San Francisco, the result of which was the formation of the firm of Goodall, Perkins & Co., which to-day is one of the leading shipping enterprises of the coast, and it may be said, of the world.

Mr. Perkins' rise to the gubernatorial office was the crowning success of his life, showing by a tremendous majority the great confidence which the people of California repose in him. Mr. Perkins is a member of many orders; he is a prominent Free Mason, and is foremost in a number of charitable societies. In opening up a steady trade between San Francisco and Alaska, Mr. Perkins became the Pioneer who made it possible for the business man and traveler alike, to visit that interesting land with comfort and at a small expense, and his splendid line of steamers, calling at Alaskan ports, is not only one of his largest enterprises, but is probably the one which is most universally known and appreciated.

JAMES W. ORNDORFF.

Among the Pioneers of California, none, perhaps, is more popular than James W. Orndorff, the proprietor of the Cafe Royal, in the Flood Building, Market street, San Francisco. Mr. Orndorff came to this State in '52, from Zanesville, Ohio. He is of good old American stock, of German and Irish descent, but both sides of his family have been Americans for generations.

Arriving in the Golden State, the subject of this sketch at once turned his attention to mining, and chose the Yuba gold field for his first prospecting operations, remaining for ten years in various parts of that locality. In Sierra County in 1854, he put in the first hydraulic pipe made of sheet iron. It was a primitive affair and would compare badly with present appliances for the same purposes, but it did its work nevertheless. During those years Mr. Orndorff was more in particular identified with Grizzly Hill, in Sierra County; and he went through all the hardships of early mining in those regions.

In 1863 Mr. Orndorff removed to Virginia City, and spent seventeen years on or about the famous Comstock mines, partly engaged in practical mining and at other times catering to the amusement and comforts of his fellow men. Thus he was at one time an overseer in the Fairview mine, while at another he conducted the Ashland Hotel. He also ran the Billiard Rooms at the Washoe Hotel, where congregated in those days all the men of note, a motly gathering, representing many nationalities and as great a variety of characters.

While in Virginia City he took a prominent interest in everything appertaining to the fire department. He was Foreman of Company No. 1, and afterwards of Company No. 6, which he helped to organize; and his popularity in that community may be judged from the fact

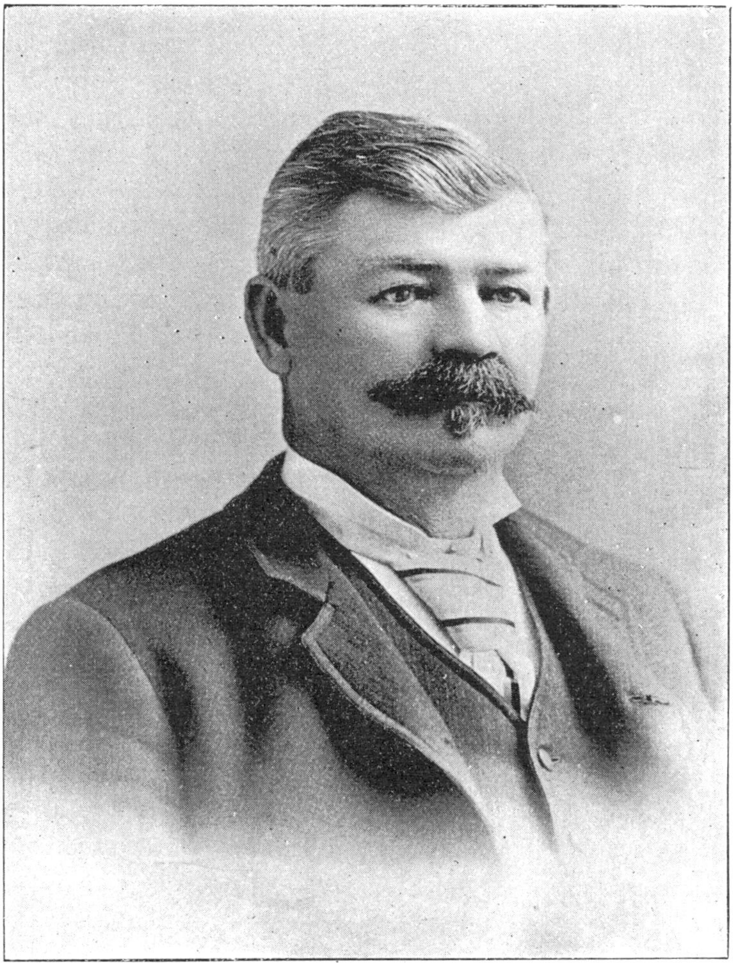

James W. Orndorff

that he was twice elected an Alderman of the city. He is now an honored member of the Veternan Firemen of San Francisco, but strangely enough does not otherwise belong to any fraternity or order.

As a business man Mr. Orndorff has been successful, principally owing to his natural attractions, his sound judgment of men and circumstance, and his even temperament. He is supposed to be second to none as an amateur billiardist and has always taken a remarkable interest in that game. He originated the idea of the patent pool table, with every ball into a common box after passing the pocket, and he had the first table of the kind built, which may yet be seen at the Billiard room of the Baldwin Hotel, San Francisco. But in all other sports Mr. Orndorfl has always taken particular interest, and from his very youth he hae been ever ready to make matches tending to the elevation of sports.

Mr. Orndorff is a great lover of animals and is one of the best read authorities on poulty in the state. He is also, a collector of curios and has a very interesting museum at his place of business. He is a very pleasant companion and his affability is calculated to make many friends for him, which, indeed has been amply demonstrated through the many years of incessant activity, he has spent on the Pacific Coast. No doubt there are many, who, reading this, will remember with pleasure their stalwart friend from ahe Gold-fields, and rejoice at once more hearing of Genial "Jim" Orndorff.

HON. EDGAR DUDNEY.

Edgar Dudney arrived in British Columbia in the early days. He was educated as a civil engineer, and turned his knowledge of this profession to good account immediately on his arrival in the new, and then mostly unknown, country.

There are few men who have more thoroughly explored the mountainous regions of British Columbia, than has Mr. Dudney. As a prospector and surveyor he penetrated early into many then unknown quarters, and located mining claims in the interior of the colony as the roads thither gradually became opened, and in this regard much credit is also due to Mr. Dudney as a gentleman whose efforts helped to bring about final settlement of large and uninhabited tracts of land.

As a result of his explorations, Mr. Dudney acquired an extensive knowledge of the nature and requirements of the country, and paid particular attention to the condition of the natives, wherefore, also, Sir John McDonald was pleased to offer him a portfolio in his cabinet as minister of Indian affairs, and in this position Mr. Dudney rendered his country important services, and proved himself an able administrator.

The final success in Mr. Dudney's career was achieved when Her Britanic Majesty appointed him Governor of the colony, an office which he still holds. In this capacity Mr. Dudney has proved himself worthy of the trust

E. Dewdney

reposed in him, and is one of the most popular Governors that ever conducted the affairs of the colony. Notwithstanding he is the last of the number, he is generally known as the Pioneer Governor, because of the many services he rendered the pioneers in the early days, and it is safe to say that among them he is held in particular esteem, and they, perhaps, more than any other class of men, appreciate those sterling qualities which have brought him to the honorable post he now occupies.

ROBERT DUNSMUIR.

As early as 1849, Robert Dunsmuir, left Ayrshire, in Scotland, under an engagement with the Hudson Bay Company. He settled in Nanaimo, Vancouver Island, as Superintendent of the local branch of this extensive Company, and soon achieved universal popularity.

Besides proving himself a business man of rare ability, Mr. Dunsmuir also engaged, from the very start, in various kinds of philanthropic movements, gaining a host of friends by his generous and charitable disposition.

One of Mr. Dunsmuir's first ventures was prospecting for coal. In his native country he had learned enough about the black diamond to appreciate its value, and recognized its existence wherever found, and it was, therefore, not to be wondered at that he met with unqualified success in a country, which is rich in coal.

He gradually extended his speculation, and bought extensive mines in Union, Komax District, which proved a most profitable speculation.

Later on, Mr. Dunsmuir built the Esquimalt and Nanaimo N. G. R. R., which became a very payable concern, and, indeed, is a great acquisition to the country through which it passes.

But the crowning success of Mr. Dunsmuir's life was when he secured a large interest in the Wellington coal mines, situated at Wellington, above Nanaimo.

ROBERT DUNSMUIR.

There are few people in America who have not heard of the product turned out so extensively at these mines, and upon the death of Mr. Robert Dunsmuir, his eldest son, Alexander, became the head of the business, and is now conducting the local depot for California in San Francisco.

The recollection of the subject of this brief sketch is dear to all who knew him, and none of his old friends can read this tribute to his memory, without remembering a good man, a faithful friend and a thorough business man.

WILLIAM IRWIN.

Among the men who have done good and honest work for California, that of William Irwin is inscribed upon one of the foremost pages of the history of this State.

Mr. Irwin was a native of Ohio, and devoted his youth to a college education and the study of law, which excellently fitted him for the important positions which he afterwards held.

In the year 1852, being then twenty-six years of age, Mr. Irwin came to California, and at once engaged in practical business is Siskiyou County. He led a most active life, and was successively a butcher, a miner, the the owner of a livery stable, and afterwards, of a line of stage-coaches, finally becoming proprietor of the Yreka *Union*, which he raised to one of the most important country papers in the State.

In 1861 he was elected to the Assembly, from Siskiyou, and although he served only one term, this was the beginning of a long and important public career. In 1869 he was elected to the Senate, and upon the expiration of his term, was re-elected, being chosen during the latter term, President *pro tem*. During that period Governoor Booth was elected United States Senator, and was succeedded by Lieutenant Governor Pacheco, while William Irwin became Lieutenant Governor by virtue of his position as President *pro tem* of the Senate.

In 1875 Mr. Irwin was elected Governor of the State,

EX GOVERNOR IRWIN.

and in 1883, while Stoneman was Governor, he was appointed to a seat on the State Harbor Commission, serving the four-year term. While holding this office he became sick, and expired on March 15th, 1886, at Hotel Bella Vista, thus ending a useful career and leaving a spotless reputation, and the memory of one who always did his duty conscienciously and fearlessly.

During Governor Irwin's incumbency, the act to take the popular vote on the Chinese question, was passed, being approved by him September 21st, 1877. At the general election in September 1879, the result showed for Chinese immigration 833 votes, and against it 154,-638. This was probably the most important measure enacted during his term of office, and was, so to speak, the first step towards the realization of the now famous Geary Exclusion Act.

CONTENTS.

CALIFORNIA.

CHAPTER I.

Introductory Remarks—At Home in Scotland—First Voyage—A Sailor on the Lakes—Lumber trade in Buffalo—The Gold Fever—Round the Horn—San Francisco—Expensive Dinners—The Glorious Fourth—Generous Gamblers—Fun With the Immigrants. 7

CHAPTER II.

On Board the Milwaukee—No Clearance Papers—Going Up the River—Sacramento—Teamsters Talk—Off For The Yuba—First Experience—War Upon Foreigners—A Silent Friend—Store Keeping—Lumpy Gold—Restless—Foster's Bar—Sick Men With Great Appetites—In Search Of a Partner. 15

CHAPTER III.

Off for the Mines Again—The Early Discovery of Gold—A Free Mason of 1820—An Interesting Document in San Francisco—Did the Priests Hold the Secret?—Captain W. H. Thomas' Account—Under the Wild Onions—"Cut Eye" Foster—A Sickly Man from Massachusetts—Jim Crow is Introduced—Over the Range—Facing the Wilds. 27

CHAPTER IV.

Through the Woods—Meeting Two Grizzlies—Across the River in a Hurry—McNair's Island—The Color of Gold—Over the Ridge—We strike the River—A Noise in the

Bushes—Round the Point—A Scene that Charmed Us—
The Forks at Last—Sullen Miners—Moving Camp—Mules
on the Hillside—Camped on the Yuba—Reminiscences of
Philo Haven. 37

CHAPTER V.

Down to Business—A Fish Story—Lead Weights and Brass
Weights—Crevicing—Breyfogle Flat—A Mule in a Hornets' Nest—Mamoo the Egyptian—A Negro from Virginia
—Rich Finds—Treacherous Friends—Mr. John Potter—
Flour Worth More Than Gold—A Very Sick Man—On
the Site of Downieville. 47

CHAPTER VI.

Death of a Friend—Andrew Goodyear—Bone Soup—At Simmons' Camp—Cooking Under Arms—Four Dead Mules
—"Cut-Eye" Out of Temper—The Ax on the Ledge—
Back at the Forks—The First Dwelling in Downieville—
Christmas—The Stars and Stripes in the Sierras—Magnificent Scenery. 57

CHAPTER VII.

Life in the Cabin—The Bill of Fare—A Prospecting Fever—
The Dangers of Traveling—Arrival of Mrs. James Galloway—A Poor Gin Mill—Jack Smith and His Jokes—Up
a Tree After Gold—Expensive Rations—William Slater
—A Rush of Miners—Taking up Claims—The Necessity
for Laws. 69

CHAPTER VIII.

Adopting a Code—Remarkable Observations—The Oh-be-joyful—Changing a Name—A Bit of Early History—Samuel
Langton—A Bag of Gold—Etiquette in the Barroom—
Corn Meal Fixings—Reading the First Newspaper—
Meeting Jim Crow—Phantom Treasures. 80

CHAPTER IX.

An Unfortunate Family—A Company of Sailors—After "Old
Downie"—Single Men and Married Men—William Slater's
Exit—A Note Due Over Forty Years—Law and Lawyers

—"Uncle Jimmie"—A Discourse About Drinking—My Claim Was Gone—The Eighth Commandment. 93

CHAPTER X.

A Spree For a Tip—Our Social Conditions—The Glorious Fourth—A Dinner at Galloway's—A Fight for Blood—A Speedy Trial—Thirty-nine Lashes—Big Logan—A Singular Suicide—Prospecting With Kanakas—A Rough Journey—Verdant Pastures. 105

CHAPTER XI.

Another Winter in the Mountains—Captain Thomas R. Stoddard—Two Well-known Millionairs—Fifteen-Hundred Dollars a Day—Gold on the Wagon Tires—Sleeping on a Fortune—Fluming a River—Poorman's Creek—Back to Downieville—Ten Bits to the Pan—Rantedodler Bar—Sunday Reminiscences. 119

CHAPTER XII.

A Severe Winter—Alexander McDonald—Close to a Fortune—A Lawsuit—Organizing a Mining District—Sluicing and Tunneling—The Summer of '58—Reports From the Fraser—A Wind-up—Now and Then—Quoting a Forty-niner. 133

YUBA SKETCHES.

LYNCHING A BEAUTY,	145
THE BLOODY CODE,	154
RIVALRY AND DEATH,	166
A FORTY-NINER'S YARNS,	172
FROM OBSCURITY TO FAME,	180
A SLAP JACK FIEND,	187
YUBA POETS AND POETRY.	190

BRITISH COLUMBIA.

CHAPTER I.

Arrival at Victoria—Sharp Practice—Indians Bring the First Gold—The Hudson Bay Company—An Energetic Governor—A Route to the Mines—Joining an Expedition—Natives Surprised—The Dame and the Bullets—Adventures on a Stream—Lilooet Lake—A Favorable Report—An Attempt That Failed. 199

CHAPTER II.

Queen Charlotte Island—Gold Harbor—Scotch Guy—The Majesty of Nature—Captain Gold—Potlatch—Political Campaigns—Totems—Architecture and Art—An Interesting People—Vanity of Savagedom—Curious Customs—The Death Dance—Myth and Legend. 210

CHAPTER III.

Fort Simpson—On the River Skeena—"Pioneer H. B. C."—A Tempting Offer—Locating A Pass—What A Gold Band Did—Red Paint—*Bon Jour*—Frank's Curly Hair—Chief Sal-tow-tow—White Men in the Wilderness—Days of Privation—A Poor Craft—Head Factor, Peter Ogden—A California Monte Bank in Victoria. 222

CHAPTER IV.

Surveying the Inlets—Looking for a Wagon Road to the Fraser—Jarvis Inlet—An Awful Ravine—Desolation Sound—All by Myself—The Bears Came Rushing Down—The Kle-na-Klene River—Bella Coola—Dean Canal—A Land Boom—False Reports—Mr. Tovalloit Prevaricates—Spearing Salmon—Indians From Fort Fraser—After Gold on the Naas. 235

CHAPTER V.

My Partners—Visiting Friends—The Village of Tsawatti—Villainous Indians—Anxious Moments—Friends in Need Bute Inlet—On the Homathco—Auxiliary Rivers—Wonderful Scenery—Glaciers Ahead—A Sick Indian—Great Hardships- The Tequahan and the Memria- Poor Luck —What a Newspaper Said. 248

CHAPTER VI.

Unscrupulous Speculators—The Pre-emption Law—The People of Westminster—Two Explorers—False Reports—A Rowdy Audience—Cariboo Mining—Trying to Pump Gold—The Money Ran Out—Waddington's Enterprise—A Camp at Bute Inlet—Treacherous Indians—A Night Of Horrors—The Avenger—The Killing of a Dear Friend. 263

CHAPTER VII.

The Gold Export Tax—Captain Evans and His Son—In the Editor's Room—The Russo-American Telegraph—Two Different Routes—How To Go To Work—Once More at Dean Canal—Some Beautiful Land—Predicting A Bright Future—Hon. John Robson—The Famous Granite Creek—Lumps of Gold—Advice to Disheartened Miners —Comparing Past and Present. 275

CHAPTER VIII.

Indians—The Value of Natives—Medicine Men and Superstition—An Incident at Yuclatan Village—Heart Disease and no Bullet—Memoir From the Naas River—Singular Customs—The Price of Flour—The White Man and the Red Man—How They Died—Scarlet Fever—Indian Mechanics—A Promising Country. 288

PANAMA.

CHAPTER I.

Taking A Rest—A New Friend—Queer Conversation—How Van Sickles Dug Gold—My Greatest Chance—Panama the Place—Departure—A Qurious Old City—Difficult Mountain Trails—Down With Fever—An Indian Graveyard—Digging For Gold—Pottery Galore—A Curious Whistle—My Collection Spoiled—Moving to Other Parts. 303

CHAPTER II.

The Chirique—Another Graveyard—More Pottery—David City—The Shuber Brothers—A Native Hog—Singular Tombs—Above the Clouds—Abandoning Grave Digging —Looking For Copper—A Perfect Hoodoo—Farewell Panama—Bric-a-brac. 314

A TRIP TO ALASKA.

CHAPTER I.

Off for Alaska—Review of the History of the Country— Russian, American and English Influences—The Tolstois and the Astors—A Wonderful Region—First Impression of Scenery—Quoting Kate Field—Mountains and Glaciers—Lieutenant Schwatska's Surveys—A Phantom City. 329

CHAPTER II.

Mining Matters—On the Stikine River—San Francisco Speculators in the Field—Large Mining Machinery—Fish Oil and Gold Dust—The Yukon Diggings—Comparison Between Past and Present—Interesting Indians—Artistic Carvings—Innocentius Veniaminoff—The End. 340

THE NATIVE SONS.

CHIPS OF THE OLD BLOCK.

The Author's Address—Pioneers and Native Sons—Two National Holidays—An Organization Established—A Moth-eaten Bear—General Winn's Efforts—A Young President—Telling Speeches—A Birthday Party—Grand Secretary and Free Mason—A Relic Saved—Men of Action. 355

SOME OF MY OLD FRIENDS.

D. T. COLE.	380
EX-GOVERNOR GEORGE C. PERKINS.	383
JAMES W. ORNDORFF.	386
LIEUT. GOVERNOR DUDNEY.	389
ROBERT DUNSMUIR.	392
EX-GOVERNOR IRWIN.	395

ILLUSTRATIONS.

FRONTISPIECE	
IMMIGRANT TRAIN NEARING THE SACRAMENTO	18
SACRAMENTO IN FORTY-NINE	20
CAPTAIN JOHN A. SUTTER,	22
SUTTER'S MILL, COLOMA, CAL.,	28
CARMEL MISSION, NEAR MONTEREY, CAL.,	31
LOOKING FOR THE COLOR,	38
WORKING THE ROCKER,	44
VIEW IN SACRAMENTO IN THE FIFTIES,	53
A LONELY MOUNTAINEER,	60
DONNER LAKE, SUMMIT OF THE SIERRAS,	67
VIEW OF LAKE TAHOE,	73
THE OLD CABIN AT DOWNIEVILLE,	86
OFF TO THE DIGGINGS,	92
AFTER OLD DOWNIE,	95
VARIOUS METHODS OF MINING,	102
VIEW OF THE SIERRA BUTTES,	108
CATCHING BREAKFAST ON THE YUBA,	114
THE DESERTED CABINS,	121

VIEW OF GOLD LAKE,	129
GROUND SLUICING IN THE EARLY DAYS,	135
DOWNIEVILLE IN THE EARLY FIFTIES,	139
DOWNIEVILLE OF TO-DAY,	144
HANGING OF JUANITA,	151
COMING OVER THE MOUNTAINS,	156
DUEL BETWEEN LIPPENCOTT AND TEVIS,	162
PHILO A. HAVEN,	169
DEATH OF MOFFATT,	177
LOUISE H. MACKAY,	183
VICTORIA BEFORE THE BOOM,	198
SIR JAMES DOUGLASS, K. C. B.,	205
HYDAH INDIAN CHIEFS,	215
MASSET, QUEEN CHARLOTTE ISLAND,	229
A GROUP OF NAAS INDIANS,	239
NANAIMO,	255
BARNARD GLACIERS, ON THE SKEENA RIVER,	269
KOSKEEMO INDIAN CHIEFS,	281
FORT SIMPSON,	291
RELIC FROM AN INCA GRAVE,	312
DANCING THE FANDANGO,	321
AMONGST THE ICEBERGS IN GLACIER BAY,	328
WRANGEL ISLAND, ALASKA,	341
GLACIER BAY, SHOWING SECTION OF MUIR GLACIER,	349
WILLIAM R. HEARST,	354
HON. STEPHEN M. WHITE,	357
HON. GEORGE C. PARDEE,	357
HON. LEVI R. ELLERT,	357
HON. THOMAS FLINT JR.,	357
ROBERT WIELAND,	357

HON. R. F. DEL VALLE,	357
FREDERICK C. CLIFT,	357
HENRY LUNSTEDT,	363
JOHN A. STEINBACH,	363
HON. C. H. GAROUTTE,	363
R. M. FITZGERALD,	363
DR. C. W. DECKER,	363
COL. C. F. CROCKER,	363
JOHN T. GREANEY,	363
HON. FRANK L. COMBS,	369
H. CLAY CHIPMAN,	369
FRANK D. RYAN,	369
M. A. DORN,	369
FRANK J. HIGGINS,	369
JOHN H. GRADY,	369
JO D. SPROUL,	369
D. T. COLE.	381
EX-GOVERNOR GEORGE C. PERKINS.	384
JAMES W. ORNDORFF.	387
LIEUT. GOVERNOR DUDNEY.	390
ROBERT DUNSMUIR.	393
EX-GOVERNOR IRWIN.	396

INDEX

Adams and Co., Express Firm, 87
ADAMS, Edwin, 186
AGNEW, Mr. and Mrs., 316
AGUILLGATH, 225
AITKEN, Dr. C. D., 181
Ale in camp, effect on lawyers and judge, 101
Alaska, History of attractions, 329-339
Aleutian Islands, 347
Alexander Fort, 232
Aliares Reo, 322
Alma Tunnel, 136
Alvarado, 33
American Flag, at the Forks, 68
American River, 19
ANDERSON, Frank, 46
ASTOR, John Jacob, 331
ASTOR, William Waldorf, 331
Astoria, 331
Avatcha, 331

Bars, drinking: BULLARD'S, 19, 21, 26, 46, 51; COX'S, 64; FOSTER'S, 24, 25, 27, 35, 62; GOODYEAR'S, 37, 45, 54, 55, 62, 79, 128; Negro, 40; RANTEDODLER, 128; ROSE'S, 19; St. JOE, 133
BANDINI, Miss, 29
Baldwin Hotel, San Francisco, patent portable, 388
Bank of Butte County (established by Geo. C. Perkins), 383
BARIO, Don Juan, 309
Bear, grizzly, 37-39
BELL, Alexander, 276
Benicia, delay over clearance papers, 17
Bering Straits, 330
Bluebanks, 43
Boston "Herald", 30
Botany Bay, 20
Boulder Creek mining, 285
Brandy, value of, to miner, 61
Brandy, for cornmeal mixing, 89
Brandreth's pills, 34
Breyfogle Flat, 40, 49, 90
BRIGGS, Mr., story of claim, 131
BRODERICK, Senator, 164
BRYANT, Dr. E., 184
Bute Inlet, 245
BUTLER, Dave, 166
Buttes Mill, 124

CAMINETTI, Anthony, 364
Canadian Pacific Railway, search for suitable pass for construction of, 210, 222
    Claiming of pass, 225
CALLIS, Albert, 40, 46
Cannon, 147
Canyons, Jim Crow, 37
    Secret, 37, 39; *Clark's*, 134
Canyon Creek Co., 136
Cape Royal, (*San Francisco*), 386
CAPIN, John, 85
Cariboo, (British Columbia), 266
Castillero, 33
Carving (of Indians), 350
Chatham Sound, 222
CHIPMAN, H. C., 373
Chirikoff, 331
Chirkchees, 329
Cherique, 314, 317
Christmas celebrations, 66
CLIFF, Frederick C., 370
COLE, Dan T., 380
COLONNA, Princess, 184
COMBS, Frank L., 365
Comox (Vancouver Island), 392
Comstock Lode, 122
Comstock Lode Mine, 386
COOK, Frank, 85
Cordilleras, 308
COSAIR, Henry, 123
COSSITT, H. B. (Downie's partner), 115, 123
Craycroft Hotel, 42
Craycroft's Sawmill, 55, 82, 168
CROCKER, Colonel Charles F., 364
CROW, Jim, 35, 48, 51, 54, 90
CROYERE, Louis de la, 331
CULTON, Jack, 46
Cut-eye FOSTER, 63, 71, 72, 77

DALL, William H., 346, 350
DAVISON, Artemis and Douglas, Downie's brothers-in-law, 303
David City, 317
Dean Canal and *Salmon River*, 283
DECKER, Charles W., 373
Deer, 42
DEWDNEY, Hon. Edgar, Lieut. Gov. of British Columbia, 389
Desolation Sound, 237
DORN, Marcellus A., 367
Doroskin, 334

INDEX

Douglas Island, 342
DOUGLAS, Sir James, Lieut. Gov. of British Columbia, 201
DOWNIE, William: incidents in in personal history of, 201; birthplace and early life, 8-10; voyage to Sydney, Australia, 8; America, Canada, Buffalo, New Orleans, San Francisco, 9-11; arrival at gold diggings, California, 33; difficulties and hardships of trail, 59, 60; ideas on temperance, use and value of brandy, 61; as cook, 62; Happy times in camp, 63; provisioning for winter, at the Forks, 64, 65; generosity to mean miner (Mr. Lord), 69; adventure at Indian Creek, 90; adventure with would-be robbers, 95, 96; law suit over claim jumpers, 101; experience with married men as miners, 103; belief in influence of environment, 107-109; prospecting for gold discovering pastoral land, 116-118; settling accounts, 119; expedition to Plumas County, 120; search for big gold, 123; work in Secret Canyon, 128; expedition to Indian Creek, Grizzly Hill, Ramshorn and St. Joe Bar, 133; constructing Alma tunnel, 136; selling out California claims, leaving for British Columbia, 140; expedition to Upper Fraser, Howe Sound and Lillvet Lake, 202-208; to Nanaimo, 208; to Queen Charlotte Islands, 210-221; Skeena River, Fort Fraser, Stewart Lake Quesnelle, 234; to Jervis, Bute Loborough and Knight's Inlet, 234-240; to Bella Coola, 241; to Chilcotin and Kithobe, 245; partners on trip up West Coast of Vancouver Island, 250; disappointing reception of report at Victoria, 266; mining in the Cariboo, 272; rest in San Francisco, 303; expedition to Panama, 306-314; expedition to Costa Rica, 314-325; trip to Alaska, 329-351; partners of H. B. Cossitt and Alexander McDonald, 125-132.
Downieville; naming of, 41, 51; and first beginnings, 66; real foundation of, 83; appointment of Justice of the Peace and constables, 83; mail service, 85; ethics of a "treat", 88; celebrations, Saturday night, 94; 4th of

Downieville; naming of, (*Cont.*) July, 110, 145, 153; lynching of Juanita Tevis and Lippencott duel, 156
DUNSMUIR, Robert, 392-394
DUTCH, Harry, 119
DUVARNEY, Michael, 34, 52, 57, 59, 60, 119
Dyah Pass, 345

ELLERT, Levi R., 372
Esquimalt and *Namaimo Railway* (Vancouver Island), 392
EVANS, Captain, 275
EVANS, Taliesin, 276

Fairweather Mountain, 338
FARLEY, Senator James, 365
FERN, F. G. W., Poet, native son, 360
FIELD, Kate, picture of Alaska Scenery, 335
FITZGERALD, Robert M., 367
Flats: Omit's, 39; Breyfogle, 40, 49, 82; Jersey, 45, 55, 66; Sumwalt, 48; Jersey, 66; Twist's, 71; Otter, 285; Hogging, 112, 115
FLINT, Thomas Jr., 374
FLOOD and O'BRIEN, 122
Forks, 41, 44, 45, 46, 49
Fort Fraser, 222
Foster's Bar, 24, 25, 27, 35
Foster's Cut Eye, 35
FRANKLIN, 334
FRANKLIN, Lady, 246
Fraser River (British Columbia), 136, 200
Freemasons loyalty in avenging death of one, 170

GALLOWAY, Mr. and Mrs. Andrew, 37
GALLOWAY, James, 72
GALLOWAY, Made J. P., 84
Gambling, faro and monte, 13, 14
GAROUTTE, Charles H., 368
Gilford Island, 240
Glasier Bay, 338
Gold: discovery of, in California, 27; cargo taken to Philadelphia by Robinson, 29, 30; papers referring to, in archives, Pioneers Hall, San Francisco, 30; knowledge of suppressed by Priests, 30; panning of, 48, 49; equipment for mining of, 49; big haul, 52; disputes, 65; daily take, 70; rich claim, 75; dishonesty over, 97; in Alaska, 342; at Butte's mill, 124;

Gold: discovery of, (*Cont.*)
  Flume above Kanaka Flat, 125;
  in British Columbia, 199; "Mining for Gold" (poem), 193
Gold Harbor, (Moresby Harbor), 210
Gold Harbor, (Mitchell Harbor), 214
Gold Lake, 120, 122, 176-179
Gobin Bay (Silver Mine), 344
Goodall, Perkins & Co., 385
GOODENOV, Marian (Mrs. Robb), 167
Goodyear's Bar, 37, 54
GOODYEAR, Miles, 57
GREAMY, John T., 366
Greenhorn Creek, 128
GRADY, John A., 376
GRIFFITH, William, 55, 57, 59
GREELY, Fred H., 375

Hagler Tunnel, 136
HAMMOND, Captain Creed, 181
HAMILTON, H. B. (trader), 229
Hanging (of the Mexican Woman), 196
HARLAN, Harry, 248
HARRISON and GORLIDGE (Explorers), 241
HARRIS, Tim, 61
Harrison Mines, 208
HARTLEY, Sam (poem), 193, 194
Hawley Simons & Co., 59
HAVEN, Philo, 45, 166, 173, 174-176
HAYES, Colonel Jack, 181
HEARST, William Randolph, 371
HEDLEY and KNIGHT (Employees of Geo. C. Perkins), 383
Hide Park, 11
HIGGINS, Frank T., 377
Hollow Log, 71
HOVENUE, Mr. Santiago, 320, 323
Howe Sound, (British Columbia), 203
Hudson's Bay Company, 199
  tribute to personnel of, 201; description of forts of, 203, 204; pioneers, 223; in Alaska, 333
HUGHES, G., 134, 186
HUNGERFORD, Colonel Daniel E., 180
HUNGERFORD, Sir Robert, 180
Incas, 305
Indians: *Kanakas*, 22; in *British Columbia*, 202; *Unamish*, 207; *Casswer Indian Village*, 211; *Hydash*, 214; customs, potlatch, totems, traditions, myths, legends, population, 216, 221; village,

Indians (*Cont.*)
  Kitchumala, 223; village *Kittoonra*, 223; *Hazelon*, 225; *Haas Glee, Tyhee, Taltowtin*, 226; *Whatatt*, 234; *Bridge River*, 235; *Fraser Valley*, 241; *Chilcotin*, 242; spearing fish, 245; tobacco for, 247; *Knight Inlet, Tswatti*, 249; *Hickhanuns* and *Homathco*, 256; Powers of endurance, 258; *Lockwatta*, 259; *Bute Inlet*, 267; diseases contracted from white men, 268; massacre at *Brewster's Camp*, 270; punishment for same, 273; special chapter on, 288, 300; burial customs of *Incas*, 311; Graveyard, 311; of *Alaska*, 346
IRWIN, Williams, 395-397

Jarvis Inlet (British Columbia), 209, 235
Jersey Flat, 45
Jokes, practical, 76
JONES, Albert F., 367
Juanita, story of, 146
JUMP, Dr., 134
JUNEAU (Alaska), 342

Kamloops (Route of Canadian Pacific Railways), 264
Kamschalka, 331
Kanaka Indians, 22, 34, 35, 51, 52, 90
  Creek, 72; Flat, 115
Kelly, 55
Kle-na-Klene River, 240

La Mesa, 307
Langley Fort, 203
LANGTON, Samuel, 85, 87, 93
Law-making and code of laws, 80, 81
LEONARD, 125
Lillvet Lake, 203, 208
LIPPENCOTT, Hon. Charles: story of duel with R. Tevis and subsequent events, 159-165
LITTLETON, Frank—pseudonym "Miner", 194
Liquor in camp, 61, 74, 100
LOGAN, Bill, 112, 114, 152
LORD, Mr., 69, 70
Lynching, 145
LUNSTEDT, Henry, 362
LUSK, F. C., 366

MACKEY, Miss Louisa, 180
Mannor, 51
MARSHALL, John, 51

INDEX

Marysville, 19
"Marysville Democrat" (Dan T. Cole), 382
McCLELLAN, General, 184
McCOMB, General John, 359
McDONALD, Alexander (Partner of Major Downie), 132, 234, 248, 252, 273
McDONALD, Sir John A. (Premier of Canada), 389
McDONALD, Calvin B. (Articles in Sierra "citizen" urging expulsion of gamblers), 155
McKAY, J. G., 202
McKENZIE, Sir Alexander, 232
McLEAN, William (Hudson's Bay Co. Factor at Kamloops, B.C.), 199
McNair's Island, 40, 45, 59
Miners' Code, 29
Miners' character of California, 109
Minerals at head of *Douglas Inlet*, 210; *Moresby Island* (copper, gold), 214; *Upper Skeena* (quartz, plumbago); *Jervis Inlet* (quartz, slate, copper), 238; *Knight's Inlet* (lead), *Simalkamein* (copper), 284; *Whipsaw Gulch* (gold), *Granite Creek* (quartz), of *Panama*, 308; *Costa Rica* (cinnabar, copper), 322; in *Alaska*, 346
MOFFAT, 16
Monterey Custom House, 29
MOLENDO, B. (for exploration of Inca sepulchres), 319
MOORE, Thomas, quotation from, 142
MORRISON, 59, 60
Mountain House, 35
Mule, accident of hornet's nest, 50

Naas Glee, 225
NANAIMO, 248, 392
Nanaimo, name of Hudson's Bay Co.'s staff, 208
Native Sons of San Francisco, 359
Native Sons of the Golden West, 359
Native Sons of Golden State, 359
Negro Bar, 40
Negro Point, 71
Negro Tent, 71
Nevada, silver mines, 122
New Westminster, 264
Nicola Valley, 285
North Fork, 40
Nye's Crossing, 62

Odd Fellows, 160
OGDEN, Peter, 230, 232

Ogden (Utah), 230
Omit's Flats, 39
Onolaska Island, 343
Ophir Flour Mill (Built by Geo. C. Perkins), 383
ORNDOFF, James W., 386-388

Pacific Fur Company, 331
PAGE (Dash, Hughes and Page), 187
Pall Mall Magazine, 331
Panama, 304
PARDEE, Dr. George C., 372-382
Parker House, 12
PAXTON, Judge, 97
Peccarico, 310, 315
PERKINS, Geo. C., 383-385
PELLET, Miss Sarah, 154
Pioneer's Hall (San Francisco), 30
POTTER, John, 54, 55, 56
Priests, 32

Queen Charlotte Islands, 210; history of, 212; description of, 213
Quesnelle River (British Columbia), 233

Red Mountains, 12, 14
Rills Mt. (Trading station of), 322
Rivers: *American*, 19; *Russian*, 332; *Sacramento*, 33; *Santa Clara*, 33; *San Joaquin*, 33; *Stikine*, 333, 340; *Yuba River*, 19, 45; *Yukon River*, 336
ROBB, Mrs. (Marian Goodenov), 167
ROBSON, Hon. John, 383
ROBINSON, Don Alfreds, 28
ROBINSON, Captain, 210
ROSE, J., 19
ROYS, Captain, 334
Russians Settlement in California, 332
Russians, mining investigation in Alaska, 334
Russo-American Telegraph Co., 331
RUSSELL, 57
RYAN, Frank D., 366

Sacramento, 16, 17
Sacramento River, 33
Salmon Catching, 48
San Francisco, 10, 12, 13
life in early days, 14
Sansome Street (San Francisco), 11
San Bernardino Mountain, 33
Santa Clara River, 33
San Diego Mission, 30
San Frascisquito, 33
St. Charles Hotel, 42

INDEX

St. Elias Mountain, 337
St. James Fort, 211
St. Louis Bay, 134
Savannah, 8
SCHWALKA, Lieut., Frederick, 336
Scurvy, 23
Sears Diggings, 120
SERRA, Junipero, 30
Settlements at The Forks and Jersey Flat (names of original settler), 66
Sexton, 57
SHUBER, John, 316
Siberia, 329
Sierra "Citizen" (Newspaper), 158
article on Roger Tevis, 159
Sierra Guards, 181
"*Sierra Buttes*" (poem), 191, 192
Simpson Fort, 211, 222
Sitka, 332, 343
Silver Mine (Gordon Bay), 344
Skeena River, 222
Skidgate Channel (description of), 211
Slate Creek House, 134
Slate Range, 35
SLATER, William (Disappearance with gold), 77, 79
Sleighville, 71
SMITH, Jack, 48, 74
"*Snow Shoe Races*" (poem), 195, 196
SPROUL, Jo Davis, 366
STEARNS, Dan Abel, 29
STEINBACH, John A., 360
Stewart Lake, 230
Stikine River, 333, 340
STODDARD, Capt. Thomas R., 119, 176, 179
Stock-keeping and sales methods, 77
STONE, Fred (Poem by), 192, 193
STONEMAN (Governor of California), 397
SUTTER, Capt. John A., 22, 51
Sutter's Mill, 28
Sydney (New South Wales), 8

TAYLOR, General Zacharias, 9, 10
TEVIS, Robert, 156
THAYER, William, 149
Thlinklets, 348
THOMAS, Capt. W. H., 30
THOMAS, quotation from letter of, 33
THOMPSON, Charlie, 119
THOMPSON, R., 200
Thorndike of Lima, 318
Tincup Diggings, 48
TOLSTOR, Count Leo, 331
TOLSTOR, Andrean, 331
Tolstor's expedition, 331
Tulameen River, and diggings, mining operations, 286
Tulameen, wild turkeys, 315

Unga Island, 343

VANSICKLES, A. T., 304
VAUGHN, Dr., 57
VENIAMINOFF, Rev. Innocentus, 351
Vernon's, 19
Village Maiden, The (Poem), 192, 193
VINCENT, Mr. Frank (description of silver relic), 318
Vineyard, 83, 84
Victoria (British Columbia): landing at, 199; Meeting at, re-projected railway, 246; Daily Press, 259; or Bute Inlet route, Major Downie's meeting to report on above, Meeting in Royal Victoria Theatre to discuss gold tax, 265, 266; "Times", 276

WADDINGTON, Alfred, 244, 246
Party murdered by Indians, 272
WAGONER and CHASE, 89
WEARE, W. K., 190; Ode to the Pioneers, 190, 191
Wellington (Coal mine Vancouver Island), 392
WHITE, Stephen M., 372
WIELAND, Robert P., 375
WILKINS, Charley, 39, 45, 52
WILSON, John, 115
WINN, General A. M., 358
Woman, first white woman in camp, 72
WOOD, Sam, 55
WRANGEL, Baron, 333, 350
Wrangle Fort, 340

Yahl or Yehl, 347.
Yakutat Bay (Black sands pay dirt), 343
YALE, Mr. (Superintendent of Fort Langley), 204
YOUNG, Dr., 123
Yreka "Union" (owned by William Irwin), 395
Yuba River, 19, 45
Yukon River, 336

Zumwalt Flat, 48